D1795209

NORMAN MAILER:
The Radical as Hipster

by

ROBERT EHRLICH

Metuchen, N.J. & London
The Scarecrow Press, Inc.
1978

Library of Congress Cataloging in Publication Data

Ehrlich, Robert, 1940-
    Norman Mailer, the radical as hipster.

    Bibliography: p.
    Includes index.
    1.   Mailer, Norman--Political and social views.
2.   Mailer, Norman--Criticism and interpretation.
I.   Title.
PS3525. A4152Z 643   813'. 5'4   78-14849
ISBN 0-8108-1160-X

For
Sidney I. Ehrlich
1914-1977

CONTENTS

ACKNOWLEDGMENTS

Quotations from the following works are reprinted by permission of the author and the author's agents, Scott Meredith Library Agency, Inc., 845 Third Ave., New York, N.Y. 10022: The Naked and the Dead; Barbary Shore; The Deer Park; The Presidential Papers; An American Dream; Cannibals and Christians; Why Are We in Vietnam?; The Armies of the Night; Miami and the Siege of Chicago; Of a Fire on the Moon; St. George and the Godfather; The Prisoner of Sex; and Advertisements for Myself.

The following publishers also granted permission to reprint brief excerpts from the titles cited:

Miami and the Siege of Chicago (copyright © 1968 by Norman Mailer). World Publishing Co. Reprinted by permission of Thomas Y. Crowell, Inc.

Advertisements for Myself (copyright © 1959 by Norman Mailer); The Deer Park (copyright © 1955 by Norman Mailer); The Presidential Papers (copyright © 1963 by Norman Mailer); Why Are We in Vietnam? (copyright © 1967 by Norman Mailer). Reprinted by permission of G. P. Putnam's Sons.

Of a Fire on the Moon (copyright © 1969, 1970 by Norman Mailer). Reprinted by permission of Little, Brown and Co.

An American Dream (copyright © 1964, 1965 by Norman Mailer). Reprinted by permission of The Dial Press.

Armies of the Night (copyright © 1968 by Norman Mailer); and St. George and the Godfather (copyright © 1972 by Norman Mailer). Reprinted by permission of The New American Library, Inc., New York, N.Y.

PREFACE

It has become almost fashionable to criticize Norman Mailer. He has been continually accused of wasting his aesthetic talents by catering to his combative needs in a never-ending series of public displays. Just as often, he has been condemned for squandering his creativity by working in so many genres (the novel, the short story, the essay, the poem, the play, the journalistic account, the film, and the biography). And finally, he has alienated virtually everyone, because he is an ideological renegade whose thought cuts across political tendencies on the Right and the Left. His stance has generally been identified with the anachronistic outpouring of the embattled male, macho to the core, intent upon preserving a minimal sense of identity in an America souring each day in an ill-defined "totalitarianism."

However, it is my feeling that these criticisms, though at times justified, fail to acknowledge fully that in the mid-fifties Mailer began to develop a "philosophy" which would be able to account for much of his aesthetic experimentation as well as his thematic concerns and public style. His "philosophy" does not have even the minimal rigor of Yeats' A Vision or Lawrence's Psychoanalysis and the Unconscious and Fantasia of the Unconscious. Rather, it is a loose discussion of matters that at different points in his life embrace psychological, political, economic, social, aesthetic, theological, mystical, and cosmological concerns, all of which are sufficiently related to allow for systematization. It is a "philosophy" which changes in amoebic fashion, the original outline continually present but always involving new emphases.

Mailer's earliest work reveals the seeds of his vision. An anarchist when he wrote The Naked and the Dead, only to embrace rather fitfully revolutionary socialism in Barbary Shore, before veering toward the apolitical in The Deer Park with its neo-Reichian hymn to sexuality at the end, itself perhaps a prelude to the more elaborate notion of the

vii

"apocalyptic orgasm" so central to his essay "The White Negro," Mailer in just the formative stages of his career appears to have undergone several major intellectual transformations.

And yet there is a consistency here, as well as in the later work, that many critics do not sufficiently acknowledge, given their concern with the various aspects of Mailer's thought: Marxian anarchism, socialism, hipsterism, existentialism, conservatism, and mysticism. For instance, Mailer has equated the concepts Hip and existential. His existential political hero was John Kennedy, "The Hipster as Presidential Candidate." His heavy immersion in mysticism, especially his theology, is an outgrowth of his "philosophy of Hip." Even his conservatism must be examined in the context of his recent description of himself as a "Left Conservative" and his desire to become Mayor of New York by forming " 'a hip coalition of the Left and Right.'" In both his writing and his public appearances, he has always stressed the need for the fullest development of the self, a process which can only take place after a long and rigorous inner journey that is continually nourished by perilous transactions in the world at large. It is not surprising that even in the earliest stages of his career his interest in politics was overshadowed by his fascination with the crippling and expanding movements of the individual in a crisis of self-exploration.

Throughout his work, Mailer has evaluated himself and his characters in an attempt to bring to his vision the intensity of a resilient moralist, a dialectician with a thirst for the dramatic and an energy which knows few limits. That vision is most clearly articulated in his essay "The White Negro." But it is in his later work, particularly An American Dream and Why Are We in Vietnam?, that Mailer develops much more fully the ideas which he offers as "reflections" in the essay. Even his journalism of the late sixties and early seventies, although clearly more subdued in tone than his previous work, draws heavily upon concepts which he had explored earlier: so much so, that he has often been criticized for his repetitious use of Manichean platitudes, a mythical God and Devil, and a no less shadowy man and woman locked in an eternal war.

The criticism is valid. What tends to be forgotten, however, is the fact that Mailer has come to place much more emphasis upon ideas which have been presented in a variety of contexts throughout his literary career. I begin with "The White Negro," then, because it is here that Mailer has made his most careful attempt to weave together many of his beliefs. If the temptation to anchor all his thought within this framework has been great, I have tried to avoid the danger of reductionism. Therefore I have considered Mailer's "philosophy" in its broadest context, beginning with the initial formal presentation in his well known essay. Then I have moved back in time to The Naked and the Dead, Barbary Shore, and The Deer Park, before exploring its full ramifications in his future work.

In all my efforts, I have been aided by James Tuttleton, presently in the English Department at New York University. In addition, I would like to thank Sylvia Paull and Andrew Gordon for reading and commenting upon parts of my manuscript.

Robert Ehrlich
Berkeley, 1977

CHAPTER 1

INTRODUCTION

I

Perhaps no other American writer since World War
II has been as concerned with the quality of American life
as Norman Mailer. Like Whitman, who catalogues his interest in the people, institutions and landscape of America,
Mailer has detailed his attitudes toward his country in an
ever-developing syncretic vision which has required continual
aesthetic experimentation.

That "philosophy" is not a highly logical system which
can be easily described. As Samuel Hux indicates, Mailer
develops an existential perspective which possesses some
similarity to the vision offered by certain twentieth-century
European philosophers.[1] Although he stated during an interview in 1960 that he had read little of Sartre and Heidegger,
Mailer reveals his interest in existentialism in his "philosophy
of Hip." If he rejects Sartre's atheism and highly rationalistic
existential philosophy with its emphasis upon "the delicate in-
volutions of consciousness,"[2] he has consistently maintained
a concern with the development of the self, the problem of
freedom and responsibility, and the proximity of death in an
increasingly alien world. Moreover, like Sartre and Heidegger, who refuse to create a neat Platonic system of essences,
Mailer has little desire either to view or judge human nature
"from a set of standards conceived a priori to the experience,
standards inherited from the past" (AM, p. 353). He is particularly interested in the complexity of the emotional life.
Therefore he states in Advertisements for Myself that "one
cannot give a lecture on Hip, one must feel it, one must
take the part of one's experience which is alive to the subject, and let it take the point" (AM, p. 389). Not "fact,"

1

but rather "nuance" is central to Hip, which can only be considered "properly with the sensuous fear of a patrol" (AM, p. 389).

The military metaphor here is quite appropriate. With Stephen Crane and Ernest Hemingway, Mailer found in war the kind of experience that would allow him to explore the nature of the self and society. World War II, in which he participated, provided the ambience in which Mailer would begin to consider some of the problems that are elaborated upon more fully in his later work. Thus in The Naked and the Dead, his first novel, Mailer focuses upon the men in an Army platoon during the Pacific campaign. Like the hero who evolves from the idea of Hip, the men in this novel are partially defined on the basis of their courage in the face of death and their willingness to probe the deepest recesses of the personality.

But unlike Hemingway and Crane, whose interest in political questions was almost always subordinate to a concern with psychological and moral problems, Mailer began with a strong commitment to radical social change. Though he considered himself an anarchist when he wrote The Naked and the Dead, that novel suggests a Marxian vision with its emphasis upon various forms of exploitation that grow out of a capitalist economy. Utilizing a naturalistic mode, Mailer presents in great detail the oppressive external conditions which are confronted by the men at home and abroad.

He translated this understanding into direct political practice by supporting the Progressive Party and Henry Wallace as a radical alternative in the 1948 presidential election. After 1948, Mailer moved even further to the Left under the tutelage of his friend, Jean Malaquais, a French Marxist, whose influence is apparent in Barbary Shore, where long political discussions are woven into a plot which centers upon the political activities of three men, two of whom are Trotskyists. And yet, in this novel, more than in The Naked and the Dead, Mailer indicates the lineaments of his "philosophy of Hip" with its emphasis upon the individual rather than society. For if Barbary Shore deals more directly with political matters than any other novel by Mailer, it is in the end a statement about the failure of radical politics in the United States and the Soviet Union.

In fact, here Mailer reveals his interest in existentialism, a stress upon the need for a transformation of the self

that runs counter to Malaquais' strong commitment to a revolution guided by the proletariat. The publication of The
Naked and the Dead created a psychological climate that undermined the certainties of Mailer's past, including his aesthetic and political beliefs. He states that existentialism
was virtually "forced" upon him, and refers to Barbary
Shore as a novel which emerged "from the bombarded cellars
of my unconscious ..." (AM, p. 94).

Barbary Shore was published in 1951, just after the
Chinese had come into the Korean War, a time when Mailer's
"libertarian socialism" could hardly flourish in an America
given to "the worship of the lifeless, the senseless, and the
safe" (AM, p. 105). The poor reception of the novel perhaps
encouraged him to seek an "interim career" as a short story
writer for established New York publications such as the
New Yorker, Harper's Bazaar, and Mademoiselle before he
regained his creative impetus in preparation "to become the
first philosopher of Hip" (AM, p. 107).

The result was the publication of The Deer Park,
which reflects Mailer's concern with the need for an intense
exploration of the self which he had begun in Barbary Shore
with the abandonment of the naturalistic mode and the use of
a first-person narrator. However, when he finished writing
The Deer Park, Mailer experienced very serious problems
with his publisher, Rinehart, who wanted to censor his work.
The crisis of conscience which Mailer experienced over this
matter made him feel like a "psychic outlaw" who "felt
something shift to murder" (AM, p. 234) in him. He was
perhaps more of an outsider than he had ever been, experimenting now with drugs, especially marihuana, and journey-
ing into Harlem, where he made new friends.

His involvement in the creation of the newspaper,
The Village Voice, during 1956 was an attempt to give public expression to his desire to see a "moral and sexual revolution" (AM, p. 278) in America. He viewed his column as
a declaration of a "private war on American journalism,
mass communications, and the totalitarianism of totally
pleasant personality" (AM, p. 278). In that column, Mailer
made his first public statements about his "philosophy of Hip. "

But it really was an exchange with William Faulkner
over the question of school integration which provided the
immediate catalyst for Mailer's elaborate discussion of Hip
in "The White Negro." Mailer stated that "the white loathes

the idea of the Negro attaining equality in the classroom because the white feels that the Negro already enjoys sensual
superiority" (AM, p. 332). For Mailer, Faulkner's rejection of this idea was tantamount to a "Biblical act of banish-
ing" (AM, p. 335) him, an act which required further response.

If "The White Negro" was initially begun as an answer to Faulkner, the essay came to encompass issues
which went far beyond the earlier exchange. Still attempting
to reconcile his interest in politics and psychology, in "The
White Negro" and its attendant pieces Mailer reveals by
means of his "philosophy of Hip" a modification of his Marxian
vision through a fuller consideration of the inner life. While
he believed that Marx offered a highly elaborate system to
examine social and political reality, he was distressed at
what he felt was Marx's failure to deal adequately with psychological experience. Mailer therefore sought a "calculus
capable of translating the economic relations of man into his
psychological relations and then back again, his productive
relations thereby embracing his sexual relations as well, until the crises of twentieth century capitalism could be understood as the unconscious adaptation of a society to solve its
economic imbalance at the expense of a new mass psychological imbalance" (AM, p. 358). Mailer continues to use
Marx's dialectical method in seeking a synthesis which will
embrace more facts and contradictions than any conservative
view could allow. But he has stated that it "might be more
'Marxist' to recognize that the superstructure of society has
attained vast autonomies outside productive relations, psychological undercurrents which often clash with material economic realities ... " (AM, p. 364).

Thus, even in The Naked and the Dead, Mailer utilizes
the psychological insights of Freud, especially in "The Time
Machine" sections, which are short personal histories of the
significant men in the novel. If Mailer was particularly sensitive in his first novel to the way childhood experience, especially parental response, molded later behavior, he quickly
developed a distaste for modern applications of psychoanalysis.
In the story "The Man Who Studied Yoga" (1952), Sam Slovoda's
paralysis of the will is reflected in his use of Freudian jargon and his dependence upon his therapist. Although Mailer
still admired Freud for being "a discoverer of secrets, mysteries, and new questions, " he was dismayed with the man's
answers, so "doctrinaire, deathlike, and philosophically most
dreary" (AM, p. 273). He was particularly concerned with

the instinctually inhibiting aspects of Freudian theory, which views human nature as primarily aggressive and in need of social control.

He turned, therefore, to the work of Wilhelm Reich. In the story "The Time of Her Time" which was written in the mid-fifties, Sergius O'Shaugnessy, the analyst in "The Man Who Studied Yoga," becomes a lay practitioner of Reichian therapy by pushing to orgasmic release Denise Gondelman, whose character armor is reflected in her endless intellectualizing, particularly her Freudian banalities. Although Mailer does not totally identify with Sergius' quest in "The Time of Her Time," the emphasis upon the need for instinctual liberation in a highly repressive society is clear.

Mailer found in Reich a psychologist who, despite the significant intellectual transformations in the course of his career, maintained the idea that society was destructively hostile to full instinctual development, especially sexual fulfillment. Reich's emphasis upon the need for emotional purgation in a therapeutic atmosphere which encouraged the expression of feeling was transformed by Mailer into a stress upon the preservation of one's emotional integrity in the face of social restrictions. Ultimately Mailer came to place a great deal of emphasis upon a transformation of the self which might take place without a corresponding alteration of society.

His "philosophy of Hip" almost naturally gives rise to the concept of a hero, the hipster, who had already been spoken of by other writers during the fifties in the context of the rising interest in marihuana and jazz. Mailer locates his hero firmly within a literary tradition. A number of critics have indicated the similarity between the hipster and Melville's Ishmael, whose willingness to experiment and desire for adventure are reflected in his voyage upon the sea, which is an attempt to purge himself of the "hypos." Mailer has constantly spoken of his desire to write a novel with the scope of Moby Dick. It is not surprising that he has also modeled the hipster upon the Dostoevskian hero who is often trapped by intense contradictory feelings in novels which explore large social, political, and even religious problems. The introspection which is the result of this emotional turmoil suggests the Proustian sensibility with its willingness to explore the roots of feeling in the past. Nevertheless, the hero created by Mailer tends to be a more robust figure than the delicate Marcel in A la recherche du temps perdu.

Inspired by the machismo of Hemingway, he offers a figure who not only demonstrates grace under pressure, but also abides by the "categorical imperative that what made him feel good became therefore The Good" (AM, p. 340). Highly sympathetic to Lawrence and Miller, he fashioned a hero whose desire for the fullest kind of sexual experience requires a long journey into the deepest recesses of the self. The fiction of Sartre and Camus provided a model for the existential man who confronts a metaphysically alien world that can only be countered through radical self-assertion. Finally, in the artists of the Beat Generation, particularly Kerouac and Ginsberg, Mailer had contemporaries who, along with him, searched for the apocalyptic encounter and the electric phrase.

In exploring the origin of the word "hipster," Mailer acknowledges his debt to Ginsberg's Howl, in which there appears the expression "angel-headed hipsters." However, he distinguishes between the beatnik, usually an intellectual renegade of the middle class, and the hipster, who tends to come "out of a muted rebellion of the proletariat" (AM, p. 373) and lives a more active, sensual life. Where the beatnik is often a "radical pacifist," the hipster is more interested "in exploring the close call of the Self ..." (AM, p. 374). In fact, Mailer states that the "rise of the hipster represents the first wind of a second revolution in this century, moving not forward toward action and more rational equitable distribution, but backward toward being and the secrets of human energy, not forward to the collectivity which was totalitarian in the proof but backward to the nihilism of creative adventurers ..." (AM, p. 363).

Similarly, in the course of his career Mailer moves away from his earlier Marxist preoccupation with the social revolution, which results in a transformation of his political radicalism as he becomes more concerned with a cultural revolution that would allow for the realization of all the possibilities in the individual, especially the fullest development of the emotional life. While Mailer continues to advocate radical social change, the individual in the guise of Mailer himself or one of his male fictional personae is usually the focus and of greatest interest.

II

As he is presented in "The White Negro," the hipster was born when the threat of nuclear annihilation, death in the concentration camps, and pressures to conform to the totalitarian state all forced man to lose concern with the future or the past and to concentrate his energy and attention on the present. In the absence of any meaningful theological, moral or political frame of reference, the hipster has been forced to forge an existential ethic in which the individual sets out "on that uncharted journey into the rebellious imperatives of the self" (AM, p. 339). It is in daily acts of courage, in a heightened consciousness of himself and the external world, and in a sensitivity to feeling that the hipster creates his identity.

In the black man, the "philosophical psychopath, " and the mystic, Mailer sees the collective embodiment of the hipster. In fact, Mailer states that the hipster "absorbed the existentialist synapses of the Negro, and for practical purposes could be considered a white Negro" (AM, p. 341). The black man constantly lives with danger and must be in a perpetual state of physical and psychological readiness in order to survive. Burdened with self-hatred and ostracized by others, he develops a "morality of the bottom" out of "all those moral widernesses of civilized life which the Square automatically condemns ... " (AM, p. 348).

Not content with a traditional rational explanation of events, the mystic relies on private vision and lives every moment with an intense awareness of the possibility of his own death. Mailer's rather personal definition of the mystic points to the religious and existential aspects of the hipster's quest, since "faith in the necessity of action is a life committed to the notion that the substratum of existence is the search, the end meaningful but mysterious" (AM, p. 341). Suggesting a Kierkegaardian perspective in which dread is paramount, during an interview in 1955 Mailer spoke of his belief in God, "but it is a very personal faith and I find in myself, as of this year, no detectable desire to join any church" (AM, p. 272). Though of Jewish origin, Mailer has not been inclined to monotheism but instead has created a theology of Hip in which man is viewed as a principal agent in an eternal war between God and the Devil. Man is both a psychological and historical voyager whose fate is tied to a God who is no longer conceived as omnipotent but as an embattled figure who tries to "impose upon the universe His conception of being against other conceptions of being very much opposed to His" (AM, p. 380).

The "philosophical psychopath" is also concerned with probing the deepest recesses of his emotional life. Unlike

his "conventional" counterpart, who lives out his infantile
feelings unconsciously and without a philosophical framework,
the "philosophical psychopath" is interested in freeing repressed childhood feeling in the hope of lessening the tension
of his infantile desires and of purging himself of certain values instilled by civilization and standards inherited from the
past. He explores "backward along the road of the homosexual, the orgiast, the rapist, the robber, and the murder-
er" and seeks the "violent parallels to the violent and often
hopeless contradictions he knew as an infant and as a child"
(AM, p. 346). Mailer emphasizes that the "philosophical
psychopath" must purge his hatred before he can love. The
aim, therefore, is not immediate gratification, but a desire
to attain "the sophistication of the wise primitive in a giant
jungle ... " (AM, p. 343).

     In his discussion of the "philosophical psychopath, " the
black man, and the mystic, Mailer emphasizes the growth
and survival of the self, always conceived in masculine terms.
Since he views himself as a collection of possibilities and the
results of his actions as unforeseeable, the hipster cannot
know if his actions are good or bad. Both character and
context are dominated by "the energy available at the moment of intense context" (AM, p. 354). Moreover, the hipster views life "as a contest between people in which the
victor generally recuperates quickly and the loser takes longer to mend, a perpetual competition of colliding explorers in
which one must grow or else pay more for remaining the
same ... " (AM, pp. 349-50). To grow means to try to contain "within oneself the implicit rhythm of the [other] person"
(AM, p. 350), a process which can take place in all acts,
including acts of violence as well as acts of love. The hipster, then, embraces a conception of life in which "incom-
patibles have come to bed, the inner life and the violent life,
the orgy and dream of love, the desire to murder and the
desire to create, a dialectical conception of existence with a
lust for power, a dark romantic and yet dynamic view of existence, for it sees every man and woman as moving individ-
ually through each moment of life forward into growth or
backward into death" (AM, pp. 342-43).

     With the black man and the "philosophical psychopath, "
Mailer acknowledges that personal survival is dependent upon
others, and he suggests the possibility of collective action.
However, the ultimate aim of the hipster's action is not the
transformation of institutions in the hope of an end to material exploitation--a traditional aim for political radicals.
Mailer seeks a revolution in consciousness.

The black man and the "philosophical psychopath" are both prevented from fully living out their instinctual lives. They are sexual outlaws, frustrated by society in their attempts to achieve the apocalyptic orgasm. Though Mailer's stress in Advertisements for Myself upon the liberating powers of sexuality was modified in his later work, where there is a concern with sin and guilt, he separates himself from the European existentialists, who were much more inclined to emphasize the anxiety which attends each human involvement. Samuel Hux speaks of the hipster's search for the apocalyptic orgasm as "the search for a metaphoric Eden": he points to the history of American literature, where "Eden was to be found, among other ways, through an Inner Light, then through intercourse with nature and the Oversoul, now through sexual regeneration."[3] Moreover, in his stress upon the sexual orientation of the black man, Mailer has been criticized, justly, by James Baldwin, who discerns in the "white Negro" one more myth of black sexuality.[4] Mailer speaks of the "instinctive apprehension and appreciation of existence" (AM, p. 314) in the black man, for whom the orgasm is one of the few positive experiences available in a racist culture. For the "philosophical psychopath," the repressiveness of any institution or work situation leads him to pursue a life outside the confines of society.

According to Mailer, in seeking the apocalyptic orgasm both of these prototypes attack the sexual mores of society, and therefore capitalism, which is based on property relations and tied to monogamy and the family. Nevertheless, Mailer does not emphasize the possibility of a transformation of property relations since he is more concerned with the transformation of consciousness. He states that the orgasm leads "to the secrets of that inner unconscious life ... that trapped, mutilated and nonetheless megalomaniacal God who is It, who is energy, life, sex, force, the Yoga's prana, the Reichian's orgone, Lawrences's 'blood,' Hemingway's 'good,' the Shavian 'life-force' ... " (AM, p. 359).

The reference to Reich is especially important here. For in his later work, Mailer's notion of the hipster's energy is explored within the context of a modified version of Reich's theory of orgone. Like Reich, who was dissatisfied with Marx's limited political emphasis, Mailer criticizes earlier revolutions which were "enacted in the name of the proletariat" but were "motivated by the rational mania that consciousness could stifle instinct and marshal it into productive formations" (AM, p. 363). But he does state that a change in consciousness can be hastened when each hipster sees that "if he would be free, then everyone must be free" (AM, p. 355).

Despite his egalitarian orientation, Mailer acknowledges the fact that the hipster may not contribute to the development of a society that is less authoritarian than our present one. He states that many hipsters are "material for an elite of storm troopers ready to follow the first truly magnetic leader whose view of mass murder is phrased in a language which reaches their emotions" (AM, p. 355). But Mailer points to the more likely possibility that the hipster will move to the Left, since conservatives impose so many social restraints. The hipster separates himself from authoritarian philosophies because of his need for maximum self-expression.

Since the only Hip morality is to do what one feels, whenever and wherever it is possible, it appears that conflicts of will are inevitable in any social system. But Mailer states that "in widening the area of the possible, one widens it reciprocally for others as well, so that the nihilistic fulfillment of each man's desire contains the antithesis of human cooperation" (AM, p. 354). At the same time, Mailer is frightening when he suggests that "no matter how brutal the act, it is not altogether cowardly" to murder a fifty-year-old candy store owner, because in the act one violates private property, enters into a new relation with the police, and introduces dangerous and unknown elements into one's life (AM, p. 347). Mailer continues to defy moral limits when he states that "To a Square, a rapist is a rapist. Punish the rapist, imprison him, be horrified by him and/or disinterested in him, and that is the end of the matter. But a hipster knows that the act of rape is a part of life too, and that even in the most brutal and unforgivable rape, there is artistry or the lack of it, real desire or cold compulsion, and so no two rapists nor no two rapes are ever the same" (AM, p. 314).

With all of his attempts to qualify his belief in the benefits that may result from the release of violence, Mailer never adequately explores the moral significance of his position. For the hipster, in any act of violence, a catharsis takes place which prepares the way for growth. The philosophical basis for this attitude toward the murder of the candy store owner and acts of rape is essentially Rousseauian since, according to Mailer, when every social restraint is removed, "man would then prove to be more creative than murderous

and so would not destroy himself" (A<u>M</u>, p. 354). And even
if violence results from the removal of social restraints,
"individual violence would still spare us the collective violence of rational totalitarian liquidations ... " (A<u>M</u>, p. 363).

This emphasis upon violence leads Kate Millett to ac-
cuse Mailer of propagating "a malign <u>machismo</u>" that is particularly destructive for women, who are often used by the
hipster in his quest for self-discovery. 5 If Millett is essentially right in this criticism, she tends to echo Mailer's remarks when she condemns the hipster's "rampant individualism. "6 He calls Hip "the all-but-despairing philosophy of
all the sensitive congeries of the defeated, the isolated, the
violent, the tortured, and the warped ... " (A<u>M</u>, p. 314).
While he states that "Hip may erupt as a psychically armed
rebellion whose sexual impetus may rebound against the anti-
sexual foundation of every organized power in America, and
bring into the air such animosities, antipathies, and new conflicts of interest that the mean empty hypocrisies of mass
conformity will no longer work" (A<u>M</u>, p. 356), Mailer implies that the hipster tends to become far too isolated to par-
ticipate in an organized political movement. He is too different in imagination from everyone he meets in the conventional world, and experiences so much conflict in the world
of Hip that his isolation is almost unbearable.

If the hipster is the result of a society that is politically, socially, intellectually, and economically oppressive,
his salvation lies in his consciousness of his condition, in a
heightened readiness to maintain the inviolability of the self,
both of which can only result from an intense, active engagement with the outside world in a unique and, most often, solitary manner. The possibility for collective political action
is limited because of the exhausting psychological demands
placed upon the hipster, and the restriction upon the fullest
amount of self-expression that is imposed in the very act of
making a serious political commitment. The result is that
when the political commitment is made, it is so rich and
confusing as to defy any existing political categories.

The aesthetic ramifications of Hip are an outgrowth
of this highly personal style. Mailer can be examined within
the context of Roy Harvey Pearce's discussion of the two traditions in American poetry, the Adamic and the mythic. 7 In
the Adamic tradition, exemplified by Whitman, the poet often
ignores or defies the past in the presentation of a self which
exists beyond social sanctions; whereas in the mythic or

"Eliotic" tradition, the poet thrives by virtue of the literary past which he utilizes, particularly the distant Greco-Roman heritage, and the self which is projected can only survive through meaningful historical connection. While he is much closer to the Adamic tradition, Mailer, like William Carlos Williams, would aesthetically and ideologically resurrect the past insofar as it has an immediate bearing upon the present. Yet, unlike Williams, who utilizes the annals of American history, Mailer focuses upon the personal and historical past within his own lifetime and that of the preceding generation. And where Williams describes past events in order to create a sense of the richness of American life or to provide resonance for the chaos of the present, Mailer emphasizes a psychological exploration in time, a journey into the self which requires a re-evaluation of past relationships. Furthermore, if the Adamic poet is oriented to time as a series of instants in which the self is continually recreated under social conditions where the egalitarian strain in American life predominates, Mailer is extremely preoccupied with the vestiges of the self that must be purged because of social inhibitions.

One of these vestiges is the worn-out language of the past. He calls Hip "a special language" that

> cannot really be taught--if one shares none of the experiences of elation and exhaustion which it is equipped to describe, then it seems merely arch or vulgar or irritating. It is a pictorial language, but pictorial like non-objective art, imbued with the dialectic of small but intense change, a language for the microcosm, in this case, man, for it takes the immediate experiences of any passing man and magnifies the dynamic of his movements, not specifically but abstractly so that he is seen more as a vector in a network of forces than as a static character in a crystallized field. (AM, pp. 348-49)

And again: "Like most primitive vocabularies each word is a prime symbol and serves a dozen or a hundred functions of communication in the instinctive dialectic of the instantaneous differentials of existence in which one is forever moving forward into more or retreating into less" (AM, p. 352). While Mailer appears to be talking here about the language of the street, he is really formulating an aesthetic for Hip. The number of words available to the hipster is limited by the very nature of his jargon: "The words are man, go, put down, make, beat, cool, swing, with it, crazy, dig, flip, creep, hip, square" (AM, p. 349). The result is that "nuance of the voice uses the nuance of the situation to convey the subtle contextual difference" (AM, p. 349).

In developing his aesthetic of Hip, Mailer ignores the fact that nuance of voice and nuance of situation are quite different when one moves from oral to written communication. And he does not discuss the obvious fact that the artist might be hindered by limiting his vocabulary. His own confusion on this point is revealed in his literary practice, which has relied upon the full resources of the vocabulary, particularly after The Naked and the Dead, since he has come to employ a language, rich in metaphor and allusion, that suggests the expansiveness of Wolfe and Faulkner. Moreover, in D. J. of Why Are We in Vietnam?, Mailer has created a narrator who employs the language of Hip, which is revealed, in part, as a banal means of expression. And in his journalism of the late sixties and the early seventies, Mailer continually indicates his dissatisfcation with the "jargon-mired children" of the Counter-Culture, whose few curt expressions, "entropies of vocabulary," are used to describe experiences which require much more elaboration.

Nevertheless, in an interview, speaking about the problems of the artist, he asserts that Hip attracts him because "it's involved with more expression, with getting into the nuances of things" (AM, p. 379). Like the hipster, who seeks out the widest variety of experience, the novelist must try to make the quality of his experience more intense. "That doesn't make for less expression: it makes for greater difficulty of expression. It makes for writing more pages about fewer episodes ..." (AM, p. 379). In employing this aesthetic, the novelist encounters "new moral complexities" which are "more interesting than anything the novel has gotten into yet" (AM, pp. 381-82). There is the possibility that the novel and other art forms may be growing into something larger at a time when everything has been getting smaller; "notions of Hip enlarge us, they make our small actions not necessarily large, but more meaningful" (AM, p. 382).

Finally, the "philosophy of Hip" leads to a didactic notion of the function of art. For Mailer, the final purpose of art is "to intensify, even, if necessary, to exacerbate, the moral consciousness of people" (AM, p. 384). The novel is the "most moral of the art forms because it is the most immediate, the most overbearing, " and "inescapable" (AM, p. 384). It is much closer "to the sense of moral command-ments, moral strictures" and explores the "interstices of moral reaction ... " (AM, p. 384).

III

My primary purpose in this book, then, is to show that Mailer's development as a novelist, journalist, and es-sayist can be understood as an outgrowth of his "philosophy of Hip. " Although he first fully articulates his idea of the hipster in "The White Negro, " Mailer's didacticism is easi-ly discernible in The Naked and the Dead, where he criti-cizes the social and political system of America and tries to formulate certain ways of responding to these conditions. In Croft, Cummings, Valsen, and Hearn, Mailer positively extrapolates from political tendencies on the Right and the Left those which he will later use in his notion of the hip-ster. That the notion is still buried and has not yet fully blossomed is indicated in the form of the novel, which is an outgrowth of work of naturalists such as Dos Passos, Farrell and Steinbeck. It is especially apparent in his use of tech-nique, for Mailer employs an omniscient observer that in no way projects the explosive energy and search for power of his later narrators, beginning with O'Shaugnessy in The Deer Park. His sensitivity to naturalistic detail, particularly evi-dent in the "Time Machine" sections of the novel, is indica-tive of his sense that the individual is almost completely weighed down by the effects of his environment. The possi-bility of political amelioration through the efforts of individ-uals is insignificant.

While Barbary Shore utilizes a first-person narrator, even here the sense of the powerful, vulnerable, emotionally explosive self that permeates Mailer's later work is missing. Yet Lovett and McLeod, both descendants of Hearn, and Hol-lingsworth, a descendant of Croft and Cummings, are embod-iments of tendencies that Mailer will later draw together in his concept of the hipster.

It is with Marion Faye and Charles Eitel in The Deer Park that we get Mailer's first full characterization of cer-tain aspects of the hipster as he appears in "The White Ne-gro. " Faye is Mailer's first full projection of the hipster who seeks after that which he most detests, continually needs to test himself with other people, and is ruthlessly honest.

In the characterization of Faye, it is evident that the hipster's emphasis upon the self tends to diminish the possibility of collective action for social change. In fact, given his mystical and theological concerns, he becomes the embodiment of the more religious side of the hipster's quest. With Eitel, Mailer is intent upon portraying the failed hipster in the world of politics and art. In the same novel, Mailer utilizes O'Shaugnessy as a narrator who has some of the energy, courage, and sense of his own power that are characteristic of Rojack in An American Dream, and even Mailer himself in The Armies of the Night and Miami and the Siege of Chicago.

The emphasis on courage particularly takes Mailer into social and political experience. It is the basis for the existential politics which Mailer develops in The Presidential Papers. His youthfulness, energy, courage, and style embodied in his war record, John Kennedy becomes for Mailer that public figure he can most easily identify as a hipster. For Mailer, Kennedy was a man of action who had the ability to touch many people's lives and move the country in a less repressive direction. However, what Mailer emphasizes in his discussion of the former President is not so much the material conditions present in America, but the strong sense of self that Kennedy projected to the American people, who he hoped would become a little more active and imaginative.

Even before Kennedy died, Mailer's faith in him dissipated. With Lyndon Johnson, who is one of the political centers of Cannibals and Christians, Mailer's hope for the appearance of the hipster on the national scene almost totally vanished. For a while it appeared that Mailer would no longer concern himself as much with social and political reality. His existential politics gave way to cosmological concerns when he began to write works such as "The Political Economy of Time," and then projected Rojack, whose concern with magic, mystery, and dread makes him the fullest embodiment of the mystical side of the hipster. He is a man far more concerned with the shades and nuances of his own feelings than he is with the social and political scene, which in fact he leaves because of his failure to reach the most profound levels of his emotional life.

D. J. of Why Are We in Vietnam? does not as readily reject the external world as Rojack. Possessing tremendous energy, D. J. is the "white Negro": part Harlem spade, part

Texas white boy. At times he is given to mystically specu-
lative flights, but these flights are grounded in the surfaces
of American experience. Unlike Rojack, who leaves for
Yucatán because he cannot survive in American society,
which makes too many demands on his individuality, D. J.
submits to cosmic powers much greater than himself, especially the urge to kill, which is reflected in his departure
for Vietnam. Despite the fact that he appears to criticize
so many of the myths that have propelled his country into
that conflict, D. J. goes with a sense of joy. There is no
indication that he is ready to engage in any form of political resistance.

    In both An American Dream and Why Are We in Viet-
nam? Mailer utilizes new aesthetic techniques which help to
illuminate his "philosophy of Hip. " His experimentation in
the use of point of view and language is integrally tied to his
concept of the self in its relation to the external world.   Similarly, in The Armies of the Night and Miami and the Siege
of Chicago, Mailer utilizes a third-person narrative device
that allows him to objectify himself and the external world.
While The Armies of the Night is a synthesis of journalism
and fiction and Miami and the Siege of Chicago is rather
straightforward journalism, both works show Mailer attempting to distance himself from experience.

    The "Mailer" of these two works is not a hipster like
Rojack or D. J.   According to Barry Leeds, "he lives by the
code of the White Negro but does so within a somewhat more
mature and sophisticated life style. "[8] Unlike Rojack and
D. J. , he does not leave the country, but he works at home
for change. Like the earlier heroes, "Mailer" challenges
basic values held by most Americans.   Unwilling to engage
in some of the alienating behavior that the earlier hipster
might have been given to, Mailer here projects a more socially oriented but less intense figure whose major concerns
still seem to be with the self and its ability to maneuver in
and out of challenging and sometimes dangerous situations.
His new restraint is particularly embodied in his designation
of himself as a "Left Conservative" in The Armies of the
Night and in the 1969 New York mayoralty race, where his
campaign slogan, "power to the neighborhoods, " reflects his
desire to cut across the political spectrum by allowing for
maximum experimentation in the practical life of the city.
Yet, despite his participation in the mayoralty race and unlike the hipster who is consumed by his quest for experience,
Mailer considers himself primarily an artist for whom events

attain their ultimate significance when an active engagement with the external world gives rise to the process of writing.

This trend is continued in Of a Fire on the Moon and St. George and the Godfather, where Mailer removes himself even further from events through the creation of a new persona. Although intent upon weaving his own experience into the events which are described, Mailer is much less a participant and more of a witness than in Armies or Miami and the Siege of Chicago. As "Aquarius," he views the existing social order through a sensibility which at times reflects the mysticism of the "white Negro," especially that of Rojack, but which preserves the integrity of the event because of a concern with external detail.

If Mailer has not made the hipster a central figure in his non-fiction of the late sixties and the early seventies, his recent work is thoroughly infused with the manner of e-valuating experience described in "The White Negro." He continues to present not only a dialectical conception of life which allows for the reconciliation and interpenetration of opposites, but an aesthetic that revelas his preoccupation with the need for offering innovations in the use of language and genre.

Notes

1. Samuel Holland Hux, "American Myth and Existential Vision: The Indigenous Existentialism of Mailer, Bellow, Styron, and Ellison," Diss. , Connecticut 1965, pp. 179-211; Robert Solotaroff, Down Mailer's Way (Urbana: University of Illinois, 1974), pp. 82-123.

2. "The White Negro: Superficial Reflections on the Hipster," Advertisements for Myself (New York: Putnam, 1959), p. 341. "The White Negro" first appeared in Dissent, 4 (Summer 1957), 276-93. Jean Malaquais and Ned Polsky then argued with Mailer about his presentation in "Reflections on Hipsterism--an Exchange of Views," Dissent (Winter 1958), 73-81. Finally, Mailer held a taped interview with Richard Stern in May of 1958 which was entitled "Hip, Hell, and the Navigator." All my citations of "The White Negro" and its appendages are to the works which appeared in Advertisements for Myself. Hereafter, page references to Advertisements for Myself (AM) will appear in parentheses after the quotation.

3. Hux, p. 208.

4. Nobody Knows My Name: More Notes of a Native Son (New York: The Dial Press, 1961), p. 220.

5. Sexual Politics (Garden City, N. Y.: Doubleday, 1970), p. 317.

6. Ibid.

7. The Continuity of American Poetry (Princeton, N. J.: Princeton University Press, 1961). I am indebted to Robert Lawler for pointing out the relevance of Pearce's study to Mailer's work in "Norman Mailer: The Connection of New Circuits," Diss., Claremont 1969, p. 82.

8. Barry H. Leeds, The Structured Vision of Norman Mailer (New York: New York University Press, 1969), p. 235.

CHAPTER 2

THE HIPSTER IN FORMATION

The Naked and the Dead

In 1948, the year of publication of The Naked and the Dead, Norman Mailer had not yet formulated his concept of the hipster. Whereas "The White Negro" deals in a direct way with the psychological ramifications of living in an authoritarian, exploitative, and racist society, The Naked and the Dead is more concerned with probing the social and political surfaces of American experience. In his first novel, Mailer did not yet believe in the heroic possibilities that are inherent in his idea of the hipster. The book is what Ihab Hassan calls a novel of "outrage"; that is, "an irrational dialectic of violence threatening the human form, the very nature of man."[1] The individuals in the novel are trapped by the social, political, and geographical conditions of the past and present. Whatever attempts are made to reclaim the self tend either to corroborate the power of existing institutions or to lack the radical emotional and intellectual energy of the hipster's quest.

In his description of social reality, Mailer was very close to Marxists and to writers such as Farrell, Steinbeck and Dos Passos, who viewed American society as highly stratified, with men of wealth occupying positions of power. Although they have little opportunity to rise above the class into which they were born, the poor constantly harbor the illusion of a mobile society in which men of discipline and shrewdness can rise to the top. Mailer is quick to criticize the hopes of the poor and shows how they never materialize. His psychological concerns are evident here and elsewhere, as he is intent upon describing the emotional results of living under oppressive conditions. Finally, the social and po-

litical critique and many of the psychological concerns which
are evident in The Naked and the Dead are reflected in Mailer's later idea of Hip.

Even before Mailer formulated his aesthetic of Hip,
he was convinced that art should serve a social purpose.
About The Naked and the Dead, he stated that "I tried to explore the outrageous proposition of cause and effect, of effort
and recompense, in a sick society. "[2] He emphasized that
writing "'moves people and affects them. '"[3] Nevertheless,
he qualified his position on the didactic function of art by
stating that "'to construct a book in terms of a message, of
an effect upon people, is disastrous. Books may accompany
social movements, but the relationship is always haphazard
and unforeseen. '"[4]

Mailer's critique of American society in The Naked
and the Dead is especially based upon the Marxian emphasis
on the importance of economic reality in shaping people's
lives. Willard Thorp states that Mailer sees the actions of
the men "almost entirely in terms of the class which formed,
or more exactly, warped and frustrated each--general, lieutenant, or private. "[5] General Cummings, the most powerful man in the novel, physically resembles "any number of
American senators and businessmen. "[6] The son of a mid-
western banker, he sees economic fear and striving as the
basis for men's motives. Since he views the mass of men
as inefficient, weak, and self-aggrandizing, Cummings believes that a society can only be governed through a strict
use of power. This belief is reflected in his admiration of
the organization of the fascists and in his desire to see the
interpenetration of the economic, military, and political
spheres of government. Therefore he engages in a transaction for his brother-in-law which involves placating the
French, so that Gibraltar is not handed to the Russians.
He does this by convincing Sallevoisseux, a businessman,
and important people in the French government to support
United States policy in return for American investments of
Leeway Chemical in the firm of Sallevoisseux Frères. It
is not surprising, then, that Cummings believes in anticommunism as the eventual power in America. He is especially
concerned with "the inertia of the masses through which the
vision, the upward leap of a culture is blunted" (ND, p. 571),
a thought which is perhaps the culmination of his marriage
into the gentility of Boston.

Cummings' perception of the nature of power in the
United States is corroborated by other characters in the nov-

el. In the mining country of the Montana hills, Red does not like the fact "that The Company owns everything" (ND, p. 222). Lieutenant Colonel Conn and Hearn's father, a very successful industrialist, vehemently oppose labor unions. For all his sympathy with the oppressed and his interest in Marxism, Hearn cannot shed the influence of his background and he is expelled from the John Reed Society at Harvard because of his "bourgeois aspirations" (ND, p. 343). Nevertheless, Hearn sees World War II as an "imperialist tossup" (ND, p. 320), and thinks that America may become a fascist country after winning. Even men from families which have had to struggle to survive echo the conservative sentiments of Cummings. Croft once served in the National Guard and took great pleasure in killing a striker. Minetta believes that a powerful man is necessary to run the country. And before entering the war, Brown, who worked for a farm machinery company, acted on the principle that every man is out for himself.

If most of the men support or are resigned to the hierarchy of power in the United States, in "The Time Machine" sections of the novel Mailer portrays the sordid effects of this condition. It is here that we are given a picture of America that suggests Mailer's later preoccupation with the decay of the urban area, the homogenization of American life, and racist attitudes among various ethnic groups. He continually reiterates the idea that the individual has little possibility of escaping or transcending the influence of forces operating in the past. The manner in which Mailer piles up one detail after another about each of the significant characters creates the feeling of entrapment and oppression. Thus "The Time Machine" is viewed by Chester Eisinger as an example of "social determinism, " and by Robert Lawler as proof that "character is fate. "7 This sense of powerlessness is echoed in the "Chorus" sections of the novel, which are random statements by the soldiers about food, women, job rotation, and other G. I. preoccupations. Both devices reflect Mailer's early Marxist view that life in the United States, particularly in the Army which is the microcosm, is brutalizing because of the authoritarianism and exploitation that grow out of the nature of material conditions, especially economic reality.

Consider, for instance, Mailer's conception of urban America. Martinez lived in San Antonio's Mexican quarter which "is unpaved, and [where] little wood lean-tos sag in the heat" (ND, p. 63). Gallagher is from the Boston area where "the gray wooden houses parade for miles in a file of drabness and desolation and waste" (ND, p. 266). A Southerner, Wilson always had to face the main street which "assumed its tawdry prosperity with discomfort; it is hot and packed with people and the stores are small and dirty" (ND, p. 373). Joey Goldstein lived in Brooklyn, where the "walls of the street fester in summer, are clammy in winter; there is an aged odor in this part of the city, a compact of food scraps, of shredded dung balls in the cracks of the cobblestones, of tar, smoke, the sour damp scent of city people, and the smell of coal stoves and gas stoves in the cold-water flats" (ND, p. 480). Polack inhabited a typical Chicago house where the lock on the door is broken, the hinges have rusted, the hallway "smells like a urinal" (ND, pp. 608-09), mice scurry through the dust, and four children must sleep in the same room. For Mailer, then, there is always "the city, lashing at one's senses," with "the cigar smoke, the coke smoke, the carbolic and retch of the el ... " (ND, p. 328).

At the same time, the poor people are often antagonistic toward one another because of racial and ethnic differences. Whereas Gallagher constantly rails about the "yids," Goldstein indulges in excessive self-pity because he is a Jew and is convinced that only the "goyim" fight. Wilson calls two black children "niggers" and proceeds to humiliate them. Those with wealth and power harbor similar resentments. Conn condemns a famous labor leader for having "a nigger woman for a mistress" (ND, p. 73). Cummings is the epitome of the sense of WASP superiority and his notion of power comes dangerously close to Norris' preoccupation with racial purity and London's notion of the superman. Minetta and Martinez, the two non-white men who are treated at length in the novel, attempt in various ways to conceal or alter their racial and ethnic backgrounds in order to survive.

While Mailer is very much concerned with social and political reality in The Naked and the Dead, throughout the novel he also explores the nature of inner experience. Robert Nadon states that Mailer "uses his background materials not so much to represent American society as to reveal the individual human personalities involved."[8] He is concerned with the way in which external reality affects the emotional lives of his characters and utilizes an omniscient third-person point of view which very often involves description of thought and feeling. However, because of the nature of the

editorializing about motive and aspiration, the narrative consciousness in the novel only contributes to the sense that the
men are powerless. Whereas the hipster places greatest
emphasis upon the power of the self through the fullest development of the emotional life, in The Naked and the Dead
almost all of the characters are preoccupied with losing a
sense of their own power because of the harsh, negative conditions of the modern world. The self which they hope to
realize, however, is much more conventional than that of
the hipster. In their desire "to be someone," the characters
in Mailer's novel seek a place within the traditional structure
of American society: a place that involves more money, authority, leisure, and conventionally beautiful women.

The platoon on the island of Anopopei in the South
Pacific is composed of men from different parts of the
United States and of varied ethnic backgrounds, all of whom,
with the exception of Lieutenant Hearn, have been brought up
in squalid environments and have suffered through the depression, but keep alive the idea that some day they will be able
to realize their dreams for success and status. A recurrent
refrain is used to describe Martinez, a Mexican-American:
"(When I am big I build fly-planes)" (ND, p. 63). Gallagher
believes that "'A man can get ahead'" and says, "'I'd see
things, and I'd know I was going to be something big'" (ND,
pp. 201, 202). Wyman remarks that "'Claire really made
me feel like I could be something,'" and "'I just knew I was
gonna be a big guy someday'" (ND, p. 256). And Goldstein
thinks that "'a man has to strike out for himself if he wants
to get ahead'" (ND, p. 449). Nevertheless, Mailer does not
allow these dreams to be realized. Like most naturalistic
writers at the end of the nineteenth and during the early
part of the twentieth century, he portrays men as victims
who have little control over themselves and events. In order to emphasize their helplessness, he uses a great deal
of animal imagery to describe the men as ants, pigs, ro-
dents, salmon, insects and sardines.

In their preoccupation with the external trappings of
success, the soldiers find themselves defeated by the debilitating effects of American society or by the obstacles of
nature. The men are constantly hindered in battle by the
heat and the terrain of the land. At one point, they are
"chafed and blistered and sunburned; already some of them
were limping on sore feet, but all these discomforts were
minor, almost unnoticed in the leaden stupor of marching,
the fever they suffered from the sun" (ND, p. 505).

Social and economic obstacles are even more insidious. Most of the men have suffered through the depression
in the 1930s. Martinez quickly realized that, because of his
race and his impoverished background, he could not become
an aviator, and instead, accepted a job as a counterman.
Goldstein's dreams of going to college were never realized,
and Roth could not get a job for two years, even though he
graduated from college. "No matter what he tried, no matter how hard he worked, " Gallagher "seemed always to be
caught" (ND, p. 6). Ridges, who lived on a farm before
the war, broods about how his work always seemed to be
ruined in one night because of the capriciousness of nature.
Having been brought up in a series of decrepit Eastern coal
mining towns, Red is convinced that "Nobody gets what he
wants ... " (ND, p. 140). Though he believes that the men
in the patrol are essentially good, Red knows that they are
going to get "'the shitty end of the stick'" (ND, p. 202).

The Army itself forces the men to avoid any expression of individuality. General Cummings worries about the
American soldier's emphasis upon personal rights. Cummings believes in creating a fear ladder since the "'Army
functions best when you're frightened of the man above you,
and contemptuous of your subordinates'" (ND, p. 176). The
soldiers react against these constrictions, often in an obscene manner. In The Armies of the Night, Mailer reveals
his belief that the "noble common man was obscene ... " and
refers to The Naked and the Dead, in which the soldiers use
obscenity "to restore the hard edge of proportion to the over-
blown values overhanging each small military existence ... "
(AN, p. 47). Therefore, Red states, "'There ain't a good
officer in the world.... They're just a bunch of aristocrats,
they think. General Cummings is no better than I am. His
shit don't smell like ice cream either'" (ND, p. 128).
Minetta dislikes the "Goddam fuggin officers, " who are "all
a bunch of bastards" and "don't give a damn about us" (ND,
p. 367). Roth resents the idea that the Army wants him
for "cannon fodder" and dislikes the officers who "'slept in
staterooms when we were jammed in the hold like pigs'"
(ND, pp. 51, 52). Even Hearn, the leader of the reconnaissance platoon, echoes the sentiments of Roth and hates the
six field officers, because "they had warped the finest minds"
of his generation (ND, p. 72).

In the face of the Army's attempt to eliminate any
trace of individual expression, some of the men try to reclaim selfhood. In this quest, they often display certain

characteristics which are common to Mailer's later projection of the hipster. Valsen in his desire to maintain an in-
violable self; Hearn in his ability to suspend judgment, analyze motive, and search for power; Croft in his love of violence and his intuitiveness; and Cummings in his huge power
needs, all represent certain facets of Mailer's hipster. If
Hearn and Valsen generally align themselves with the poor
and the exploited, while Cummings and Croft generally identify with the rich and the powerful, the fact that Mailer portrays these men in terms of their shifting political allegiances is a reflection of his awareness of the complexity of
any political commitment, and corroborates what he states
later in "The White Negro," that the hipster can align himself with any political tendency, depending upon his immediate needs and the socioeconomic conditions of the moment.

The hipster is more likely to be a picaro, a man
"on the road," for whom life is a sprawling (if sometimes
dangerous) feast. 9 But in The Naked and the Dead there is
little of the intense emotional involvement or exuberant expectation that Mailer attributes to his later fictional characters, who move from one situation to another. Red "never
found anything. All he knew was what he didn't like" (ND,
p. 14). His first departure is from the Montana coal mines;
yet "In 1931 all the long voyages end in a hobo jungle" (ND,
p. 225), where he will not accept the cries for revolutionary
action. Although he slows down by taking a job in New York
and living with a woman for a few years, he wants "no en-
tangling alliances"; "if you stop and quit moving you die"
(ND, p. 234). Hearn leaves Chicago's Lake Shore to wander in and out of many jobs and relationships with women before finally joining the Army, which gives him some relief
from the sterility of his daily life in the United States. He
desperately tried to preserve his instinctual life by refusing
the deadly trappings of convention and custom, only to find
himself in the end an emotional shell, as self-sufficient as
the kelp with which he is intrigued. "Style" becomes for
Hearn the measure of success. Wary of committing himself, he does not possess the hipster's desire to "swing"
with the other person or situation; rather, he is distant,
hoping always to retain that sense of superiority which has
been bred into him.

Grace Witt remarks that for each of the men in The
Naked and the Dead, strength cannot be mixed with sentiment; they are cold and will not show emotion. 10 In fact,
at times the novel tempts one to agree with D. H. Lawrence,

who stated that "The essential American soul is hard, iso-
late, stoic, and a killer. "11 The "white Negro's" thirst for
confrontation often takes on murderous proportions here.
Croft is not only a highly intense, cruel, and vicious fighter;
he is sexually sadistic. Most critics view him as a representative of fascism, but Ihab Hassan sees him as a nihilist
characterized by frenzied self-affirmation and psychopathy. 12
While possessing attributes of both nihilist and fascist, Croft
is neither, because his political perspective is totally overshadowed by his psychological needs. The roots of his violence lie in his Texas past. In a situation which foreshadows
an experience between D. J. and Rusty in Why Are We in
Vietnam?, Croft is humiliated by his father, who shoots a
deer that the boy has tracked himself. He tries to strike
his father, who then hits him across the face, a recurrent
reaction if we are to believe Jesse's statement that "'Ah'd
beat the piss out of him, and he'd never make a sound.
Jus' stand there lookin' at me as if he was fixin' to wallop
me back, or maybe put a bullet in mah head'" (ND, p. 157).
The men who surround Croft as a child are prone to be violent, reminiscent of his ancestors who "pushed and labored
and strained, drove their oxen, sweated their women, and
moved a thousand miles" (ND, p. 164).

If Mailer suggests that the frontier experience has
transmitted styles of violence into contemporary American
life, he is equally concerned about the less obvious, urbane
forms of expression. "A Peculiarly American Statement, "
Cummings had been sent to military school by his father,
who would make a man out of his son. Before he becomes
a tyrannical General, he loses himself with his wife in his
need to "subdue her, absorb her, rip her apart and consume
her" (ND, p. 415). Hearn's father loved to watch his son
box and set him up for those football games in college, especially that "instant of complete startling gratification when
he knew the ball carrier was helpless, waiting to be hit"
(ND, p. 344). As the platoon leader, he likes the tension
of battle and command which produces in him "a suppressed
joy and excitement" (ND, p. 509), a feeling quite close to
the hipster's heightened sense of himself before the possibility of a violent confrontation and its sequel, his own death.
If he is virtually lured to death by Croft, Hearn feels that
his leadership of the platoon is "one of the most satisfying
things he had ever done. He could understand Croft's star-
ing at the mountain through the field glasses, or killing the
bird. When he searched himself, he was just another Croft"
(ND, p. 580).

The last part of this statement is not entirely true, for Croft's love of violence is far more deeply rooted than Hearn's. Croft's personality has hardened, so that he is characterized repeatedly by the statement, "I HATE EVERY-THING WHICH IS NOT IN MYSELF" (ND, p. 164). Without the philosophical vision of the hipster, who wishes to purge the darkest urges of his personality in order to grow, Croft compulsively repeats his earlier behavior. Facing the Japanese, he screams wildly, "'COME AND GET ME YOU SONS-OFBITCHES'" (ND, p. 150). When the reconnaissance platoon is assigned to beach detail during the first week of the campaign, he is dejected and longs to be in the battle that is taking place inland. He does not have the "white Negro's" courageous acceptance of the terror which surrounds death. Instead, he "believed a man was destined to be killed or not killed, and automatically he had always considered himself exempt" (ND, pp. 444-45).

There is little fear in Croft until he climbs the mountain which he considers "a personal affront" (ND, p. 527). Just as Ahab feels the need to battle Moby Dick, Croft must overpower and conquer the large, alien mountain. But unlike Ahab, whose search for the White Whale involves him in important metaphysical speculations, and pushes him into an understanding of some of the motivation behind his quest, Croft, until possibly the very end of the novel, pits himself in a much more blind and unconscious manner against the brute force outside himself. The relief that he feels when he has been unable to climb the mountain is perhaps a dim realization of how much energy he has wasted in trying to subdue everything outside himself. He is "rested by the un-admitted knowledge that he had found a limit to his hunger" (ND, p. 701). Still, in the end, "Croft kept looking at the mountain. He had lost it, had missed some tantalizing revelation of himself. Of himself and much more. Of life. Everything" (ND, p. 709).

Underlying the intensity of Croft's assault upon the external world is his intuitiveness, which foreshadows the mystical side of the hipster, especially Mailer's later exploration of Rojack. Croft possesses "a crude unformed vision in his soul but he was rarely conscious of it" (ND, p. 156). He is given to hunches, as in the early part of the novel where he is playing cards and "had a sudden and powerful conviction that he was going to win the pot" (ND, p. 8). He is wrong about this, but is able to intuit the death of Hennessey, which opens him to a sense of "omnipotence" and tantalizes him "with odd dreams and portents of power" (ND, p. 40). When he climbs the mountain Croft has the ability to know how to move from ridge to ridge: "He had the mountain in his teeth as completely and excitedly as a hound which has picked up the scent" (ND, p. 635).

In his desire for power, Croft is similar to Cummings. He is deeply resentful when Hearn assumes leadership of the platoon. When he does have power he challenges any man to usurp his authority. But unlike the General, Croft is not nearly as conscious of his own power needs and their political implications. He cannot say, as Cummings does, that "'Your average man never dares suspect that the men in power have all the nasty impulses he has, except they're more effective about carrying them out'" (ND, p. 313).

Red and Hearn are even more introspective, "philosophical psychopaths" without the latter's need to act out repressed feelings. Red has an urge to hit Stanley, but controls himself because he realizes that his anger is really directed at Croft, with whom he has just had a quarrel. He acknowledges that he wanted to ge a corporal, but he is also aware of the source of the desire. Similarly, when his power needs are aroused in an encounter with Croft, Hearn is disgusted with himself. While he is aware that he does not want to give up his commission, he knows how he has come to accept this power, and realizes that he must resist the influence and control which is offered him by the Army. Like the hipster, he sees the ambiguities inherent in every experience and continually reappraises his motives. But he does not utilize his constant search into the "rebellious imperatives of the self" in order to extend his field of action. Rather, he becomes confused, less able to act, and resentful of those whose choices appear to be simplistic. Although he is attracted to the General's "unique ability to extend his thoughts into immediate and effective action," and to the magnetism of Cummings' power, he senses his difference from the tyrant, who believed that the "'root of all the liberals' ineffectiveness comes right spang out of the desperate suspension in which they have to hold their minds'" (ND, pp. 77, 174).

The General has a vision, a sense of purpose, and the ability to act in order to realize his goals; and all of this tends to remind Hearn of his own indecisiveness and passivity. Robert Lawler states that Cummings is an existentialist "because for him every moment is a moment of crisis in which his private destiny as a leader is bound inextricably with the death-like destiny of his culture."[13] As a general he is free to make choices among the existing avenues to power. However, unlike the existentialist, for whom the present is the only reality, Cummings cannot fully exercise his freedom, because his choices have been curtailed and his attitudes defined by his past experience, especially his relationship with his parents. Therefore, toward the end of the novel, when Cummings fires the howitzer, he reveals once more his complusive need to control others and to commit violence. This is embodied in the nature of his ecstasy, a sexual enchantment with "the sharp detumescent roar of the gun, the long soaring plunge of the shell through the night sky, its downward whistle, and the moments of complete and primordial terror for the Japanese at the other end when it landed" (ND, p. 565). Yet Cummings is able to move beyond the highly personal connotations of the experience and can view it with more distance when he sees the "screaming burst of a shell" as a symbol for "All the deep dark urges of man, the sacrifices on the hilltop, and the churning lusts of the night and sleep ... " (ND, p. 566). One could argue that even here he is still projecting his psychological needs, as he does when he begins to theorize about the phallic dimensions of the shell and the earth, or contemplates the idea that men are like machines. However, he draws an asymmetrical parabola to image the rise and fall of all cultures: "It is the curve of the death missile as well as an abstraction of the life-love impulse; it demonstrates the form of existence, and life and death are merely different points of observation on the same trajectory" (ND, p. 570). To the extent that, in this instance, Cummings does not merely synthesize his experience out of a need to compulsively and unconsciously recreate earlier childhood feeling, he is close to the hipster, who seeks the widest vision and hopes to recapture and give form to his repressed impulses. For a moment, Cummings seems to have crossed the Nietzschean abyss, which he posited much earlier by stating that "'man is in transit between brute and God'" (ND, p. 323). In his desire to "mold the curve" (ND, p. 571), Cummings, perhaps, has become the "philosophical psychopath. "

Cummings' political attitudes are based upon his need for power. Robert Lawler astutely criticizes those who without qualification picture Cummings as a fascist; he is rather a "desperate opportunist"[14] who carefully calculates

that the "route to control could best masquerade under a
conservative liberalism. The reactionaries and isolationists
would miss the bell, cause almost as much annoyance as
they were worth" (ND, p. 718). His political position reflects the hipster's ability to move where the power lies.
Cummings will not be misled by the use of such words as
"liberal" and "reactionary," but will strike to the heart of
power, calculate his "profit and loss" (ND, p. 717). It is
among the reactionaries that he knows he will be able to
survive, but he is aware of their failings.

At the conclusion of the novel, Cummings has not
yet achieved the power which he seeks, even if he receives
credit for defeating the Japanese on Anopopei. While Major
Dalleson is actually more responsible for the victory, his
decisions are less important than the depletion of Japanese
military resources and a subsequent victory by masses of
American enlisted soldiers. That Dalleson has a vision, on
the last page of the novel, of what he believes is a brilliant
military innovation--a teaching device which consists of "a
full-size color photograph of Betty Grable in a bathing suit,
with a co-ordinate grid system laid over it" (ND, p. 721)--
indicates that Mailer does not yet believe that heroism is a
viable possibility.

While many critics argue that either Valsen, Hearn,
Croft, or Cummings is the hero of the novel, Richard Foster is closer to the truth when he states that The Naked and
the Dead lacks a true hero or forceful protagonist. 15 Mailer's emphasis upon man's capacity for autonomous action,
which is so central to the concept of the hipster, is not presented here. Instead, man appears to be relatively helpless
before the insidious geographical, social, and political conditions of the present. Mailer's belief that the novel "offers
a good deal of hope" is undermined by his determinism. 16

In fact, The Naked and the Dead is a fine novel precisely because of Mailer's ability to detail in a relentless
manner the horrible conditions with which the men must
struggle. His attempt to soften his determinism through the
creation of a hero who combines the endurance of Sisyphus
with the powerful self-assertion of Zarathustra is not at all
convincing. At the beginning of Part III, he presents an existential paradox from Nietzsche's Thus Spake Zarathustra:
"Even the wisest among you is only a disharmony and hybrid
of plant and phantom. But do I bid you become phantoms or
plants?" Certainly Mailer, like Nietzsche, is pushing for a

new kind of synthesis of mind and body in order to create a higher self. 17   The hipster is that synthesis, but his presence is only felt in the tendencies displayed at times by a few men, tendencies which are generally counteracted by a poisonous political and psychological atmosphere, if not by the brute physical world.   In the end, Hearn is lured to death by Croft, who regains command of the reconnaissance platoon only to exhaust himself attempting to carry out the General's grandiose military plan, which itself proves to be unnecessary.   And when he gets out of the Army, Red is hopelessly resigned to do "the same fuggin thing I always did.   What else is there?" (ND, p. 710).

The visions of both Cummings and Croft, which appear in Part III, are inadequate, given the reality before them.   In referring to Cummings' lengthy speculations, which are shallow and tonally stiff, Robert Solotaroff speaks of Mailer's "penchant for instant, borrowed philosophy,"18 a problem which haunts Mailer's later writing, where it is almost always suggested that man attains noble stature merely in the act of searching for a comprehensive vision.   Compelled by that belief to move further away from the naturalistic tradition and its emphasis upon the external limitations confronted by man, Mailer will come to create a more symbolic fictional world in which the complexity of inner experience is the focus.   In The Naked and the Dead, then, if he is more derivative than in his future work, Mailer at times uses the naturalistic tradition skillfully in order to present a world in which man is "corrupted, confused to the point of helplessness...."19

Barbary Shore

The Naked and the Dead suggests the bankruptcy of liberalism because of the failure of Hearn and Valsen to preserve their democratic values against the power and violence of Cummings and Croft.   However, Norman Podhoretz has remarked that while Cummings and Croft are reactionaries, "they demonstrate (as reactionaries often do) the workings of the radical spirit--which is to say that the principle of their behavior is a refusal to accept the limitations inherent in a given situation as final...."20   Podhoretz also states that "In Marx and Trotsky, Mailer found a system that brought the courage, vision, and uncompromising determination of Cummings and Croft into the service of freedom and

equality rather than class and privilege.... "21 This observation is especially true of Barbary Shore, where Mailer utilizes Marx and Trotsky in the form of political experience
and ideology to which each of the characters must relate.
As in The Naked and the Dead, no one survives as a successful political radical or as a hipster, but in the creation of
McLeod, Lovett, and Hollingsworth, Mailer embodies once
again ideas that he is later to use in "The White Negro."

Of greatest significance is his departure from a realistic rendering of events through the use of Lovett as a first
person narrator. Both devices indicate Mailer's dissatisfaction with the Marxian version of reality, which depends upon
a constant recognition of the primary importance of the material world. As reported in 1948, even "In the author's
eyes, The Naked and the Dead is not a realistic documentary;
it is, rather, a 'symbolic' book, of which the basic theme is
the conflict between the beast and the seer in man."22 John
Stark remarks that the surrealistic devices of Barbary Shore
"lead to a conclusion about the world that is the opposite of
the Marxists' belief that the world is solidly material, orderly, and comprehensible by means of reason. Similarly, the
aura of temporality in the novel, which is caused by the
characters' difficulty in recalling their pasts, contrasts viv-
idly with the Marxists' belief that there is an inexorable historical process moving forward in time."23 More than in
The Naked and the Dead, Mailer is concerned with the complexity of inner experience. In Advertisements for Myself,
he views Barbary Shore as a novel with "a kind of insane
insight into the psychic mysteries of Stalinists, secret police-
men, narcissists, children, Lesbians, hysterics, revolutionaries ... " (AM, p. 94). And he senses "that the direction
I took in Barbary Shore was a first step toward work I will
probably be doing from now on" (AM, p. 107).

His conception of character alters, to the extent that
the naturalistic portraits of people in The Naked and the Dead
now give way to a richer conception of personality in which
the past still plays a dominant role, but no longer totally
shapes the individual. In Cannibals and Christians, Mailer
states that Lulu Meyers of The Deer Park "is a being rather
than a character. If you study her closely you will see that
she is a different person in every scene."24 Mailer's sense
that Lulu "seemed right in her changeableness" (CC, p. 212)
is also applicable to the characters in Barbary Shore, where
the men and women are no longer developed in terms of what
D. H. Lawrence called "the old stable ego of character,"

but begin to suggest "another ego, according to whose action
the individual is unrecognisable, and passes through, as it
were, allotropic states which it needs a deeper sense than
any that we've been used to exercise to discover are states
of the single radically unchanged element. "25   Lawrence's
conception of the ego is perhaps the basis for Mailer's idea
that in the language of Hip, man is viewed "more as a vector in a network of forces than as a static character in a
crystallized field" (AM, p. 349).

Despite his increased emphasis on the nature of inner
experience, Mailer is still very much concerned with social
and economic conditions.   In Barbary Shore, as in The Naked
and the Dead, he is quick to portray the decay of modern,
urban life.   Lovett thinks of "the Negro slums ... where
children sleeping on the fire-escape would turn in their slum-
ber as the train passed, moaning a little in acceptance of
its fury even as artillery men will drowse beside their howitzer while a night mission is fired."26   The setting is
Brooklyn, where tramps are evident and charwomen scrub
all day in tenements which are falling apart.   The apartment
house inhabited by Lovett "had been a modest mansion, but
now it was partitioned into cubicles" (BS, p. 19).   Reminiscent of Polack's Chicago dwelling, Lovett's room has not
been painted for years and "had soiled to the ubiquitous yel-
low-brown of cheap lodgings.   Its surface blistered and
buckled, large swatches of plaster had fallen, and in a corner the ceiling was exposed to the lath.   Cinders drifted up
from the dock area below the bluffs to cover the woodwork.
The sash cord was broken, and the window rested in all its
weight upon two empty beer cans which served as support"
(BS, pp. 8-9).   While Lovett has great difficulty discerning
his past, he is convinced that he "was always poor" (BS,
p. 4).   For Guinevere, reportedly a former burlesque queen,
McLeod, a radical who has a job as a window dresser, and
Hollingsworth, a government police agent who claims to be
working as a clerk on Wall Street, the temptation to sell the
valued but dangerous "little object" points out the essential
economic poverty of their lives.

Lovett's sense of external conditions is overshadowed
by his inner experience.   In Cannibals and Christians, Mailer
indicates that after writing The Naked and the Dead he no
longer believed he could utilize again a third-person narrative device until he developed "a coherent view of life" (CC,
p. 209).   According to Samuel Hux, in his use of Lovett as
a narrator Mailer comes close to the existential vision of

the hipster for whom reality is grounded in the perceptions
of the individual. 27 Mailer himself calls the novel possibly
the "first of the existentialist novels in America ... " (AM,
p. 106).

The despair and anxiety of the existentialist are deeply rooted in Lovett's inability to comprehend his past, which
is so clouded that he "could never judge whether something
had happened to me or I imagined it so" (BS, p. 4). Like
the hipster, who experiences the terrible freedom of the
present, Lovett has virtually no past and therefore little
sense of the future. He can recognize nothing, not even his
age, but he is certain that his parents are dead and that he
grew up in Brooklyn. James Scott indicates that Mailer utilizes the orphan device in The Naked and the Dead, where
Valsen and Polack are essentially parentless, having left
home so long ago that they have no family ties. However,
Scott adds that the orphans of Mailer's first novel are not
"existential heroes, " but "subconscious prophets of and trans-
itions to the radically altered style and content of his second
two novels. "28 To the extent that Lovett experiences what
Heidegger describes as the sense of being thrown into the
world, he is the existentialist who must continually create
himself through his own actions.

Lovett's search into the past for his childhood and
youth is not like the hipster's attempt to release repressed
childhood impulses in order to achieve psychological growth.
Stripped of any identity, Lovett is engaged in a more fundamental search. Whereas the hipster tries to enliven his
emotional life and to widen the possibilities for himself,
Lovett attempts to hypostatize his existence by locating himself in time and space. His condition is apparently the result of wounds suffered during World War II in Europe, but
he is not even certain about that. His preoccupation with
his shattered face, which he believes has been patched up
by surgery, and his attempts to recapture the past, which
so often end up in speculations about his life in the Army,
all tend to corroborate his war experience; yet, he remarks
that Willie Dinsmore "made the assumption that I was a war
veteran, and I never bothered to explain there might be some
doubt" (BS, p. 9).

The ambiguity of Lovett's life brings him quite close
to the hipster's sense that character is amorphous and constantly changing--what Robert Jay Lifton calls "protean. "29
Lovett himself is cynical about Dinsmore, a writer who pi-

geonholes people. Preferring the hipster's "negative capability," Lovett criticizes Dinsmore for having "the kind of
mind which could not bear any question taking longer than
ten seconds to answer" (BS, p. 10).

As a novelist, Lovett is extremely self-critical and
often tears up pages very quickly, since "New ideas were
forming ... confused and often destructive" (BS, p. 58).
Possessing Hearn's ability to suspend judgment and examine
motives, Lovett continually searches out his past and evaluates his memories and perceptions, to the point where he
is rarely certain of anything. His final commitment to
McLeod and the "little object" reveals his ability to stand
alone, with faith in a highly unique and orthodox version of
political radicalism that has no institutional sanction, though
firmly based upon freedom and equality.

Because he is apparently not hemmed in by the emotional weight of the past, as all the characters in The Naked
and the Dead are, Lovett has much more of a possibility of
giving himself fully to the present. Yet he constricts himself. Unlike the hipster, who seeks the widest possible experience and utilizes the richness and diversity of the city
to aid him in his quest, Lovett spends most of his time in
his tiny room and works on a novel which he describes as
an "absurd" story with a "sentimental" (BS, p. 58) concept.
But he does get involved with the people in his apartment
house. While he grows in the novel, since he is able to recapture his earlier political radicalism and symbolically commits himself to building a better society by accepting the
"little object" from McLeod, his life does not have the dynamic emotional quality of the hipster's.

He is incapable of searching for the apocalyptic orgasm, and all of his sexual encounters are either incomplete
or not very satisfying. In fact, his sexual experience, like
the rest of his activity, reveals his precarious identity, so
that he must continually convince himself that he is real,
rather than attempt to develop some sense of mutuality with
another person. Possessing a name that really is an ironic
comment on his inability to love, only once does he remember
giving pleasure to a woman. And he becomes so involved
with her that he refuses to leave the room where they are
staying, a dim reminder of the way in which he has limited
his life to the shabby apartment house where he now spends
so much of his time.

His political experience is similarly dissatisfying.
He finds "'politics among the most pathetic'" ways that man
"'attempts to express himself'" (BS, p. 35). In the course
of the novel, he appears to remember his earlier political
involvement in a Trotskyist organization. His belief in the
possibility of spreading the revolution has dissipated because
of his sense that state capitalism and bureaucracy have e-
roded the Marxian vision in Russia. While he does not accept conditions in the United States, he does not foresee im-
provement. Lovett therefore takes the "little object" not so
much because of his political commitment, but in order
"'to elect to have a future!'" (BS, p. 304). He seeks to
establish an identity by making his past political radicalism
a present and future reality. Once the choice is made, he
appears ready to engage in serious work and study, not, as
earlier, in service of a particular organization, but alone
and with little hope. Lovett ends the novel as he does the
first chapter, repeating the same words of despair: "So
the blind will lead the blind, and the deaf shout warnings to
one another until their voices are lost" (BS, p. 312). If
Mailer has drawn from the teachings of Jesus here, the
words and rhythm of this passage also suggest the end of
The Great Gatsby, where Fitzgerald writes, "So we beat on,
boats against the current, borne back ceaselessly into the
past."[30] The sense that history is cyclical and the despair
about America's future at the end of Gatsby are transformed
by Mailer into a bitter and hopeless cry about the future of
mankind.

If Lovett represents one aspect of the political Left
in Barbary Shore, Hollingsworth represents the political
Right. Yet while many critics have attempted to read the
novel allegorically, the shifting allegiances of the complex
characters make it questionable to call Lovett the Trotskyist, and Hollingsworth the fascist. Even though most of the
characters possess a specific political orientation, Barbary
Shore possesses too much density to allow for the easy definitions of a political allegory. The book is closer to Kafka's
method in The Trial, of presenting large social phenomena
through individuals whose density of perception and feeling
explodes the boundaries of any simple political equation.

As a clerk in one of the large brokerage houses on
Wall Street and as a government agent, Hollingsworth suggests the interpenetration of the economic and political levels of control in the United States. His attempt to obtain
the "little object" from McLeod is one step in his search

for power. Nevertheless, while he works for the United
States government, Hollingsworth's politics, like Croft's and
Cummings', are a matter of expediency, given the nature of
his personality. At the end of the novel, his willingness to
sell the "little object" (should he receive it), rather than
turn it over to his superiors, makes his political commitment highly questionable.

In keeping with his departure from the naturalistic
tradition, Mailer details not Hollingsworth's past but his current life, which is characterized by emotional vacuity and
periodic violent outbursts. While the hipster's urge for the
apocalyptic orgasm is revealed in Hollingsworth's feeling that
sex is much duller the second time with the same woman,
he is too submerged in anger to experience the kind of intense gratification which the hipster seeks in "swinging"
with a woman. Moreover, there are intimations of homosexual impulses in his interrogation of McLeod, which often
brings him into close physical contact and leads him into an
emotional involvement which is at least partially the basis
for Mailer's statement in Advertisements for Myself that
Hollingsworth's "sadism and slyness were essentially com-
bined with his sexual deviation" (AM, p. 223). Like Croft
and Cummings, Hollingsworth is sadistic with women. Lannie enjoys being beaten by him. Hollingsworth acknowledges
that he has "'forced'" a woman "'to do it'" (BS, p. 110).
Lovett overhears him telling Guinevere

> how he loved her, his speech containing more ob-
> scenity than I had ever heard in so short a space,
> and in rapid succession with a gusto which could
> have matched Guinevere's description of the doc-
> tor, he named various parts of her body and des-
> cribed what he would do to them, how he would
> tear this and squeeze that, eat here and spit there,
> butcher rough and slice fine, slash, macerate, pil-
> lage, all in an unrecognizable voice which must
> have issued between clenched teeth, until his ap-
> petite satisfied, I could see him squatting beside
> the carcass, his mouth wiped carefully with the
> back of his hand. With that he sighed, as much
> as to say, 'A good piece of ass, by God.' (BS,
> p. 203)

With women, then, as with his job, Hollingsworth
searches for power and opportunities to release his violence.
However, he is extremely unconscious of his needs, and does

not even believe that any attempt to probe the nature of motivation is valuable, "'Cause we never know what's deep down
inside us ... and it plays tricks'" (BS, p. 269). Without a
desire to integrate repressed childhood feelings with the aim
of becoming more vulnerable and expansive, Hollingsworth,
nevertheless, foreshadows Mailer's presentation of the hipster because of his desire for power and the pressure of
his violence and sexuality.

McLeod is much closer to the "white Negro." He
continually searches for an ideology and a life style which
are adequate to his needs. Near fifty, he has a long history
of radical political activity, based on a Marxian perspective
which itself has undergone close scrutiny. While at first he
maintained strong organizational ties, he now refuses to submerge his own individuality for the sake of the greater cause.
In Spain and in an unnamed Balkan country he murdered
friends, because the Party believed them to have betrayed
the revolution. The guilt which he now feels over this activity is an indication of his new sense that the individual's
moral, psychological, and intellectual freedom is just as
important as the demands of the Party apparatus. In addition, he comes to believe that the revolution must alter man's
consciousness as well as material conditions. In his last
conversation with Hollingsworth, he foresees a catastrophe
unless the people in Russia and the United States can deal
with the "'fantastic atrocities and inequalities of state capitalism'" (BS, p. 284). While he believes in socialism, his
earlier Marxian vision has become more flexible, to the
point where he states that "'There is no dogma we can carry with us, no legal machinery we can invoke'" (BS, p. 285).
He envisions the revolution as "'the first time in history that
man freed of hostile environment shall be able to discover
his real dilemmas and real fulfillment if there is any'" (BS,
p. 286). Skeptical of the value of marriage, family, and
religion, he shares with the hipster the idea that human be-
ings need the greatest freedom to develop. He is especially
hopeful that socialism will make it possible for any two people to find warmth together.

In his relationship with Guinevere and Monina, McLeod
reveals his new emphasis upon the self and feeling. He married Guinevere because of a sense that he was "'frozen'" and
wanted "'to be laid against a body that's nice and warm'"
(BS, p. 76). However, he could not accept the constrictions
of family life, and found his passion for his wife and child
turning into hatred. Now he consciously attempts to nurture

his feelings for both Guinevere and Monina, although admitting "'that I must always fight with myself to keep from looking for the first train west'" (BS, p. 172). He never really lays to rest his fear that a revolution will reduce "'the brotherhood of man'" to "'a world of stinking baby carriages'" (BS, p. 249). When Guinevere demands that he sell the "little object," any possibility of a renewal of their relationship is ended. The murder at the end of the novel is not merely a reflection of McLeod's willingness to confront "'the possibilities within death' which Mailer claims in 'The White Negro' provide the 'curious community of feeling in the world of the hipster.'"31 If McLeod knowingly walks to his death, this act is also the result of his feeling that he will never be able to capture the emotional aliveness which he seeks, and is a way of convincing himself of the seriousness of his political commitment.

In Barbary Shore, then, Mailer indicates the precarious position of the radical sensibility in America. At the end of the novel, not only is McLeod killed but Lovett flees from one rooming house to another with the "little object." The fate of the radical is also revealed in the isolation of a devoted follower of Trotsky, Lannie Madison, who has been confined to a mental hospital, because for her everything becomes symbolic. Thus she merges with all that suffers, as in her identification of Ophelia, Christ, and Wing Biddlebaum. She distorts reality to the point where her finger becomes that of an exploited worker and is used as a window lock in a wealthy Newport house. Burdened by a sense of guilt for all the exploitation and oppression which exists, she often humiliates and inflicts pain upon herself as recompense. Her conception of the future is that of a tremendous prison, a reminder of the German concentration camps. In desperate need, she cannot turn to McLeod because of his past atrocities, or to Lovett, whose own identity is too precarious; instead, she seeks protection and love from Hollingsworth, whom she recognizes as the future of America.

Lannie is the most dramatic demonstration of Mailer's belief in the early fifties that an individual's commitment to radical politics is perilous and futile. Without any adequate organizational vehicle, the radical is left to shift alone in an increasingly repressive environment which can only exacerbate whatever psychological turmoil is brought to the political quest. Power in America resides in the collective sensibility of Cummings, Croft and Hollingsworth.

If Barbary Shore suffers from a sense of unreality, as has been suggested by a number of critics, Mailer's attempt to portray the plight of the radical justifies his use of the disoriented narrator and the ideological debate. Too often, however, the characters in this novel, especially McLeod, tend to become merely vehicles by which Mailer can present political and social theories. It is then that the novel loses its emotional impact and becomes extremely tedious to read. Barry Leeds is right when he states that the political views which color Mailer's first two novels "are better expressed in The Naked and the Dead, where they are often implicit and almost always integrated with the characters and situations involved, than in Barbary Shore, where they are expressed primarily in lengthy, explicit, polemical passages."32

Although he detailed the complexity of experience to a greater extent in Barbary Shore than in The Naked and the Dead, Mailer cut himself off too quickly from his aesthetic roots. He acknowledged that the literary fame which attended the publication of his first novel "had been a lobotomy to my past, there seemed no power from the past which could help me in the present, and I had no choice but to force myself to step into the war of the enormous present, to accept the private heat and fatigue of setting out by myself to cut a track through a new wild" (AM, p. 93). In the process of utilizing techniques other than those which he learned from the naturalists, Mailer did not achieve the fictional integration which he sought in Barbary Shore. He recognized his failure and stated that he "was obviously trying for something which was at the very end of my reach, and then beyond it, and toward the end the novel collapsed into a chapter of political speech and never quite recovered" (AM, p. 94).

But Mailer must be admired for his willingness to move beyond the safety of his earlier success. Like the hipster, he began the process of endless redefinition. Barbary Shore not only reveals his willingness to engage in aesthetic experimentation, but also his recognition of the limitations of his political vision. The implicit conclusion of the novel is that the individual might be better off seeking salvation without making any political commitment. Speaking before the Progressive Party in 1949, Mailer stated that neither Russia nor the United States was close to his conception of socialism, and that "people should not believe in countries and patriotism anyway" (AM, p. 410). In his concern with the limitations of Marxian theory, despite his constant preoccupation with the deteriorating economic, social, and political conditions in the United States, and in his sense of the importance of the violent and the orgiastic, it is evident in Barbary Shore that Mailer is moving toward his notion of the hipster, and an emphasis upon a transformation of the self rather than of society.

Notes

1. "The Novel of Outrage: A Minority Voice in Postwar American Fiction," American Scholar, 34 (1965), 240.

2. "The Talk of the Town," New Yorker, 23 Oct. 1948, p. 25.

3. Harry Warfel, American Novelists of Today (New York: American Book Co., 1951), p. 276. Warfel quotes Mailer here.

4. Ibid. Warfel quotes Mailer here.

5. American Writing in the Twentieth Century (Cambridge: Harvard University Press, 1960), p. 136.

6. The Naked and the Dead (New York: Rinehart, 1948), p. 81. Hereafter, page references to The Naked and the Dead (ND) will appear in parentheses after the quotation.

7. Chester E. Eisinger, Fiction of the Forties (Chicago: University of Chicago Press, 1963), p. 33; Robert W. Lawler, "Norman Mailer: The Connection of New Circuits," Diss., Claremont, 1969, p. 14.

8. "Urban Values in Recent American Fiction: A Study of the City in the Fiction of Saul Bellow, John Updike, Philip Roth, Bernard Malamud, and Norman Mailer," Diss., Minnesota, 1969, p. 346.

9. James B. Scott, "The Individual and Society, Norman Mailer versus William Styron," Diss., Syracuse, 1964, p. 101. Scott first formulated the idea of the similarity between the hipster and the picaro.

10. "The Bad Man as Hipster: Norman Mailer's Use of

the Frontier Metaphor, " Western American Literature, 4 (Fall 1969), 208.

11. Studies in Classic American Literature (New York: Thomas Seltzer, 1923), p. 92.

12. "The Way Down and Out: Spiritual Deflection in Recent American Fiction, " Virginia Quarterly Review, 39 (Winter 1963), 87.

13. Lawler, p. 21.

14. Ibid.

15. Norman Mailer (Minneapolis: University of Minnesota Press, 1968), p. 11.

16. "The Talk of the Town, " The New Yorker, 23 Oct. 1948, p. 25.

17. See Robert Solotaroff's book Down Mailer's Way for a discussion of the relationship between Nietzsche and Mailer, pp. 16-17.

18. Ibid. , p. 17.

19. "The Talk of the Town, " p. 25.

20. "Norman Mailer: The Embattled Vision, " Partisan Review, 26 (Summer 1959), p. 376.

21. Ibid. , p. 378.

22. "Norman Mailer, " Current Biography (New York: The H. W. Wilson Co. , 1948), p. 410.

23. John Olsen Stark, "Barbary Shore: The Basis of Mailer's Best Work, " Modern Fiction Studies, 17 (1971), 406.

24. Cannibals and Christians (New York: Dial, 1966), p. 212. Hereafter, page references to Cannibals and Christians (CC) will appear in parentheses after the quotation.

25. The Collected Letters of D. H. Lawrence, ed. Harry T. Moore (New York: The Viking Press, Inc. , 1962), I, 282.

26. <u>Barbary Shore</u> (New York: Rinehart, 1951), p. 127. Hereafter, page references to <u>Barbary Shore</u> (<u>BS</u>) will appear in parentheses after the quotation.

27. Hux, p. 191.

28. Scott, p. 11.

29. "Protean Man," <u>Partisan Review</u>, 35 (Winter 1968), 13-27.

30. F. Scott Fitzgerald, <u>The Great Gatsby</u> (New York: Chalres Scribner's Sons, 1925), p. 218.

31. Max F. Schulz, <u>Radical Sophistication: Studies in Contemporary Jewish-American Novelists</u> (Athens: Ohio University Press, 1969), p. 81.

32. Leeds, p. 99.

CHAPTER 3

THE HIPSTER

The Deer Park

Just one year after Barbary Shore was published,
Norman Mailer indicated in a symposium for the Partisan
Review that he was extremely dissatisfied with the movement
of America's major novelists "from alienation to varying de-
grees of acceptance, if not outright proselytizing for the A-
merican century" (AM, p. 188). He admired the artist who
would attempt to describe America's war economy and increasing authoritarianism. 1 In 1954, he reviewed the work
of David Riesman, whom he criticized for failing to explore
adequately the nature of power and capitalism in America. 2
It is not surprising that in 1955, a month after the publication of The Deer Park, he revealed his continuing concern
with the didactic function of art. Mailer stated that he wanted "to reach people and by reaching them, influence the history of my time a little bit" (AM, p. 269). However, in the
same interview, he also revealed his belief that "politics as
politics interests me less today than politics as a part of
everything else in life" (AM, p. 271).

Diana Trilling remarks that by the time Mailer was
fully involved in The Deer Park, "he realised that politics
was failing him as the material of fiction, as it had failed
him as a means of saving the world. "3 Eisenhower's Republican version of state capitalism and the erosion of democratic liberties in the anticommunist assault of Senator
Joseph McCarthy intensified Mailer's despair about American political life. Without faith in the effectiveness of radical politics, and yet with a sense of the oppressive social
and political conditions in America, in The Deer Park Mailer

44

continues to explore more fully the psychological aspects of human experience.

Synthesizing techniques and conceptions of character employed in the highly naturalistic The Naked and the Dead and the more symbolic Barbary Shore, Mailer carefully creates a real, yet phantasmagoric world where people have more of an opportunity to define themselves than in his previous work. While The Deer Park describes a world that is as oppressive as that of the first two novels, in Sergius O'-Shaugnessy Mailer projects a self-conscious narrator whose grasp of the external world and sense of his own strength are far greater than Lovett's. Not yet experienced enough to be the hipster, O'Shaugnessy's mentors are Marion Faye and Charles Eitel, who embody respectively the mystical/theological and political/artistic aspects of the hipster's quest.

Like Fitzgerald's The Last Tycoon and West's The Day of the Locust, novels which describe the corruption and decadence which permeate the American film industry, central to The Deer Park is a movie colony outside Hollywood whose name, Desert D'Or, suggests its desolation and artificiality. Unlike his two previous novels, which detail at some length the squalid conditions of life in urban America, here Mailer is concerned with the trappings of wealth and power in a more rural environment. Robert Nadon remarks that "The small town, with its proclaimed morality masking the basically immoral social ethos behind its movie-set like facade, provides the metaphor more appropriate of the human condition than the city with its admitted amoral social ethos."[4] Once inhabited by prospectors for gold, Desert D'Or is an outgrowth of this earlier materialistic venture. It is "all new" and was built "out of no other obvious motive than commercial profit."[5] With stores whose interiors resemble modern living rooms, with trees that do not bear leaves, and with hotels that consist of garishly colored bungalows and artificial creeks, Desert D'Or possesses an air of unreality and is an example of what Mailer later calls the totalitarian American landscape. Sergius directly experiences this sterility in his fenced-in house, which is "like living in a room whose walls are mirrors" (DP, p. 3). In a bar, this world is so insubstantial that one "never knew whether it was night or day ... " (DP, p. 4).

When he first arrives in Desert D'Or, Sergius feels compelled to lie about his life in order to fit in socially.

The story which he tells about himself mirrors the artificial environment: he poses as the product of a wealthy Eastern family and in the midst of a broken marriage which he can only escape by drinking. In reality, as a youth growing up in an orphanage, Sergius acknowledges that he never was sure of himself; he even doubts that he came from a particular place. Although he always feels "like a spy or a fake" (DP, p. 21), he is not as cut off from the world as Lovett. While he, too, is an orphan and has suffered from his participation in the Korean War, Sergius always retains a firm sense of the past and therefore creates a more real world, where choice is possible.

The energy of the hipster is embodied in his father's life, which was highly picaresque and included a brief stretch in prison as well as service in the Merchant Marine. Not content with his "mongrel sailor blood" (DP, p. 20), his father assumed the name of O'Shaugnessy and paraded his false Irishness. Sergius himself had many nicknames in the orphanage and, as a youth, constantly found himself fighting over his attempt to be called by his proper name. While the aristocratically sounding "Sergius" reflects his intelligence and nobility, "O'Shaugnessy" points to his capacity for feeling and his identification with the working man. His full name suggests Mailer's idea of the hipster: that vision which, according to David Helsa, is "a synthesis of intellectuality and sexuality, mind and body, sentiment and courage, experience and vitality, and also of the traditions and cultures which make up the American life."[6]

It is not in Sergius' political commitment that this synthesis is revealed. Even though he admires Eitel for having stood up to a McCarthy-like congressional investigating committee on subversion, Sergius cares "little enough about politics ... " (DP, p. 24). While by the end of the novel he has spent two months reading Das Kapital, he cannot embrace socialism. A declared anarchist, Sergius has been influenced by his father, who would talk of Bartolomeo Vanzetti, "the martyrdom in Boston and how religion was for women and anarchism for men" (DP, p. 22). Like the hipster whose anarchism allows him to embrace either end of the political spectrum, depending upon which orientation provides for the greatest amount of self-expression, Sergius is not only sympathetic to the oppressed working man--a feeling which is revived when he takes a job as a dishwasher--but is drawn to the power of the FBI, in which for a brief period of time he contemplates a career.

Nevertheless, like his father, Sergius is a picaro whose allegiances shift continually. After his father died, he ran away from the orphanage five times in three years. When he read, he chose books "about English gentlemen, and knights, and adventure stories, and about brave men and Robin Hood" (DP, p. 22). As a member of the Air Force, he not only loved combat, but also boxed in the enlisted men's tournament. Externally, his life reflected the hipster's attempt to test himself against other men and to seek out dangerous situations. Internally, however, it is not until Sergius becomes more vulnerable to people and to himself that he begins to engage in the hipster's psychological quest for more intense feeling and expanded awareness.

His machismo as well as his lack of feeling for people are undermined when he views the burned arm of a fifteen-year-old Japanese boy. He begins to realize the human implications of dropping napalm on oriental villages. While pondering a career in the Air Force, he has a breakdown and comes to Desert D'Or in order to escape the "real world" of "wars and boxing clubs and children's homes on back streets where orphans burned orphans" (DP, p. 47). Since Sergius does not deal with the political implications of his activities in the Air Force, but concentrates on detailing his moral and psychological reactions, he reveals the shift in Mailer's thinking away from political radicalism and toward the possibilities for inner transformation.

One can dispute Mailer's claim that Sergius fails to grow despite his bravery, because "he is not brave enough ..." (AM, p. 238). Sergius transforms himself to the extent that through his experience he comes closer to the "real world," which he partially masters in his growth as an artist. This mastery is also reflected in the development of Mailer's conception of his narrator.

In describing a major rewrite of the novel, Mailer states that he moved away from "a poetic prose which was too self-consciously attractive and formal," and created a voice which was more "abrupt and muscular" (AM, pp. 235, 236). Aware of his tendency to create first-person narrators who were "overdelicate, oversensitive, and painfully tender," he then decided to shape an "adventurer," a "confident young man" who possessed some "stubbornness and belligerence" (AM, p. 237). While the major changes were stylistic, Mailer was concerned with projecting a narrator who was more forceful than Lovett.

A similar process is evident in Sergius' growth as an artist. After working on a novel about the orphanage and then on one about bullfighting, he finally becomes the narrator of The Deer Park, which apparently is the book that he does write. His experience has forced him to broaden his subject matter, until finally he uses his entire life as the basis for his book. Therefore he shares with the hipster the sense of having engaged in a long inward journey that has forced him to touch his deepest impulses, all of which he uses artistically.

Moreover, Mailer's conception of the artist's aesthetic options appear to have undergone a change. As a novelist, Sergius is unlike Lovett, who describes what he sees in the limited environment of a boarding house and, in the last part of the novel, is given to recording lengthy ideological debates. The narrator of The Deer Park, in contrast, imaginatively recreates much that he has not witnessed, especially Eitel's relationship with Elena Esposito, in a more open setting. This imaginative recreation is closer to the hipster's emphasis on feeling and breadth of vision than to Lovett's more realistic, yet passive and confined, method of recording experience as it occurs. Though his presentation possesses a symbolic richness, Lovett is incapable of the more expansive vision of Sergius, whose sense of the world would be inappropriate for an amnesiac without a past and therefore with little sense of the future.

Yet, in the beginning of the novel, O'Shaugnessy appears to be as immobilized as Lovett. While he possesses some of the intuition of the mystical side of the hipster, which is revealed in the fact that he won $14,000 in a poker game just before he came to Desert D'Or, O'Shaugnessy is too weak to engage in the hipster's intense encounters with other people. If Jake Barnes of Hemingway's The Sun Also Rises is sexually impotent as a result of wounds suffered in a war, the physical results of which are emphasized as much as the vast spiritual malaise of the early twenties, Sergius finds himself incapable with women for psychological reasons only. He views Eitel, his closest friend, as one of the "few kind and honest men in the world" (DP, p. 23), a conception which Sergius is able to recognize as much too limited after his move to New York City. In fact, according to Robert Lawler, Sergius' growth is evident in his "successful escape from the older, historically charged father-figure" which corresponds, in 'The White Negro,' to the rejection of all traditional life styles."[7]

His sexuality returns in his relationship with Lulu Meyers, a movie starlet, but he is still too weak to assert himself after the manner of the hipster. He is manipulated by Lulu, whose mood and behavior continually change. Without engaging in the overt violence of Croft, Cummings, or Hollingsworth, in his painful dependency upon Lulu, Sergius indicates the sadomasochistic nature of their relationship. His comparison of their first sexual encounter with his thrill at flying a plane suggests Cummings' sexual pleasure upon firing the howitzer. Later, Sergius "could feel her as something I had conquered, could listen to her wounded breathing ..." (DP, p. 130).

Nevertheless, he does not like Lulu's suggestion of marriage, which, like the hipster, he views as a constraint upon his freedom. Ultimately Lulu leaves him, but her decision is inspired by Sergius' refusal to yield to Hollywood's attempt to capitalize on the melodrama of his life by making a movie about him in which he would have the lead role. After recognizing the way in which Hollywood played upon his worst impulses, and despite the portection offered by Eitel, who would be the director of the movie, Sergius commits himself to becoming a writer. If he makes love to Lulu again, only to be invaded by thoughts of "bursting flesh, rotting flesh, flesh hung on spikes in butcher stalls, flesh burning, flesh gone to blood" (DP, p. 229), this night is concluded with their finest rapport when he tells her of his horrible life in the Air Force. But Lulu cannot enter the "real world" with Sergius and continues to pander to the American public by having an affair with Tony Tanner, the actor with the high "Bimmler" rating, and by making movies that serve the fantasies of the American public.

Sergius, then, begins to develop the sensibility of the hipster who will not allow himself to be manipulated by others but will create for himself a life style that pushes him into direct and emotionally charged contact with the world. At the same time, like his predecessors, Hearn and Lovett, Sergius develops the ability to see the nuances in experience. In the rewrite, Mailer tried to communicate Sergius' "hard eye for the world, and his cool sense of his place in it" (AM, p. 239), and this often meant giving him more of an ability to see than in the earlier conception of the novel.

His decision to leave his home of mirrored walls and to take a job as a dish washer pushes him even closer to the "real world" as he learns of poverty again and, in his isolation, repossesses the earlier experience of being an orphan. In an interrogation by two FBI men, who have come to him after Eitel has testified before the congressional committee, Sergius shows his strength and does not allow himself to be bullied. Moreover, he realizes that part of him is a reflection of his interrogators' sensibility, a compound of force and ignorance. He acknowledges that "I touched the bottom myself, there was a bottom that time. I returned to it, I wallowed in it, I looked at myself, and the longer I looked the less terrifying it became and the more understandable" (DP, p. 326). However, as Barry Leeds indicates, Sergius "knows what he must defy and reject, but not what he must affirm and commit himself to. The social ills which Sergius sees continue to exist, and he, feeling unable to rectify them, leaves America."[8]

After a brief stay in Mexico, where he becomes interested in bullfighting and has an affair with the mistress of a novillero, two situations in which he actively courts danger and violence, he goes to New York and opens a bullfighting school. There he sees "a few girls who made for some very complicated romances" (DP, p. 353), including Dorothea Faye, whose offer to keep him he rejects. Like the hipster, he has come to embrace a dialectical conception of experience and a life of action. He thinks in "such couples as love and hate, and victory and defeat ... " (DP, p. 325). And "living with the opposites in ourselves, we move to a decision" (DP, p. 327). But "finally one must do, simply do, for we act in total ignorance and yet in honest ignorance we must act, or we can never learn for we can hardly believe what we are told, we can only measure what has happened inside ourselves" (DP, p. 326). He has earned what perhaps can best be described as an incentive for the weary, the idea that "sex was time and time the connection of new circuits" (DP, p. 319). This is a highly personal and apolitical vision which points to the hipster's credo of the apocalyptic orgasm. Richard Foster states that Sergius "has come to terms with the world that has wounded him, and like the good Emersonian fatalists that all such Mailer heroes are, he affirms it as his destined inheritance from nature and history."[9] Yet Sergius parodies the idea of destiny and is too ahistorical to feel his roots in the past. Tony Tanner, the critic, captures the solitary, apolitical quality of the final vision when he states that the "important transferences and linkings of power will in future be very private affairs, with the ostensibly important power circuits of society counting for less than the mysterious forces which work behind and through them. "10

In the end, Sergius never fully measures his revelation against his experience, because he is too young. Older than Sergius, Charles Eitel has been the major catalyst for his transformation. Eitel is the failed hipster: a man who has knowingly lost his integrity to the demands of a congressional investigating committee on subversives and to the lure of Hollywood wealth and status. On the last pages of the novel, Sergius envisions Eitel's loss of artistic desire in terms of his failure to confront and shape the real world. This vision accurately describes not only Eitel's refusal to develop his artistic powers, but also his inability to tap the deepest resources in himself which earlier he acknowledges is the most fundamental task of every person. To Sergius, he says that people should cultivate their "buried nature-- 'the noble savage' he called it--which was changed and whipped and trained by everything in life until it was almost dead" (DP, p. 121). His rejection of Eitel's recent choices and his admiration of Eitel's earlier life, especially his vision of 'the noble savage' and his capacity for self-criticism, allow Sergius to move forward.

In the past, Eitel had made many attempts to retain his political, artistic, and sexual integrity despite his need for the security of a continuous relationship with a woman and the safety of his position as a director of second-rate movies for a large Hollywood studio. Unlike the hipster, however, he cannot shed his old habits. After much anguish, he yields to his desire for money and status by popularizing his most recent serious movie script and by cooperating with the congressional investigating committee. As Robert Solotaroff indicates, even Eitel's concept of the "buried nature" is vitiated, an essentialist's vision of "a constant entity which will offer man a refuge, a kind of cleft in the rock of the world if he can only get in touch with another nature like it. "11 Therefore, with people, Eitel tends to be manipulative. Like Dick Diver in Fitzgerald's Tender Is the Night, he holds out to others a sense of their importance, only to turn them away in the end. He is consumed by the need to shape people to his own ideals, and does not possess the hipster's ability to accept and absorb the other person in the hope of changing himself. Despite his willingness to adopt many roles, character for Eitel is static, something to be molded and fixed to an ideal conception. Ironically enough, while it is impossible for him to love Elena Esposito, be-

cause she fails to live up to his expectation of a refined and
intelligent woman, he marries her out of pity, thereby mock-
ing the belief which he shares with the hipster, "that one
must grow or else pay more for remaining the same" (DP,
p. 346).

Still, Eitel's identity is protean, which is revealed in
his voice that "had a hundred things in it, " and "more than
one accent, " as well as in his reputation, that at different
times he "was an alcoholic, a drug addict, a satyr ... an
espionage agent" (DP, pp. 28, 29, 28). He likes roller
coasters, because the first drop is "'Like the black hole of
death'" (DP, p. 83). He insists that "'everything you learn
is done by fighting your fear'" (DP, p. 102). And the essence of spirit, he believes, is "to choose the thing which
did not better one's position but made it more perilous" (DP,
p. 257). He not only possesses the hipster's sense of the
possibility for growth through confronting danger and death,
but also searches for the apocalyptic orgasm: "The unspoken purpose of freedom was to find love, yet when love was
found one could only desire freedom again. So it was. He
had always seen it as a search. One went on, one passed
from affair to affair, some good, some not, and each provided in its own way a promise of what could finally be
found" (DP, p. 205).

Like the hipster, Eitel seeks out feeling for the sake
of its intensity. To lose his jealousy of Elena "was to lose
his knowledge of how she could hurt him, blessed woman
who could cause him pain after so many dozen who had
caused him nothing" (DP, p. 124). And he searches out
his motives, often with the aid of coffee and drugs, even to
the point where he uses liquor to defuse the "too large, too
complex, too directly dangerous" (DP, p. 168). He is bored
by people who will not continue a discussion because they
might "have to give up something they had decided in advance
they would continue to believe in" (DP, p. 172). After he
testifies before the congressional committee, he tells Sergius
that the only kind of self-respect is "'To be able to say to
yourself that you're disgusting'" (DP, p. 306).

No longer involved politically, Eitel is more concerned
with surviving psychologically, artistically, and morally. He
does not lend his name to any political committee, and his
latest film, which he ultimately alters, is not directly concerned with political matters. Rather, it is a study, in the
tradition of Nathanael West's Miss Lonelyhearts, of a "mod-

ern saint, " a man who gives up a successful television show,
refusing any longer to ease the suffering of his viewers, and
wanders through the slums, where he is destroyed by those
with whom he would be honest. But Eitel's temptation to ex-
ploit his mastery of Hollywood technique is too great and prevents him from developing his honest creative impulses. He
allows Collie Munshin to persuade him to make a profitable,
dishonest movie in which there is a hero acceptable to the
public.

To Marion Faye, Eitel has become despicable precisely because of the dishonesty that permeates his life.
With the courage and integrity of the hipster, Faye's life
consists of successive attempts to probe the deepest recesses of himself and others. As with O'Shaugnessy and the
older Eitel, Faye's search is apolitical. Given to extremes
of thought, feeling, and behavior, Faye creates a theology
of the devil and flirts with arcane rites, at the same time
that his job as a pimp brings him into contact with every
kind of person. Donald Kaufmann states that Faye's name
is close to ofay, the black's term for a white person, and
points to Mailer's conception of the "white Negro's" desire
for power, psychopathic disposition, and love of violence. [12]
While the quality of his thinking and experience parallels
the dynamic life style of the hipster, Marion's desire for
power is not for the realization of all the possibilities of
the self; it is a reflection of his need to control and humiliate others. Committed to total honesty of perception and
feeling, Faye cannot enter a relationship fully, since the
other person always falls short of the ideal. Thus, Faye
also lacks the hipster's desire to appropriate the best in
others and cannot maintain his enthusiasm for the apocalyptic orgasm.

As an illegitimate child, Faye was immediately cast
in the hipster's role as an outsider. With a mother from
the lower class who later became an actress and nightclub
singer, and a father who was a Prince, Marion's past suggests those extremes which later characterize his life.
Dorothea could not handle her "high strung choir boy" and
was "pleased to spoil her son, to forget him, to love him,
and to match his tantrums with her own" (DP, p. 13). His
extreme sensitivity is particularly revealed in his intense
anger. Like the hipster, he can be quite violent: in his
first fight, "he had been pulled screaming off the other boy's
neck" (DP, p. 14). Always he pitted himself against his
teachers, "smoking, drinking, doing whatever was not al-

lowed" (DP, p. 14). However, he was also a very specula-
tive boy, drawn to theology. His interest in religion involved
him in a continual search for a state of purity that could only
be attained after a willed submersion in "sinful" pursuits, including witchery and the Devil.

Like the "philosophical psychopath," Faye lives out
his earliest feelings in the hope of purging himself. While
his mother wanted him to work at a movie studio where she
had found him a job as an assistant to a well-known executive, Marion adopts Dorothea's picaresque mode of life. As
a pimp he continues to operate on the fringe of society, but
he refuses to be a slave to his business: "he kept his freedom and used it to drink, to push dope on himself, and to
race his foreign car through the desert ... " (DP, p. 15).
And he continues to stay close to violence through his job,
which makes it necessary for him to keep a gun. Although
he knows he has enemies, he refuses to sleep with his door
locked, in order to discipline himself into feeling the fear.
When an acquaintance, Paco, desperately seeks money for a
fix, Marion refuses, because he believes his compassion is
either an extension of the guilt which has been bred into him
by the social order, or the result of his fear of being physically threatened. He even admires Sergius for having killed
people and almost being killed himself, "emotions he considered interesting" (DP, p. 16).

While he possesses the hipster's need to cultivate intense feeling, his need for the apocalyptic orgasm is transformed into an obsession with the painful aspects of sexuality.
He tells Sergius, "'You find a hundred chicks, you find two
hundred. It gets worse than dull. It makes you sick. I
swear you start thinking of using a razor. I mean, that's
it ... screwing the one side, pain the other side. Killing.
The whole world is bullshit. That's why people want a dull
life'" (DP, p. 17). Marion turns to homosexuality and brief
encounters with women in order to pursue the pain that his
honesty entails, and his belief that "'There is no pleasure
greater than that obtained from a conquered repugnance'"
(DP, p. 146).

Unlike Croft and Cummings, whose sexual cruelty is
rooted in unmet childhood needs, Faye has a larger purpose,
given his religious concerns, which are close to the theology
of Hip. He projects a Manichean vision in which he would
serve either God or the Devil, "God-in-banishment" (DP, p.
331), each engaged in a war for men's souls. The conflict

between the needs of his body and his yearning for a spiritual calm is so great that he decides to try to coax Elena to
kill herself.

He becomes a synthesis of Ihab Hassan's prototypes
of saint and criminal anarchist whose historical roots are
embodied respectively in Calvin's emphasis upon conscience
and Rousseau's emphasis upon hope. [13] While ultimately he
intervenes before Elena can take the sleeping pills he has
given her, this act comes to possess more than religious
significance for Faye; he also views it as part of the hipster's attempt to search for new experiences beyond the conventional moral order. While earlier he understood his relationship with her in a manner that suggested the fin de
siècle conflict between sensuality and Catholicism, he moves
closer to Dostoevsky's Raskolnikov or Nietzsche's Superman,
for whom intensity of feeling was tied to the idea of challenging moral absolutes with the sanctity of individual belief.

As with the hipster, for Faye there is no morality,
because the conventions of society are superseded by the individual's need to cultivate intense feeling: "'Nobility and
vice--they're the same thing. It just depends on the direction you're going. You see, if I ever make it, then I turn
around and go the other way. Toward nobility. That's all
right. Just so you carry it to the end'" (DP, p. 147). He
searches for a new world, beyond nobility and vice; therefore, he imagines an atomic blast that purifies the present
of "the stench and the stink" and "the world stands clear in
the white dead dawn" (DP, p. 161).

Displaying no consciousness of social conditions, Faye
is perhaps the culmination of Mailer's search for a self that
can withstand all social exigencies and yet experience the
most intense feelings. Even with his picaresque adventures,
for Marion the external world is merely a vehicle for his
psychological explorations. The self has turned inward to
the extent that he rents a furnished house where the "furniture meant as much to his eyes as stones and cactus on the
desert flats" (DP, p. 151). He pursues the interests of the
mystic as he studies "odd books," and lays "new arrange-
ments of his Tarot cards ..." (DP, p. 148).

Faye's vision, his automobile accident, and his imprisonment at the end of the novel all suggest his inability
to survive in America. While his honesty and courage, as
well as his mystical/theological concerns, make him a full

projection of certain facets of the hipster, in the intensity of his feelings Marion becomes too isolated from others and fails to grow. Moreover, unlike the "philosophical psychopath" who experiences his inmost desires in the hope of mastering them, Marion is never able to transcend the pressure of his feelings, which drive him to a consuming self-hatred and contempt for others.

Having absorbed the experience of Faye and Eitel, Sergius O'Shaugnessy remains the only viable hero in The Deer Park. Norman Podheretz indicates that Sergius and Faye resemble Hearn, who tried to get by on style and personal integrity. 14 The Deer Park, then, explores the nature of sexual experience and inquires into mystical and theological matters, all of which suggests that Mailer has moved away from the political and social concerns of his earlier work. However, while Alfred Kazin states that "Mailer's interest in the external world has dwindled to the point where sexual power and delight ... has become a labyrinthine world in itself, "15 the novel still demonstrates that Mailer has not divested himself of his earlier political interests. The wasteland of Desert D'Or, the anarchism of Sergius and the political past of Eitel are all indications of Mailer's social and political orientation.

If in The Deer Park Mailer has created a more interesting novel than Barbary Shore, which fails to avoid the aesthetic trappings of political ideology, Mailer still has a tendency to belabor the grand idea. Just as Cummings and Croft constantly speculate about the future in terms that are hastily pulled from the western philosophical tradition, Faye, Eitel, and O'Shaugnessy offer up important ideas which are not adequately explored and therefore sometimes weigh heavily upon the novel as metapsychological bloat. Character and event become so inflated that the realistic base which is established quite early in the book is violated. Neither the demonic energy of Faye nor the exhaustion of Eitel is particularly convincing.

The fault perhaps is with the narrator. Too often Sergius extracts from his own experience and that of others a meaning that has the quality of a Joycean epiphany. Unlike Joyce, Mailer does not allow the insight to emerge organically from the experience. The notion that "sex was time, and time the connection of new circuits" is not an adequate ending to a novel in which sexuality has torturous, if not murderous, dimensions. Thus, throughout Advertisements

for Myself, Mailer suggests that he began to write essays
partly because of his inability to find an adequate fictional
form in which to embody his ideas.   In his concept of the
hipster, Mailer incorporates many of the ideas which appear
to be appendages to The Deer Park.   After fully presenting
his notion of the hipster in his essay "The White Negro, "
Mailer's next task is to locate his hero in the public arena.

The Presidential Papers

While Mailer's preoccupation with politics continued
to be equaled by his psychological interests after he wrote
The Deer Park, he was sufficiently sensitized to social and
economic problems to admit in Advertisements for Myself
that "I have been running for President these last ten years
in the privacy of my mind ... " (AM, p. 17).   His sense of
failure, however, is acute: "Defeat has left my nature divided, my sense of timing is eccentric, and I contain within
myself the bitter exhaustions of an old man, and the cocky
arguments of a bright boy" (AM, p. 17).   In addition, he
has come to believe that the forces of totalitarianism in
America have done everything to prevent a writer with any
critical acumen from surviving with integrity.   "The shits
are killing us, " he says, with "little institutional lies from
the print of newspapers, the shock waves of television, and
the sentimental cheats of the movie screen" (AM, p. 23).

Mailer is still sufficiently interested in Marx to draw
directly from Das Kapital, which provides the basis for his
ideas about the relationship among the media, commodities,
and leisure time.   Like Marx, who was concerned with the
"fetishism of commodities, " Mailer speaks more specifically
of the sexual aspect of this process: "every commodity is
festooned with sexual symbol, " so that the consumer tends
"to leave his desire to mate for the desire to hunt down his
happy and faithful fetish" (AM, pp. 431, 432).   Then, in his
discussion of what Marx called "surplus value, " the profit
that results because of the difference between the value of
what is produced by the worker and the value of his own
labor power, Mailer transforms the meaning of the concept
by taking into account the increasing importance of leisure
time and the media.   The consumer, he believes, now pays
"a disproportionate amount for the desire to work a little
less in his leisure time" (AM, p. 435).   The process is further complicated since the consumer can spend less and less,

given the taxation necessary in a war economy. What he
does spend is controlled by the influence of television, radio, and the newspapers.   Unlike the capitalism of the nineteenth century, which destroyed the body of the worker, in
the twentieth century one's capacity to respond autonomously
is limited by the power of the media.

In his attempt to change America, Mailer came to
center his attention upon the consciousness of the individual,
rather than upon the institutions which govern people's lives.
Though bitterly exhausted, he "will settle for nothing less
than making a revolution in the consciousness of our time"
(AM, p. 17).   He will "defend courage, sex, consciousness,
the beauty of the body, the search for love ... " (AM, pp.
23-24).   He is not only the hipster in the guise of the novelist, but also a journalist who "would cut the smog of apathy, gluttony, dim hatred, glum joy, and the general victory
of all that is smug, security-ridden and mindless in the A-
merican mind" (AM, p. 284).

Throughout Advertisements for Myself, Mailer writes
that he has been searching for a style adequate to what he
feels.   Frederick Hoffman remarks that Mailer moves away
from his earlier interest in the ideological, so that what is
important is not "an ideational ordering of fact, " but a "sit-
uational 'integrity. '"16   Like Whitman, who states in the
Preface to the 1855 edition of Leaves of Grass that "A great
poem is no finish to a man or woman, but rather a beginning, "17 Mailer continually redefines himself in the act of
creating a style and therefore experiments with different
writing techniques, all of which he demonstrates in the heterogeneous collection of fiction, poetry, essays, and plays
that comprise Advertisements for Myself.

In 1956, he even turned to drugs as a means of
blasting away the habits of the past, including the "heavy
unhappy prose of three generations of great radicals, and
radicals not so great (let us not mention the brick walls and
plumbers' waddings of the psychologists and sociologists I
also studied) ... " (AM, p. 284).   As a journalist for the
Village Voice, he complains that his language has become
"arch and pious, self-righteous and pompous, overambitious
and imprecise" (AM, p. 283).   More generally, he warns
that the fatal thing for a writer is "to shrink, to be interested in less, sympathetic to less, desiccating to the point
where life itself loses its flavor, and one's passion for human understanding changes to weariness and distaste" (AM,
p. 225).

Therefore he now calls himself the "General" (AM, p. 278) and is ready to battle all the pieties of his time, regardless of their political origin. For Mailer, there is "no communication unless action has resulted ... " (AM, p. 286). Yet, in an article about Beckett's Waiting for Godot, he states that "man's consciousness has increased at an incredible rate and yet his capacity to alter history, to make change, has never been more impotent" (AM, pp. 324-25). With a sense of his own historical powerlessness, he presents in one of his last columns of the Village Voice and in his essay, "The White Negro, " his "philosophy of Hip, " which emphasizes the development of the individual but in no way precludes a concern with politics.

In 1960, he considered running for Mayor of New York; at about the same time, he began to develop his notion of existential politics which, in Existential Errands, he suggests is really the politics of Hip: "I came to use the words existential and existentialism rather than Hip. Hip, I knew, would end in a box on Madison Avenue. "[18] In his stress upon the hero with a face, "a consecutive set of brave and witty self-creations" (PP, p. 6), Mailer retains the idea of the importance of the self, at the same time that he explores the nature of the social order.

The notion of existential politics is central to The Presidential Papers, a collection of essays written between 1959 and 1963, and addressed to the potential hero, President John Kennedy. Richard Gilman points out that in The Presidential Papers the personal crises treated in Advertisements for Myself "become more of a public possession, its public subject more specific and detailed. "[19] While the contents of the book are clearly political, Mailer is more concerned with the revitalization of the inner experience of Americans than with a transformation of the social order: "What is at stake in the twentieth century is not the economic security of man--every bureaucrat in the world lusts to give us this--it is, on the contrary the peril that they will extinguish the animal in us. "[20] In America, life "becomes more economically prosperous and more psychically impoverished each year" (PP, p. 4). At a time when we have used up our physical frontier, Mailer would have us explore a psychological frontier, a "subterranean river of untapped ferocious, lonely and romantic desires, that concentration of ecstasy and violence which is the dream life of the nation" (PP, p. 38).

He continues to develop his argument, advanced first in Whitman-like terms in Advertisements for Myself, that the survival of the nation is dependent upon the existence of artists who "still feel rage at the cowardice of our time which has ground down all of us into the mediocre compromises of what had been once our light-filled passion to stand erect and be original" (AM, p. 23). In The Presidential Papers, he echoes Whitman's Democratic Vistas, which laments the failure of America to develop spiritually and creatively at a time when the economic base of the country was being strengthened. Mailer states that art is "as essential to the nation as technology," and is the "last force to stand against urban renewal, mental hygiene, the wave of the waveless future" (PP, pp. 92, 145). But without Whitman's messianic sense of the destiny of American democracy, Mailer believes in the subtle and existential quality of the democratic voice which sometimes emerges from beneath the totalitarian facade.

In a preface to a later edition of The Presidential Papers, Mailer indicates that the book was inspired by his desire to be that voice and "to have [his] influence."21 No longer as concerned with problems of class as he was in The Naked and the Dead, he is more interested in the way in which both the rich and the underprivileged lose their identity by becoming part of the undifferentiated mass. Lawrence Goldman states that in The Presidential Papers Mailer sees the greatest danger not in any specific political force, but in the cultural effects of what has come to be called mass society.22 Mailer argues that television, radio, and the newspapers have an insidious effect by fostering the "mediocritization of psyches" (PP, pp. 129-30), thereby forming people as similar as commodities. This effect is nowhere better demonstrated than in American architecture, where it is often impossible, especially in urban areas, to distinguish one building from another. America, then, has become totalitarian by destroying individuality and dissent in all areas of experience and by encouraging a homogeneous style of thought, feeling, and behavior.

According to Mailer, what America needs is a political hero with a face, in order to combat the facelessness of American institutions. Without Pound's love of the aristocratic and the classical, Mailer seeks a man with the diverse abilities of a renaissance prince. The hero's politics must be existential, which argues that "if there is a strong ineradicable strain in human nature, one must not try to suppress it or anomaly, cancer, and plague will follow" (PP, p. 22). Mailer is even more emphatic when he states that "no President can save America from a descent into totalitarianism without shifting the mind of the American politician to existential styles of political thought" (PP, p. 5).

Unlike the Marxist focus on the dialectical operation of economic forces, Mailer's politics are now completely tied to his concept of the hero. In fact, he states that "At bottom the concept of the hero is antagonistic to impersonal social progress, to the belief that social ills can be solved by social legislating ... " (PP, p. 42). Foreshadowing his platform in the New York mayoralty campaign of 1969, Mailer believes that government exists to provide the individual with the opportunity to better his life. Therefore he would give people in the slums the materials and the manpower to rebuild their apartments, rather than urge the government to put up new housing projects. Economically, he is enough of a Marxist to suggest that in a period of local economic crises with rising unemployment, he would explore "the concealed nature of the waste within the industry," the roots of which lie in the "mode of production" (PP, p. 270). But while "Waste is a proper obsession for existential politics," he would descend even further into "the root of the matter-- man's private elimination of his private waste" (PP, p. 270).

Maintaining his emphasis upon the self, he tells radicals that it is better to work alone, "subtly, silently, steelfully, against the state" by joining the mass media, "not to sabotage so much as to shift and to turn and to confuse ... and hold the mirror to its guilt ... " (PP, pp. 135, 136). While he would not eliminate all legal structures overnight, he is a "constitutional nihilist" (PP, p. 144) who would dissolve them with art. In his debate with William Buckley, he acknowledges the dangers of collectivism, whether from the Right or the Left, because of its failure to allow for the fullest amount of self-expression. He criticizes the Communists who "liquidate the life of millions and argue they are the imagination of the future" (PP, p. 71). And his politics even cut through the "furious pips of protest from the Peace Movement's Left," which is totalitarian in its own way, because it utilizes "dull, moral, abstract force" (PP, pp. 26, 126).

Existential politics does not encourage "safe" slogans like "'Ban the bomb'" (PP, p. 126), but rather synthesizes different aspects of experience. Robert Lawler points out that for Mailer the "destiny of a body cell may illuminate the destiny of a nation," or the "condition of food in the digestive tract may testify to the sickness of American economics."[23] Like the hipster, Mailer seeks a politics that is concerned not only with social and economic problems but which pushes psychologically into areas of experience where the possibility of dying is greatest: "A politics devoted exclusively to the immediate needs of society murders death as absolutely as theology once massacred the possibilities of life" (PP, p. 215). He is concerned with mystery and courage, and not merely with the facts and statistics that preoccupy the bureaucrat. He is impressed, then, with the courage and search for adventure of the Southern freedom rider in the civil rights movement, and with Fidel Castro in the mountains of Cuba, before the overthrow of Batista.

Earlier, in 1956, Mailer wrote in the Village Voice that Hemingway should be drafted for President by the Democrats for his war record and his stimulating language. In the same article, he urges a "return to voting for individual men (or individual women) rather than for political ideas, those political ideas which eventually are cemented into the social network of life as a betrayal of the individual desires which gave birth to them--for society, I will argue, on the day I get the wit, is the assassin of us all" (AM, p. 312). With a war record that reveals his bravery, a mind that can digest large blocs of information, and a physical presence that projects youth and vitality, John Kennedy becomes for Mailer the potential political hero in America. In the Democratic Party of 1960, Stevenson is closest to Mailer ideologically but is too simplistic, idealistic and innocent in comparison to the "unpredictable dynamic" (PP, p. 57) of Kennedy. And Nixon·is the "apotheosis of opportunistic lead," of "ugliness," while Kennedy is as "handsome as a prince," the "heir apparent to the psychic loins" (PP, p. 59). However, without imagination and politically neuter, Kennedy must grow before he can cope adequately with American totalitarianism.

As if to corroborate his emphasis upon the self, Mailer likes Kennedy's personality and not his conventional politics. In "Superman Comes to the Supermarket," he calls him "The Hipster as Presidential Candidate," because he is not only a war hero, but his manner suggests "the poise of a fine boxer" (PP, p. 44, 45). He is a man with "a dozen faces," and possesses the "air" of one "who has traversed some lonely terrain of experience, of loss and gain, of nearness to death, which leaves him isolated from the mass of others" (PP, pp. 47, 48). Mailer hopes that he will inspire Kennedy to encourage large numbers of Americans to combat the growing sterility of their lives and reawaken instincts and feelings that have been buried so long in a totalitarian environment.

However, Kennedy fails to realize fully Mailer's conception of the hipster as political hero. Written after Kennedy had been assassinated, the preface to The Presidential Papers refers to Kennedy as the "outlaw's sheriff," who may possibly have believed "that the health of America (which is to say our vitality) depends in part on the inventiveness and passion of its outlaws."24 While his time in office was "neither conclusive nor legislatively active," it was still a period "when writers could speak across the land in intimate dialogue with their leader."25 In the essays of The Presidential Papers, Mailer is more critical of Kennedy, especially of his conventional public mind, most dramatically revealed in his willingness to allow the invasion of Cuba by an army whose "roots are in United Fruit and the Commissars of Decency ..." (PP, p. 76).

As if to echo Hearn, Lovett, and O'Shaugnessy, Mailer states that Kennedy may have lacked "some of the necessary and vital emotions of most people" (PP, p. 74). Even before Kennedy took office, Mailer revealed that he had constructed a myth in order to get him elected. He fitted Kennedy with the clothes of the hipster, not only with the hope of getting him elected, but also with the desire of moving him in the political and psychological directions suggested in "Superman Comes to the Supermarket." After Kennedy defeated Nixon, Mailer felt as if he had diluted the strength of the Left by helping to elect a man who would perpetuate the "compromises and hypocrisies of a new Democratic administration" (PP, p. 61). In one of his last papers, written in 1963, he calls Kennedy "the embodiment of the American void, that great yawning empty American mind which cannot bear any question which takes longer than ten seconds to answer" (PP, p. 183). And he adds that "we have moved as a nation, under his regime, deeper into totalitarianism ..." (PP, p. 183).

The totalitarianism "beheads individuality, variety, dissent, extreme possibility, romantic faith, it blinds vision, deadens instinct, it obliterates the past" (PP, p. 184). Americans are mired in a rootless present whose blandness is the result of the failure to take responsibility for the violence and injustice of the past. Commenting on Jackie Kennedy's television tour of the White House, Mailer regrets the unreality of her fact-cluttered presentation and says it divests the past of its emotional tone. If James, Cooper, and Hawthorne lamented the absence of an American past which could provide the historical density of established institutions against which novelists might measure the self, Mailer is more concerned about attempts by the institutionally powerful to destroy what vestiges of the past remain. This failure to take full responsibility for the past is "a defense against eternity, an attempt to destroy that part of eternity which is death, which is punishment or reward" (PP, p. 176).

Kennedy therefore perpetuates a totalitarianism which, according to Mailer, has theological as well as political ramifications. Mailer's belief, that death is not the end of life but a new beginning for the soul which has endured courageously, is reflected in his discussion of the dread which permeated America on the eve of the Cuban missile crisis. Without the courage of the hipster, who makes certain that he will not, at the time of the crisis, die badly and end in "some unendurable stricture of eternity," most Americans experienced dread, "disproportionate terror" (PP, p. 151) at the thought of death; a terror brought about by the deadness of their lives and a fear of their destiny in the hereafter. Mailer uses his theology of Hip to describe Americans who were not courageous agents of God, but had struck a pact with the Devil, the agent of bureaucracy and authoritarianism. Afraid of death, they also ignored the essential terror of life which can inspire the courageous. They approached possible extinction with apathy, and the hope that death itself would be destroyed as completely as life in a nuclear holocaust.

Mailer's discussion of dread, death, and totalitarianism, in The Presidential Papers, suggests that he now viewed his political concerns in the context of a larger cosmological vision. He states that the true war is no longer "between capitalism and communism, or democracy and totalitarianism; it is rather the deep war which has gone on for six centuries in the nature of western man, it is the war between the conservative and the rebel, between authority and instinct, between the two views of God which collide in the mind of the West ..." (PP, p. 172). The "ceremonious" conservative believes that the form of society is created by God. Given this view, the man who is born poor may be more fortunate than the rich, "since he may be judged less severely on his return to eternity" (PP, p. 172). In accord with his theology of Hip, Mailer states that the opposing view portrays man serving as God's agent and attempting to allow the poor to develop the talent, creativity, and strength which have been dulled for so long by the inequities perpetuated by the oppressor, the Devil. Mailer, then, understands the experience of the concentration camps in World War II as the depletion of the power of God--here the embodiment of inspiration and intuition--by a Devil, a representative of the institutional and the bureaucrat of repetition.

Not content to create a Manichean view, Mailer acknowledges the creative powers of the Devil insofar as that conception derives from our puritanical past. His discussion of John Kennedy emphasizes the demonic quality in the charismatic power of the President. In his description of a heavyweight championship fight, Mailer views Sonny Liston as the agent of the Devil, imaged as the "King of Hip" (PP, p. 267) and the purveyor of magic, who transcends ordinary politics as an extension of the criminal underworld of the Mafia. Mailer regrets the dried-up circuits of the past which have pushed him into rooting for Patterson, the agent of an institutionally sanctioned God, imaged as goodness in the guise of the underdog who embodies the politically liberal values of discipline, responsibility, security, and guilt.

By the time Mailer finished writing the articles which comprise The Presidential Papers, the ground of his political thinking had shifted considerably because of his new emphasis upon cosmological concerns. While his earlier analysis of material conditions, especially economic reality, gave way to his psychological interests, here he projected problems which extended beyond his attempt to explore the nature of inner experience and began to develop more fully the mystical side of his thinking which was intimated in The Deer Park and "The White Negro." When he began to try to understand psychological, political, and social phenomena by creating a cosmology, his ideas were unconvincing, if not idiosyncratic. That he was not merely using theological metaphors to describe experience, but actually believed in the supernatural, became evident in his next two works, An American Dream and Cannibals and Christians.

Notes

1. Mailer, Advertisements for Myself, pp. 187-90.

2. Ibid., pp. 190-204.

3. "Norman Mailer," Encounter, Nov. 1962, p. 51.

4. Nadon, p. 353.

5. The Deer Park (New York: Putnam, 1955), p. 2. Hereafter, page references to The Deer Park (DP) will appear in parentheses after the quotation.

6. "The Two Roles of Norman Mailer," in Adversity and Grace, ed. Nathan A. Scott, Jr. (Chicago: University of Chicago Press, 1968), p. 213.

7. Lawler, p. 67.

8. Leeds, p. 114.

9. Foster, Norman Mailer, p. 18.

10. City of Words: American Fiction 1950-1970 (London: Jonathan Cape; New York: Harper and Row, 1971), p. 355.

11. Solotaroff, p. 61.

12. Donald L. Kaufmann, Norman Mailer: The Countdown (Carbondale: Southern Illinois University Press, 1969), pp. 32, 73.

13. Hassan, "The Way Down and Out," pp. 84-86.

14. Podhoretz, p. 388.

15. "The Alone Generation," Harper's, Oct. 1959, p. 130.

16. Frederick J. Hoffman, The Mortal No: Death and the Modern Imagination (Princeton: Princeton University Press, 1964), p. 481.

17. Walt Whitman, Prose Works 1892, ed. Floyd Stovall, II (New York: New York University Press, 1964), 455.

18. Existential Errands (Boston: Little, Brown and Co.,
1972), p. 210. Like earlier compilations, this one
contains short works written mainly between 1966 and
1971. Hereafter, page references to Existential Errands (EE) will appear in parentheses following the
quotation.

19. The Confusion of Realms (New York: Random House,
1969), p. 129.

20. The Presidential Papers (New York: Putnam, 1963),
p. 200. Hereafter, page references to this edition of
The Presidential Papers (PP) will appear in parentheses after the quotation.

21. The Presidential Papers (1963; rpt. Harmondsworth,
Middlesex, England: Penguin Books, 1968), p. 7.
Hereafter, this edition of the work will be referred to
as The Presidential Papers (1968 rpt.).

22. "The Political Vision of Norman Mailer," Studies on
the Left, 4 (Summer 1964), 133.

23. Lawler, p. 118.

24. The Presidential Papers (1968 rpt.), p. 8.

25. Ibid.

CHAPTER 4

THE HIPSTER IN RECOIL

An American Dream

An American Dream is the fictional culmination of
Mailer's need to cast experience in the largest possible
mold. In the "Introduction" to Cannibals and Christians, he
distinguishes between writers who view each of their works
as separate entities and their adversaries whose "writings
are part of a continuing and more or less comprehensive
vision of existence into which everything must fit" (CC, p.
xi). Like the hipster, who seeks a new synthesis of thought
and feeling after each previous equilibrium is shattered by
his vulnerability to experience, Mailer is clearly the second
kind of writer, his growth based upon successive attempts
to widen his vision and to develop his aesthetic resources.
He states that in the very act of writing he shapes his character and pushes toward new moments of intellection. [1]

Mailer initially projected his previous novel, The Deer
Park, as the first in a series of eight books in which Sergius
O'Shaugnessy, the hipster as picaro, "would travel through
many worlds, through pleasure, business, communism,
church, working class, crime, homosexuality and mysticism"
(AM, p. 154). He hoped that the book would embrace a conception of life so broad that it would maintain the interest of
such disparate figures as Dostoevsky, Marx, Joyce, Freud,
Stendhal, Tolstoy, Proust, Spengler, Faulkner, and Hemingway. [2] Before finishing The Deer Park, Mailer decided to
allow the novel to stand alone. However, he did continue to
work on his longest book, and four fragments remain, three
of which were published in Advertisements for Myself: "The
Man Who Studied Yoga," "The Time of Her Time," and "Ad-

vertisements for Myself on the Way Out. " The other piece, "Truth and Being; Nothing and Time," appeared in The Presidential Papers. In experimenting with a first-person narrator whose vision is more expansive than Lovett's or O'Shaugnessy's, in utilizing a language that pushes beyond narrow realistic canons into broadest metaphor, and in continuing his assault on the traditional American values of success and status, as opposed to a more instinctive and emotionally vulnerable life style, Mailer reveals in these fragments the germination of the aesthetic and thematic concerns of An American Dream.

In the beginning of the novel, Rojack is similar to Sam Slovoda, from "The Man Who Studied Yoga. " Like Slovoda, who cannot fully experience his sexuality with his wife and has given up his creative impulses "as an overworked writer of continuity for comic magazines" (AM, p. 158), Rojack is bound by his success as a former congressman, television personality, author, and teacher, and is at the mercy of his wife's control over him. However, while the narrator of "Yoga" has a protean identity, in that he does not possess the same name from night to night, the fragment still focuses upon the surfaces of Sam's life, especially his relationship with his wife, and therefore mirrors Mailer's naturalistic mode in The Naked and the Dead.

Expanding upon the symbolic richness of Barbary Shore and The Deer Park, in An American Dream Mailer is unwilling to become merely "the quiet master of his craft" but ventures even further "into the jungle of his unconscious ... " (CC, p. 108). Because it lacks verisimilitude and is given to flights of melodrama in which the irrational and violent predominate, An American Dream is in the tradition of what Richard Chase calls the romance. 3 While much of the melodrama and coincidence are effects of Mailer's attempt to write a novel beyond the confines of realism, supernatural forces not only contribute to the symbolic heightening of experience, but exist, independent of the form of the novel, as part of Mailer's developing cosmological vision. If many critics have referred to the novel's title as an ironic commentary on the American dream of success and status, and as a positive assertion about the frontier dream, the title also suggests Mailer's need to create a world more real than the mythologized impulses of the past, and therefore points to a catastrophic psychological transformation, with an emphasis upon greater vulnerability to cosmic, supernatural forces.

In The Presidential Papers, Mailer states that when the western frontier ended, "the expansion turned inward, became part of an agitated, overexcited, superheated dream life" (PP, p. 39). Despite attempts by those in power in the fifties to tame the thirst for adventure, violence, freedom, and the unexpected, by emphasizing the menace of communism, Mailer believed for a while that the charisma of Kennedy might encourage an end to repression and the beginning of new growth for many Americans. Kennedy's failure to unify the life of politics and the life of myth led Mailer to project Rojack as a narrator whose concern as a psychology professor with magic, mystery, and dread supersedes his earlier work as a congressman. On the edge of a very significant psychological transformation, Rojack creates highly elaborate symbolic constructs that have cosmological import to allow for the expression of his most intense feelings. Both Mailer's and Rojack's earlier political concerns are subsumed by a new vision, a panoply of biology, politics, and psychology, and an even larger theological/cosmological frame of reference in which God, the vagina, the self, and intuition war dialectically with the Devil, the anus, institutional power, and reason.

Asked if there is a secret or hidden pattern worked out in his novels, Mailer replied: "I have some obsession with how God exists. Is He an essential god or an existential god; is He all-powerful or is He, too, an embattled existential creature who may succeed or fail in His vision?" (CC, p. 214). Moreover, his interest in Hasidic tales, which is evident in The Presidential Papers, is continued in Cannibals and Christians, where he states that "our taste for miracles has left us. Man in the Middle Ages lived with dread as a natural accompaniment to his day. His senses uninsulated by the daily use of daily drugs ..., his mind not guarded by a society which was antisupernatural, medieval man was therefore able to live with gods, devils, angels, and demons, with witches, warlocks, and spirits" (CC, p. 377). Mailer is so convinced of the legitimacy of his new emphasis that he criticizes Joseph Heller, Mary McCarthy, and James Jones for their failure to deal with the mystical side of experience, and with ontological questions about the nature of anxiety and dread. [4] For Mailer now conceives the major illness of the twentieth century to be the war between being and nothingness; yet not even Sartre and Heidegger explore sufficiently "The new continent which shows on our psychic maps as intimations of eternity ..." (CC, p. 215). And scientists, who once acknowledged the mystery of the universe by relying on intuition and metaphor, are now engaged in experiment and research in order to further the limited end of technological development. [5] Mailer therefore likes Bellow's Henderson the Rain King, which inches closer to the "Beast of mystery" (CC, p. 127) than any earlier American novel. In An American Dream, Rojack believes that men are afraid of murder, "not from a terror of justice so much as the knowledge that a killer attracted the attention of the gods; then your mind was not your own, your anxiety ceased to be neurotic, your dread was real. Omens were as tangible as bread." [6]

Close in conception to Marion Faye, of "Advertisements for Myself on the Way Out," whose concern with growth leads him to commit a murder in the hope of becoming emotionally reawakened, Rojack murders his wife and encounters one dangerous situation after another in order to free himself from the pressure of the past. Unlike Bellow's Herzog and Malamud's Levin in A New Life, two fictional characters whom Mailer criticizes for being "passive, timid, other-directed," and "pathetic" (CC, p. 100), Rojack is the "philosophical psychopath" who must purge himself of violence and test his courage in order to love beneficently.

However, Rojack's control over his life is severely limited, since he so often merely reacts to the feelings and behavior of others. He does not consciously journey into himself, but is literally thrown back into the past to relive situations which he has refused to deal with courageously. The central experiences were an encounter with a German soldier in World War II and a variety of confrontations with his wife, all of which tend to reappear in different guises, many of them metaphorical, when Rojack becomes emotionally involved in the present. In addition, like Sergius O'Shaugnessy of "The Time of Her Time," Rojack seeks the apocalyptic orgasm only to find himself blocked by the pressure of his anger, which, in its intensity, recalls the battles of a child with its parents. With Deborah, and even Cherry, he seeks maternal protection, which is suffocating but also allows him a modicum of security. As for Barney Kelly and the other less powerful men in the novel, they promise Rojack only treacherous authority. While his childhood is never described, Rojack must purge himself of the feelings aroused by these "surrogate" parents before he is capable of the apocalyptic orgasm.

In order to communicate Rojack's tumultuous experience, Mailer utilizes his hero as a first-person narrator
with a gift for language, especially metaphor, that pushes
the novel to a mythic and allegorical level. Mailer's use
of metaphor echoes his earlier admiration of Picasso, who
bridged "the animate and the inanimate, to recover the infantile eye which cannot distinguish between a pitcher and a
bird, a face and a plant, or indeed a penis or a nose, a
toe and a breast" (AM, p. 461). He likes Picasso's circu-
lar exploration which "moves along the route of the association, and so any exploration of reality must travel not from
object to object but from relation to relation" (AM, p. 462).
The artist is constantly sinking back "into that ocean of e-
quivalents" (AM, p. 462) where everything is interchange-
able. The first literary projection of this artist is Marion
Faye in "Advertisements for Myself on the Way Out," who
possesses "the fluid consciousness of a God," and can travel "from the consciousness of one being to the emotions of
another--a house, a tree, a dog, a cop, a cannibal, all e-
qual to my hunter's eye and promiscuous ear" (AM, pp. 513,
515). In "Truth and Being; Nothing and Time" the narrator
remarks that "meaning dissipates, sound presents its attrac-
tions," and "metaphors live ... with the power of mechanical laws" (PP, p. 272). Both fragments and the essay on
Picasso point to An American Dream, where Rojack's psychological crisis shatters his usual sense of his relationship
to people, objects, and events. The traditional boundaries
between the self and the external world are severed, so that
the vision is often close to that of a child for whom the
world is one vast sensorium, dominated by intense feelings
of love, anger, and fear.

Unlike his first three novels, where Mailer is more
likely to remain within the boundaries created by the deno-
tative quality of words, An American Dream draws on the
more connotative resources of the language and pushes toward
the looser mode of expression of Why Are We in Vietnam?
Like the language of Hip, which relies upon nuance and elaboration to capture the intensity of experience, Rojack's language is often highly suggestive, very rhythmic, and almost
poetic in the texture of its imagery. Howard Harper speaks
of Mailer's new "organic prose style": "From the earlier
fidelity to rhythms of everyday speech he has moved to a
new synthesis of rhythm, sound, and emotional tones, and
overtones."7 However, at times, interlocking clusters of
images often suggest the surrealists, whom Mailer criticizes
in The Presidential Papers for failing to communicate pre-

cisely. If he accuses them of allowing "The charge" to
come "more from sound than from meaning" (PP, p. 211),
a similar observation holds true for some of the more rhap-
sodic passages in An American Dream. Betrayed by the
absence of meaning in their civilization, the surrealists
shift the aesthetic act "from the creation of meaning to the
destruction of it" (PP, p. 211). In An American Dream, as
Mervyn Rosenthal states, Mailer's language becomes "anti-
social in its refusal to communicate with that society it feels
so much contempt for."[8]

Alienated from America, Rojack has recourse to a
vision that is barely intelligible. However, in "The Metaphysics of the Belly," which appeared in The Presidential
Papers, Mailer states that "the modern condition may be
psychically so bleak, so overextended, so artificial, so plas-
tic--plastic like styrene--that studies of loneliness, silence,
corruption, scatology, abortion, monstrosity, decadence,
orgy, and death can give life, can give a sentiment of beauty" (PP, p. 282). Mailer's sense of the diseased social order now turns into an interest in scatology, in which the
quality of feces reflects the quality of man's life and the social order in which he lives. According to the narrator of
"Truth and Being; Nothing and Time," in the twentieth century "We are drawn to shit because we are imperfect in our
uses of the good" (PP, p. 274). Rojack's disaffection is so
great that at the end of the novel he leaves the stench and
rot of America's personal and physical landscape for Guate-
mala and Yucatán.

Rojack's retreat from America and the world begins
in the first chapter of the novel. As a former war hero and
friend of the late President, John Kennedy, he is well situated for public life. However, his sensitivity to the psychological "abyss" (AD, p. 2) distinguishes him from the former
President, who pursued a life of power and prestige. Once
an overly intellectual college student with a "sweaty near-
adolescent style" (AD, p. 2), Rojack does not develop the
hipster's need to test himself in dangerous situations and to
confront the possibility of his own death until he is pinned
down before two German machine guns in World War II.
Unlike Croft, who instinctually climbs the mountain and kills
the Japanese without externalizing the basis of his power,
Rojack locates his power and desire to kill the Germans in
an outside force, especially the moon. When he loses a
sense of this force, his courage dissipates. The experience
ends with the haunting reminder that at the charge of the last

German soldier, Rojack failed to encounter him bayonet to bayonet as the force dictated, but instead fired at close range.

In the process of developing more fully his concern with cosmological powers to which the individual must be sensitive if he is to become the hipster, Mailer comes to embrace a modified version of Reich's conception of orgone energy. Not only does Rojack move "from fantasy as a psychological illusion about the world to the use of fantasy as a somewhat self-conscious but exuberant display of his own inventive powers," as suggested by Leo Bersani, [9] but he experiences an energy radiating from without, and at times it controls his feelings and behavior.

Andrew Gordon has already pointed out that in An American Dream Mailer takes Rojack through a Reichian journey in which "'social mask' and Freudian 'unconscious' are penetrated in an attempt to reach the 'biological core.'"[10] But Mailer goes further: he draws upon Reich's belief in the existence of a bio-energetic, plasmatic moving substance inside the individual. For Reich, self-realization could take place only if the individual were allowed to come into contact with the streaming "orgonotic sensations" within.[11] In his essay, "The Schizophrenic Split," he describes the emotional turmoil of a woman by stating that she is terrified of these sensations which she transforms into a delusion of forces from beyond. Roger Ramsey has indicated that in Why Are We in Vietnam? Mailer has drawn directly from this essay in his presentation of D. J., whose fascination with the lights of the Aurora Borealis and concomitant desire for his friend, Tex, coincide with the woman's preoccupations in Reich's clinical study.[12]

In An American Dream, Mailer pictures Rojack not only as a man who can achieve psychological equilibrium by allowing himself to experience the Reichian "orgonotic sensations," but as capable of coming through his dilemma only when he can fully acknowledge the existence of outside forces. The pressure to avoid these forces is quite great because of the accompanying physical and psychological dangers as well as the social ostracism that is likely to result. Rojack's quest in the novel is to rid himself of the repressed feelings which transform the powers into a malign influence capable of pushing him to suicide and destruction. By pointing to an indefinable force outside man, Mailer moves even further away from his earlier Marxian viewpoint which had grounded

all power in the material world.   The emphasis upon the
mystical side of the hipster gives even greater thrust to
Mailer's concern with a transformation of the self rather
than the social order in his attempt to bring about a revolution in his time.

It takes many years for Rojack to open himself again
to the influence of the powers which moved him in the confrontation with the Germans.   With the help of Eleanor
Roosevelt, he is elected to Congress, but loses a crucial
part of himself to the demands of public life.   He is haunted, however, by the eyes of the fourth German, and finally
departs from politics to become a professor of existential
psychology at a university in New York.   There, he advances
the thesis "that magic, dread, and the perception of death
were the roots of motivation" (AD, p. 8).   The author of a
book, The Psychology of the Hangman, Rojack also has his
own television show.   It once catered to the counter-culture
of his time, but he has succumbed to the pressure of the
broadcasting industry, which has forced him to transform
the show from a dynamic platform for dissent into just another popular program.   As much as he has tried to retain
his integrity, he is trapped by the intellectual demands and
the discipline of his job as well as by his relationship with
his wife, Deborah.

His marriage was a planned attempt to obtain institutional power.   Deborah's ancestry clearly reveals her ties
to various levels of power in business, church, aristocracy,
and state.   Alternately murderous and suicidal, Rojack
clings to Deborah, despite her constant criticism and man-
ipulativeness, because of his "secret ambition to return to
politics" (AD, p. 17).   But he also possesses the hipster's
desire to retain the best of another person.   And Deborah
has "a winner's force" (AD, p. 18), a strength which Rojack extracts to make himself more vital.   She has so much
power that Rojack envisions her control over him as a reflection of her psychic abilities, which he tends to equate
with the power of the more beneficent moon.   But he also
senses that the moon possesses a force that can take him
to his own death as well as to new levels of growth.

Before his first walk on the parapet, he speaks to
the host at a party and wonders about Deborah's faithfulness,
which he doubts to the point of such frustration that he vomits the food of the evening over the balcony.   Feeling the
pressure of the moon, the "platinum lady with her silver

light" (AD, p. 12), he once again experiences the dissolu-
tion of his ego that took place in Germany. On the balus-
trade, he feels the urge to jump radiating from the moon,
but he also experiences the feeling that he has not yet done
his life's work. Later, with Deborah, he states: "There
are killers one is ready to welcome, I suppose. They offer a clean death and free passage to one's soul. The moon
had spoken to me as just such an assassin. But Deborah
promised bad burial" (AD, p. 26). He recognizes that the
moon pushes him to heighten his life through a confrontation
with the possibility of his own death in a fall from the balus-
trade, while at the same time reinforcing the urge to suicide
developed in his relationship with Deborah.

To combat that urge to suicide, he murders Deborah
after she announces the end of her love for him, boasts of
the prowess of another man, and demeans Rojack for his experience with the Germans, his ragged appearance, and his
relationships with other women. Utilizing the aesthetic of
Hip, which emphasizes the moral complexity of experience,
Mailer makes this murder a central situation in the novel.
Unlike Clyde Griffith in Dreiser's An American Tragedy and
Raskolnikov in Dostoevsky's Crime in Punishment, Rojack
experiences no remorse after the act. Many critics have
claimed that An American Dream is morally outrageous, because Rojack escapes unpunished, and the reader is manipulated to sympathize with him. Philip Rahv certainly passes
accurate moral judgment upon the act: "Only in a hipster's
phantasy is society so easily cheated of its prey and only in
his phantasy can the self become so absolutized, so unchecked
by reality, as to convert itself with impunity into the sole
arbiter of good and evil."[13] Alive, Deborah gives him her
energy and social connections, both of which he is terribly
dependent upon at the time of the murder. Killing her makes
it impossible for him ever to return to the security which
she offered and pushes him even further into the "rebellious
imperatives of the self." Afterwards, Rojack feels like a
pleased twelve-year-old, his hatred passing from him "in
wave after wave, illness as well, rot and pestilence, nausea
..." (AD, p. 31).

Like the hipster, who seeks the apocalyptic orgasm,
Rojack's quest is at least partially a sexual one. Caged by
her Catholicism and an aristocratic idea of grace, Deborah
cannot conceal the anger which is aroused by a lusty encounter. Her sense of "the swish of the devil" is a symbolic
transformation of impulses denied for so long that she has

even convinced Rojack to believe in "devils, warlocks, omens, wizards and fiends ... " (AD, pp. 35, 37). For Deborah, the cosmological forces are always malign, an extension of her own repressed past which confuses Rojack, who would open himself to the unseen but in her bed finds only "oppression close to strangling on my throat" (AD, p. 37). Making love with her leaves Rojack "with no uncertain memory of having passed through a carnal transaction with a caged animal" (AD, p. 34).

In murdering Deborah, Rojack tries to reclaim himself sexually and experiences "some desire to go ahead not unlike the instant one comes in a woman against her cry that she is without protection ... " (AD, p. 31). After the murder, he seeks out the maid, Ruta, in two separate encounters, the second of which results in "one hot fierce streak of fierce bright murder, fierce as the demons in the eyes of a bright golden child" (AD, p. 56). In the initial encounter, his sense of being a "healthy alley cat" (AD, p. 42) is also lost in his anger. Given his need to view everything in its metaphorical and cosmological richness, he is preoccupied with her anus, imaged as a "raid on the Devil," rather than with her vagina, the seat of the "Lord" (AD, p. 45). Penetrating both anus and vagina, Rojack ultimately ejaculates in the former. In this choice, he finds that "A host of the Devil's best gifts were coming to me, mendacity, guile, a fine-edged cupidity for the stroke which steals, the wit to trick authority" (AD, pp. 44-45). If he is not consciously frightened of the police at this moment, he is still searching for the resources with which to survive. More importantly, he is too consumed by his hatred of Deborah to be able to choose Ruta's vagina. At a moment of entry, he even says, "'You're a Nazi'" (AD, p. 44). Here, he suggests his homosexual impulses, which are revealed in his experience with the Germans, one of whom he laboriously describes as possessing an "overcurved mouth which only great fat sweet young faggots can have when their rectum is tuned ... " (AD, p. 4). When killing this man, Rojack "pulled the trigger as if I were squeezing the softest breast of the softest pigeon which ever flew, still a woman's breast takes me now and then to the pigeon on that trigger ... " (AD, p. 4). Rojack's meetings with Shago Martin, the black entertainer, and Barney Kelly are suffused with a similar combination of violence and sexuality.

With Cherry, however, Rojack moves closer to the sexual experience of the hipster. The sense of being in control and maintaining power over another, so evident in his relationship with Deborah and in his encounter with Ruta, is replaced by a new sense of equality where Rojack and Cherry meet on a Lawrentian plane beyond ego and will. Before they make love, Rojack visits her in the bar where she sings. There he opens himself to the cosmic powers made available to him by her energetic presence and his sensitivity to himself. His brain "had developed into a small manufactory of psychic particles, pellets, rockets the length of a pin, planets the size of your eye's pupil when the iris closes down" (AD, p. 97). He engages in what might ordinarily be construed as a paranoid response to the people in the bar, but, because of his own exuberance, is more likely meant to be understood as a statement about his newly found strength. Yet he still must purge himself of the past and vomits "with all the gusto of a horse on a gallop, cruds, violations, the rot and gas of compromise, the stink of old fears, mildew of discipline, all the biles of habit and the horrors of pretense ..." (AD, p. 101). And in bed with Cherry he moves through a series of moods, including the sense that "the membrane of my past had collected like a dead skin to be skimmed away" (AD, p. 127).

Fortified by the regurgitation of his past, the murder of Deborah, the encounter with Ruta, and his ability to outwit the detectives and a prize fighter, Rojack now has the hipster's ability to sense the mood and feeling of another person. He possesses a new sense of power that is fully realized in what for him is his finest sexual experience, and for Cherry, her first orgasm. No longer preoccupied with the anus, he seeks her vagina. Having dispensed with her diaphragm, which Mailer indicates throughout The Prisoner of Sex is one more technological contraption that prevents both man and woman from assuming full responsibility for their acts, Rojack is convinced that Cherry will conceive a child from this experience, in stark contrast to Deborah's sterility. He has a greater sense of his past defeats, a realization which extends beyond himself to a knowledge of "all the compromised souls of the dead up from the river and cobblestones permeated with the horse wagons of the last steep century ..." (AD, p. 131).

With Cherry, he has moved beyond the social world of class and status which he experienced in his sexual encounters with Deborah. Possibly a double agent for Mailer's totalitarian adversaries, Russia and the United States, Deborah "smelled like a bank" and possessed a womb which is described as "the filthy-lucred wealth of all the world" (AD, p. 34). From the lower class, Ruta "deadened the head of my heat," because she presents to him "A virulent hatred, a detailed specification of the hardest world of the poor, the knowledge of a city rat ..." (AD, p. 44). Immediately after his first orgasm with Ruta, he has a vision of "a huge city in the desert.... For the colors had the unreal pastel of a plastic and the main street was flaming with light at five A. M." (AD, p. 46). This description suggests Las Vegas, that "jeweled city on the horizon" with "spires rising in the night," where the "jewels were diadems of electric and the spires were the neon of signs ten stories high" (AD, p. 269). Yet, with Cherry, he moves closer to "some quiver of jeweled cities shining in the glow of tropical dusk" (AD, p. 31), a vision Rojack first had after he killed his wife. As Tony Tanner states, these different jeweled cities "may indicate the two aspects of the creative-destructive dream which man has imposed on the American continent in his continuing loving and raping of the land."14 But Rojack also rejects the small town, with its hypocritical morality and its dulled sensibility. His description of Cherry's Southern past includes not only his sense of "raw red promise" but also "stubborn will, something compromised, inert, and full of gas, something powerful and dull as her friends ..." (AD, p. 109). Like Huck Finn and Natty Bumppo, Rojack ultimately casts off all his social ties and is left at the end of the novel ready to light out for the territory.

The murder of Deborah not only forces an investigation by the police, but brings Rojack into contact with other representatives of American society: the producer of his television show, the chairman of the psychology department, a Mafia leader, and an international business magnate (his father-in-law), all of whom are portrayed as cowardly, manipulative, and dishonest. The detectives will use any means to extract a confession from Rojack, who is interrogated close to another room where a black man is beaten for failing to admit to an alleged criminal offense. Too repressed to acknowledge his own hostility, one patrolman has the kind of face one sees among "young killers who never miss a Mass until the morning after the night they go berserk ..." (AD, p. 88). And Roberts, the chief detective, beats his wife for no explained reason the night after he arrests Rojack. The photographers who huddle outside the police station possess a different kind of rapacity. Reminiscent of the paparazzi in Fellini's movie La Dolce Vita, they are "a pack of twelve-year-old beggars in some Italian town, hys-

terical, almost wild, delighted with the money they might be
thrown, and in a whinny of fear they would get nothing" (AD,
p. 73).

Both the producer of his television show and the chairman of the psychology department try to force Rojack into re-
signing. A caricature of the psychoanalyzed, Arthur, the
producer, uses the phone conversation to discuss his own
anxiety and the needs of the television industry. Dr. Tharch-
man, "Good old Protestant center of a mad nation" (AD, p.
143), talks of how he has defended Rojack's esoteric academic interests in the past, and asks him to take a leave of absence.

While he is not a blatant conformist like Rojack's immediate supervisors, Ganucci has given up his life to the
world of crime and is now dying of cancer. For Mailer,
cancer is the biological result of repression; that is, the
wild eruption of similar cells is the body's answer to a continual loss of self which takes place through a failure to a-
chieve honest emotional expression. If Ganucci is a member of the underworld and, therefore, like the hipster must
live with danger constantly, he has confined his life to the
demands of organized crime, which forces him to be as disciplined and dishonest as if he were the head of a large corporation. At the end of the novel, Rojack views the face of
a man who died of cancer: "It could have been the face of
a man who owned his own farm or had been the local banker. It was lustful and proud, much hate in it, but disciplined. A general could have been cousin to that face. Maybe the discipline did him in; all that desire and all that com-
pression of the will clamped on one another in some spew of
the private states, the pressure continuing into that instant
when the dissecting knife went into the belly" (AD, p. 266).

An autopsy indicated that even before her murder,
Deborah had been dying of cancer. But her father, Barney
Kelly, the most powerful man in the novel and perhaps the
most disciplined, is alive and well. From a working class
Irish family, Kelly has become wealthy by stealing $3000
from his father and speculating on the stock market. Then
he opened an interstate trucking concern with another man
in Kansas City, where he met Leonora, whom he married
because of her wealthy and aristocratic relatives. Now Kelly
has "'strings in everywhere from the Muslims to the New
York Times" (AD, p. 237), including the CIA and the Mafia.
Physically, he has a "pronounced resemblance to a particular

president and particular prime minister ... " (AD, p. 219).
His home contains tapestries, sculptures, paintings, musical instruments, and furniture from all over the world. "Aristocrats, slave owners, manufacturers and popes had coveted these furnishings until the beseechments of prayer had passed into their gold" (AD, p. 235).

However, unlike Cummings, whose power is rooted in the material world, Kelly's control has satanic dimensions. In his portrayal of Kelly, Mailer reveals once again a cosmological vision which embraces his earlier social and political concerns. For Mailer, even the smell which emanates from an individual indicates a particular disposition. If Kelly's Waldorf apartment encourages Rojack to sense "some antechamber of Hell" (AD, p. 234), the smells emanating from Kelly suggest the Devil and the anus, both of which are linked in an associative chain with Kelly's institutional and financial power. Rojack describes the "deep smell" which "came off Kelly, a hint of a big foul cat, carnal as the meat on a butcher's block, and something else, some whiff of the icy rot and iodine in a piece of marine nerve left to bleach on the sand. With it all was that congregated odor of the wealthy, a mood within the nose of face powder, or perfumes which leave the turpentine of a witch's curse, the taste of pennies in the mouth, a whiff of the tomb" (AD, p. 217). On the parapet, "a gout of the stench which comes from devotion to the goat came up from him and went over to me" (AD, p. 253).

Impressed with Rojack's theology of Hip, Kelly even conceives of himself as the Devil. In order to maintain his financial and power base among the Caughlins, he "drilled" his "salt" into Leonora, and "took a dive deep down into a vow ... 'Satan, if it takes your pitchfork up my gut, let me blast a child into this bitch!'" (AD, p. 240). If Leonora's difficulty in conceiving suggests the similar problems of her daughter, Deborah, Kelly's entire life mirrors Rojack's to the extent that both utilize almost any means to obtain wealth and power. Yet Kelly's sense of cosmic powers is always tied to his desire to obtain institutional control, while Rojack's concern with the ultimate mysteries is the result of his need to return to a more pristine self. After Kelly begins an affair with Bess, Leonora's distant cousin, he uses her powers, imaged in witch-like terms, in order to increase his holdings on the stock market. With the belief that "'There's nothing but magic at the top,'" he is tempted to engage in an incestuous sexual pact with Bess and her daugh-

ter, so that he might have "'the opportunities of a president
or a king'" (AD, p. 246).

Unlike Rojack, Kelly never gives himself fully to his
frightening feelings. When he experiences incestuous desires
for Deborah and then suicidal impulses to jump from a building, Kelly immediately decides to send his daughter to a con-
vent. Rojack's walk around the parapet contrasts starkly
with Kelly's unwillingness to engage in a similar act and his
attempt to cause Rojack to fall; the walk is also the culmination of Rojack's assault upon the cosmic, institutional, and
personal power of Deborah and her father.

In the confrontation with Kelly, Rojack possesses the
courage of the hipster, who will not shrink from dangerous
physical and psychological situations. Earlier, he is tempted
to confess out of fear of the new psychological and cosmological forces to which he has become vulnerable. Rojack, nevertheless, comes to feel like "some new breed of man" (AD,
p. 81). Like the hipster, he is energized by danger and experiences "the sweet panic of an animal who is being tracked
..." (AD, p. 75). As Barry Leeds states, Rojack possesses
the legacy of the American black, a sense of dread which allows him to survive. 15 At the police station, he identifies
with the black man who is beaten in an adjoining room. In
his encounter with Shago Martin, Cherry's former lover, Rojack becomes the "white Negro" at the same time that his
black counterpart is beginning to capitulate to the white world.
Allan Wagenheim speaks of Rojack's recognition that "the Hip
philosophy is not only psychopathic but 'deranged and doomed,'
that it is a decision to court defeat, to choose for suicide,
all of which is underscored by the fate of Shago Martin."16

Yet Shago does not fail as a hipster. As if to assume
Shago's earlier and more natural role, Rojack wears the robe
of the singer, who is now dressed in a conservative suit.
Merely a month away from taking over Rojack's spot on television, Shago is a famous entertainer who has sought to please
by developing many voices, until he finally became harsh,
his "mind racing between separate madnesses, like a car
picking its route through the collision of other cars" (AD, p.
183). He realizes that he has become a "'lily white devil in
a black ass,'" with a "'heart'" that has been "'snatched'" (AD,
p. 189). Purging himself of the violence that has been contained for many years in his relationship with Deborah and
in his highly cerebral and controlled public life, Rojack confronts the jealous, taunting Shago, who is armed with a knife,

and beats him decisively. Believing Harlem to be shaken by
the black man's defeat, Rojack feels compelled to face retribution, but allows himself to be taxied to Kelly's apartment.
With the hipster's knowledge that "God was not love but courage" (AD, p. 204), Rojack believes that his failure to make
this journey is partially responsible for Cherry's death, even
though he obeys "the message" and walks the parapet before
Kelly, to whom he has confessed the murder of Deborah.

Depressed and disoriented at the end of the novel, to
the point where he tries to telephone Cherry, Rojack is ma-
rooned in Las Vegas, the end of his final journey through A-
merica, before he leaves for Guatemela and Yucatán. After
his first sexual encounter with Cherry, Rojack heard the
whistle of a locomotive and speculated about the first trains
which one hundred years ago "had torn through the prairie"
(AD, p. 131) and ravaged the natural landscape. In Las
Vegas he is subjected to endless billboards, mass-produced
cars, and monotonous hotels, air-conditioned to make the
one hundred and ten degree heat sufferable. Since America
is ultimately imaged as hell, Mailer becomes one more modern novelist for whom the very landscape has become an assailant. 17

Still possessing the intuition of the hipster, Rojack
wins enough money to pay off his debts. However, totally
isolated and shattered, he appears unable to purge himself
of the emotional vestiges of the past. To argue, as Tony
Tanner does, that Rojack is "moving out beyond the world's
mirror towards some placeless city of his own imagination"18
is to suggest too strongly a resolution of his anguish. In
South America, he will still have to deal with his failure to
save Cherry, his reluctance to go to Harlem, and his inability to walk the parapet a second time with Kelly. If he has
achieved his finest orgasm, purged his violence, and momentarily loved, he is drained of energy at the end of the novel.
His decision to leave for South America is a reflection of his
inability to survive in the United States, where the pressure
of external reality is too great for his ravaged sensibility.
In Yucatán, he seeks an isolation which may be able to temper his pain. Thus, despite his sudden willingness to explore his terrifying feelings and to confront physical danger,
all of which is embraced by his cosmological vision, Rojack
is the hipster who fails to achieve a dynamic equilibrium because of the alien nature of his environment and, given the
terms of the novel, the limited nature of his courage.

Cannibals and Christians

While highly critical of many aspects of American society, An American Dream describes people of wealth and position without probing into the complexities of life at the bottom. In Cannibals and Christians, Mailer laments the failure of the aristocratic tradition of the novel of manners to merge with the proletarian tradition of the realistic novel, so that a more comprehensive vision of American life could be developed. 19 Reminding writers that they are "the last liberators in the land" (CC, p. 103), Mailer develops more fully his notion of totalitarianism in a collection of essays, interviews, poems, short stories and book reviews, most of which had appeared earlier in a variety of magazines. However, unlike The Presidential Papers, Cannibals and Christians describes the deterioration of America in apocalyptic terms: "The sense of a long last night over civilization is back again; it has perhaps not been here so intensely in thirty years, not since the Naxis were prospering, but it is coming back" (CC, p. 2). The possibility for the appearance of a hero or the development of a movement capable of resisting the forces of American totalitarianism is considered by Mailer to be minimal. According to Donald Kaufmann, for Mailer, totalitarianism has become "so rooted in American life that any 'Resistance' through politics would cover too small a part of the culture. "20

Thus Mailer's conception of his own role as a catalyst for change has altered. Intending to analyze "an unknown illness, a phenomenon which partakes of mystery, nausea, and horror," he sees himself more as a "physician" than as a "rifleman" (CC, p. 5). Where he spoke in Advertisements for Myself of his private desire to become President, in Cannibals and Christians he states, "I don't know if I want power any more" (CC, p. 255). Yet he is critical of writers like Faulkner and even Hemingway, who are not concerned with saving "souls," or the "nation" (CC, p. 99), a task which in our time has been taken over by the conservative Luce magazines. Mailer is still concerned with making a raid on the "Godawful Time Magazine world ..." (CC, p. 221). But he is more interested in being "clear in my mind," since "The compromises one has to make in acquiring power dull the brain irreparably" (CC, p. 255).

Continuing his search for "metaphors to fit the vaults of modern experience" (CC, p. 310), Mailer never fails to remind his readers of the cosmological vision which embraces his social critique. Wilfrid Sheed refers to the "hallucinogenic" quality of Cannibals and Christians. 21 And Max Schulz suggests that Mailer's "shift from advocacy of social action to enthusiasm for spiritual nodes" is at least partially the result of his growing doubt that the individual can withstand the pressure of the totalitarian state. 22 In fact, the longest piece in Cannibals and Christians, "The Political Economy of Time," is a metaphysical dialogue in which all of Mailer's concerns appear associatively linked. Here, and in other essays, Mailer's notion of the hipster and his political interests become even more deeply embedded in a mystical conception of life.

While the totalitarian "plague" is first presented as a "mysterious force" (CC, p. 3), Mailer does describe its visible manifestations quite fully. "Aesthetically emaciated buildings," "nonspecific diseases," deadened sexuality, poisoned food, deteriorated products, an electrified landscape, surrealistic wars of carnage, and faceless politicians, all are the result of a world which consists of "Cannibals" and "Christians" (CC, p. 3). Just as he maintains that God and the Devil are good or evil, depending upon the perspective of the viewer and the forces operating in a given situation, Mailer reveals his dialectical conception of experience in his definitions of "Cannibals" and "Christians." Born Christian, yet titillated by violence, the "Cannibals" are the political Right Wing, whose various elements share the belief that the world can be saved "by killing off what is second-rate" (CC, p. 4). With little interest in Christ, but maintaining faith in the goodness and perfectibility of man, the "Christians" are left-liberals on a political spectrum that includes Lyndon Johnson and Mao Tse-tung, as well as moderate Republicans and Bolsheviks. Since the "Christians" have much greater power, Mailer holds them responsible for the wars of the last twenty-five years and the deteriorating environment. 23

As in The Presidential Papers, Mailer is particularly sensitive to the physical quality of his surroundings. An airplane reminds him not only of a "child's plastic nursery," but suggests "another of the extermination chambers of the century--slowly the breath gives up some microcosmic portion of itself, green plastic and silver-gray plastic, the nostrils breathe no odor of materials which existed once as elements of nature ..." (CC, p. 7). In describing a room in the San Francisco Hilton hotel, he speaks of the "huge puff of a modern chandelier made up of pieces of plastic," a carpet of "electric plastic green," and bridge seats "covered in

a plastic the color of wet aspirin ... " (CC, p. 13). In the
city itself, Mailer notices the "monstrous boxes of Kleenex
ten, twenty, thirty stories high through the downtown section,
and the new view from Telegraph Hill had shards of glass
the size of a mountain wall stuck into the soft Italian landscape of St. Francis' City" (CC, p. 6). By emphasizing the
theological connotations of the city's name, Mailer transforms
his architectural criticism into a religious observation about
the tendency of Americans to divorce themselves from any
real concern with ultimate questions. He is even more direct when contemplating American buildings which are flat at
the top, unlike the towers, gables, and spires of the past,
which are reminders "that every previous culture of man attempted to engage the heavens" (CC, p. 234). Building cities
up into the sky would not only stop the growth of the megalopolis, but also would once again arouse in man the hipster's
sense of "awe and elation, of dignity and self-respect and a
hint of dread ... " (CC, p. 237). As if to recall Rojack's
walk on the parapet, Mailer acknowledges that most people
would be unwilling to venture so high off the ground for fear
of the feelings that would be aroused in them.

Even with his religious concerns, in considering the
source of the environmental plague Mailer constantly points
back to his earlier Marxian emphasis in his description of
"Monstrous corporations in combine with monstrous realtors"
(CC, p. 6), who are not only intent upon making a profit,
but upon creating a world that reflects the monotony and
deadness of their lives. In no way encouraging the development of a truly vital sensibility, according to Mailer, the
institutionally powerful make it more likely that the hipster
will survive in the slums which, in their decrepit buildings
and dirty streets, at least demand that an individual mobil-
ize some of his best resources. Without the courage of
Franklin Delano Roosevelt or John Kennedy, Lyndon Johnson
cannot offer "high style to the poor" (CC, p. 52). He is en-
visioned as the modern dictator, who will cater to the tendency to erect "faceless buildings and roofless roofs ... " (CC,
p. 51).

In Cannibals and Christians, Mailer virtually abdicates
any hope for the survival of the hipster as a political figure.
If he became disenchanted with John Kennedy, at least that
man provided artists with an atmosphere in which their work
might receive a hearing from the most powerful in America.
In 1968, Mailer called a miscellany of his writings on the
Kennedy and Johnson administrations The Idol and the Octopus,

a title he once planned to use for The Deer Park: "The Idol was to represent Charles Francis Eitel, the artist; the Octopus was Herman Teppis, the producer, and the man of power. Here I use it to characterize two administrations.... "24 No doubt remembering his 1965 anti-war speech at Berkeley, in which he suggested that the president's picture would soon be found everywhere, upside down, he dedicates Cannibals and Christians to Lyndon Johnson, with the cynical caption, "whose name inspired young men to cheer for me in public" (CC, p. vii). In fact, the last piece in the book is "The Last Night: A Story," which possesses a brief introduction indicating its applicability to Kennedy and not to Johnson. Here, the unnamed president must consider the possibility of destroying the earth, made radioactive by the atom bombs of another United States president and other world leaders, and of sending one hundred people, including himself, to some distant region of the solar system. With a sense of his awesome responsibility, the president asks all Americans to vote on the proposal.

Imaged as Caesar throughout Cannibals and Christians, Johnson is not interested in participatory democracy, but represents the worst of a "liberal Establishment obeisant to committees, foundations, and science ..." (CC, p. 43). Unlike the hipster, who seeks power that comes from continually redefining himself in dangerous situations, Johnson tries to solidify an ego, nourished by his political manipulation in the past. With "vast competence, no vision, and the heart to hold huge power," Johnson erects forty-foot-high posters of himself at the 1964 Democratic convention, and proceeds to become the "organization boss to whom all mafias, legit and illegit, all syndicates, unions, guilds, corporations, institutions, cadres of conspiracy and agents for health, Medicare, welfare, the preservation of antibiotics, and the proliferation of the Pentagon could bend their knee" (CC, p. 43).

No longer a country of adventurers, the United States produces public figures without sufficient imaginative or emotional reach for Mailer. Scientists do not possess the diversity of interests and ability of their counterparts in the nineteenth century, but are laboratory technicians, trapped by their love of the rational and incapable of thinking intuitively and metaphorically. Most literary figures have compromised their vision, so that the "aristocratic impulse clawed at the remaining fabric of a wealthy society it despised ..." and the realistic tradition failed to produce a novel "which would ignite a nation's consciousness of itself' (CC, pp. 102, 101-

02). Finally, with a sense of the "ambiguity present in the hard Marxist front of [his] ideas" (CC, p. 55), given his emphasis on personalities and mysterious forces and not on material conditions, especially economic reality, Mailer continues to look for the hero on the political scene but fails to find him.

The men about whom Mailer speaks positively are Robert Kennedy and John Lindsay, not so much because of what they offer, but out of fear of the political alternatives. In analyzing the 1965 New York mayoralty campaign, Mailer announces that he will vote for John Lindsay since William Buckley of the Right is too out of touch with the poor and obsessed with bombing Communist China, and since Adam Clayton Powell of the Left, although an "undisputed genius" (CC, p. 63), makes unfortunate political alliances. In the New York senatorial contest, Mailer is frightened that Robert Kennedy will become a powerful leader of the Right. But unlike his mediocre opponent, Kenneth Keating, Kennedy is an active principle. With the hipster's ability to sense the ambiguity of political allegiances, Mailer will vote for the possible hero: "a hero, even a failed-hero, or a hero-as-monster, is more likely to create other heroes, by his example or by opposition to him, than a man who gains power and has never been anything at all" (CC, p. 58).

Similarly, in describing the 1964 Republican national convention, Mailer evaluates the famous and lesser personalities according to the standards established in his earlier pieces on the hipster and the existential political hero. He is highly critical of Goldwater and his followers, the "Cannibals" from "Main Street" (CC, p. 16), who in the guise of freedom cling to the authoritarian values of the family and the nation with a tenacity that can only lead to a violent confrontation. With the literary eye of a Marxist intent upon a class analysis, he describes them as "the old doctors of Pasadena with their millions in stock and their grip on the A. M. A. , the small-town newspaper editors, the president of the second most important bank, the wives of Texas oil ..." (CC, p. 16). Scranton, Goldwater's major adversary, represents the liberal wing of the Republican party, the "Christians," who are composed of eastern corporate interests, especially Wall Street, and alienated young people, the descendants of Holden Caulfield.

Utilizing his dialectic, Mailer, whose sympathies are almost always with the Left, admires "the heft of a political

jockstrapper like Goldwater," as he does not Scranton, part
of whose soul "seemed to live in the void" (CC, p. 15).
Mailer likes Goldwater, whose raw and rugged projection of
himself suggests the hipster's need to purge his violence.
Earlier, in The Presidential Papers, Mailer spoke of "his
obsession with violence" in The Naked and the Dead, and
his "secret admiration" (PP, p. 136) for characters like
Croft, who were extremely violent. If Goldwater is the descendant of Croft, Scranton is reminiscent of Hearn and embodies the suicidal impulses of the beatnik who "wished for
immolation rather than power ..." (CC, p. 28). Moreover,
Goldwater has a face, a clear political position and a personality to embody it, which in its iron totalitarianism might
give birth to an underground. Mailer has the sense that "The
heart of the beast had loosed a primitive call. Civilization
was worn thin in the center and to the left the black man
raised his primitive cry; now to the far Right were the ma-
niacal blue eyes of the other primitive. The jungles and the
forests were readying for war" (CC, p. 34). For a moment,
he even hopes that Goldwater might win the election in order
to avoid four more years of Johnson, whose remedial pre-
scriptions for the poor and the alienated might co-opt dissent.

If Mailer has little hope for the appearance in America of political figures who will move the country in a desirable direction, he is even more pessimistic in his evaluation of the international scene. As in Barbary Shore and The
Presidential Papers, he still views America and Russia as
two totalitarian states, "malignancies upon the spirit of honest adventure and open inquiry which developed across the
centuries from primitive man to the Renaissance ..." (CC,
pp. 79-80). He acknowledges that America has "grown rich
because of one fact with two opposite interpretations: There
has been a cold war. It has been a cold war which came
because communism was indeed a real threat to our freedom,
or a cold war which came because capitalism could not survive without an economy geared to war; or is it both--who can
know?" (CC, p. 78). De-emphasizing external threats to A-
merica, Mailer believes that the survival of communism depends upon an aggressive adversary from the capitalist world
and primitive economic conditions, all of which necessitates
the discipline only an entrenched bureaucracy can provide.
While still admiring Marx, Mailer criticizes post-Marxian
ideology, "which cannot change remotely so fast as reality
and so must be insulated from reality by war" (CC, p. 87).
He is certain that contradictions in ideology within and among
various Communist countries can only lead to internecine war-

fare. Even if they solve economic, social, and political problems, Mailer is certain that the Communists will find that their ideology does not speak to the deepest needs of man.

Implicit in his criticism of both Russia and the United States is the idea advanced in The Presidential Papers that the future does not belong to the superstates, but to that third force emerging slowly around the world of brave, talented, and generous people. The audience that he would "like to be good enough to write for" is not only the politically and ideologically disenfranchised, but those who have "no tradition by which to measure their experience but the intensity and clarity of their inner lives" (CC, p. 220). Given his cosmological orientation, he is especially interested in the "Wealths of primitive lore" possessed by "backward lands" (CC, p. 8).

Therefore, in "The Political Economy of Time," Mailer attempts to transcend ideology and to speculate about his political and aesthetic concerns in a philosophical framework which focuses upon mystical notions such as "soul" and "spirit." Interestingly enough, this piece was written during the same year as An American Dream, in which both Rojack and Cherry enliven the world by using these terms in the course of their quest for authenticity. It is tempting to believe that in the early sixties Mailer moved in a totally new direction to embrace an other wordly mysticism. And yet, read closely, "The Political Economy of Time" reveals that Mailer presented in metaphysical guise ideas which were offered earlier in The Deer Park and "The White Negro." He utilizes the interview as his mode, because it is "dialectical" (CC, p. 250). Seeking people to create inventive forms, Mailer notices only the expression of the totalitarian sensibility, the passion "to abstract form into monotony" (CC, p. 368). Elaborating upon the metaphysical dimensions of the hipster's struggle, he acknowledges that everything which "is alive, or intent, or obsessed, must wage an active war: it creates the possibility for form in its environment by its every attempt to shape the environment" (CC, pp. 370-71). Only in the art of the absurd does Mailer see any interest in the complexity of form. And yet this art is based upon the annoyance and interruption in a totalitarian world cluttered with the dissonance of automobile horns and construction noise. In one of his interchapters, Mailer states that we live in a time "which interrupts the mood of everything alive ... " (CC, p. 248), and then, in "The First Day's Interview," refers to the importance of mood which, for him, unlike the Marxists, takes precedence over matter.

Moreover, in his discussion of form, Mailer focuses upon the soul and moves even further away from the material world. Form is dependent upon the perceiver, human or inhuman, whose soul, through memory, shapes an object, person, or event. The highest form is the "Vision" which "may be beatific, heroic, epic, contemplative, tragic, harmonious, or even Faustian," and is dependent upon the instinct of the soul to sense or comprehend, and the resistance thrown up "by all those forces in the world, whose desire is to frustrate every soul in this attempt" (CC, p. 329). A transcendental counterpart to the courageous self of the hipster, the soul obtains nourishment "from growth and victory, from exploration, from conquest, from pomp and pageant and triumph, from glory" (CC, p. 341). Echoing the hipster's quest in "The White Negro" and Eitel's vision in The Deer Park, Mailer states that if the soul "does not grow, it must pay more for remaining the same" (CC, p. 346). The death of the body in which it was housed forces the soul into "the most existential of conditions ... a time of voyages and anguish, and loss, the diminution of its properties" (CC, pp. 331-32). With the hipster's urge to impinge on people and events, the soul, although passive and acted upon by its environment, tries to locate itself in an object or person in order to perpetuate the form of its being.

After his discussion of the nature of soul, Mailer turns to his idea of spirit. Without form, but possessing a function, a spirit is never really alive and tends to be without a delineated existence. In a spirit, something vital has died, so that habit rather than innovation predominates. Extending his metaphysical speculations into the realm of the political, Mailer refers to the spirit of the total corporation as "A mind without a body. A soul which died forever" (CC, p. 356). The plague in America ultimately becomes for Mailer a more powerful force standing beyond spirit but sharing its tendency to deaden the soul.

While not alluded to in "The Political Economy of Time," the Vietnam war is mentioned repeatedly in Cannibals and Christians as America's attempt to relieve the plague through the massacre of an alien people. After dismissing the political and economic arguments usually offered by the United States government and its critics about the

Vietnam war, Mailer, in accord with his increasing emphasis upon the self, offers a more psychological explanation.
Speaking existentially about minority groups, Mailer does
not refer to racial or religious categories but to men who
possess a particular sense of their own lives. "What characterizes a member of a minority group is that he is forced
to see himself as both exceptional and insignificant, marvel-
ous and awful, good and evil. So far as he listens to the
world outside he is in danger of going insane. The only way
he may relieve the unendurable tension which surrounds any
sense of his own identity is to define his nature by his own
acts ..." (CC, p. 77). In Vietnam, then, Lyndon Johnson
merely acts for all America, since nearly everyone is a
member of a minority group. Bombarded with an "impossible mix of camp, redneck, civil rights, street violence,
playboy pornography, and all the glut which bugs our works"
(CC, p. 89), Lyndon Johnson and many other Americans
were pushed to an intolerable level of frustration which could
only be relieved by a violent external engagement such as the
Vietnam war.

As in his discussion of the sensibility which provided
the energy for this military engagement, Mailer is very critical of the American people. Despite the recurrent refrain
that the time may give rise to a new kind of man or sink
into cancerous conformity, the tone of almost all the pieces
in Cannibals and Christians suggests that Mailer really believes that the American government and a majority of the
people seek to eliminate dissent and diversity and provide a
home for mass man. When Mailer resurrects the hipster
in his future work, he does so with an even greater sense
than before of the almost insurmountable perils of surviving
with any degree of emotional and intellectual honesty in contemporary America.

Notes

1. Mailer, Cannibals and Christians, pp. 107, 221.

2. Mailer, Advertisements for Myself, p. 477.

3. The American Novel and Its Tradition (New York:
   Doubleday, 1957).

4. Mailer, Cannibals and Christians, pp. 113, 118-19,
   139.

5. Ibid., p. 308.

6. An American Dream (New York: Dial, 1964), p. 204. Hereafter, page references to An American Dream (AD) will appear in parentheses after the quotation.

7. Howard M. Harper, Jr., Desperate Faith: A Study of Bellow, Salinger, Mailer, Baldwin and Updike (Chapel Hill: University of North Carolina Press, 1967), p. 118.

8. "The American Writer and His Society--The Response to Estrangement in the Works of Nathaniel Hawthorne, Randolph Bourne, Edmund Wilson, Norman Mailer, and Saul Bellow." Diss., Connecticut, 1968, p. 122.

9. "The Interpretation of Dreams," Partisan Review, 32 (Fall 1965), 606.

10. Andrew Mark Gordon, "A Psychoanalytic Study of the Fiction of Norman Mailer," Diss., Berkeley, 1973, pp. 30-31.

11. Wilhelm Reich, Character Analysis, trans. Vincent R. Carfagno, 3rd ed. (New York: Farrar, Straus, 1972), p. 421.

12. "Current and Recurrent: The Vietnam Novel," Modern Fiction Studies, 17 (1971), 427-29.

13. "Crime Without Punishment," New York Review of Books, 25 March 1965, p. 3.

14. Tanner, City of Words, p. 361.

15. Leeds, p. 145.

16. Allan J. Wagenheim, "Square's Progress: An American Dream," Critique, 10 (1967), 67.

17. Frederick Hoffman uses the expression "the assailant as landscape" throughout The Mortal No.

18. Tanner, City of Words, p. 364.

19. Mailer, Cannibals and Christians, pp. 95-98.

94 / Norman Mailer

20. Kaufmann, Norman Mailer: The Countdown, p. 66.

21. "One-Man Dance Marathon," New York Review of Books, 21 Aug. 1966, p. 33.

22. Schulz, Radical Sophistication, p. 100.

23. Mailer, Cannibals and Christians, p. 4.

24. The Idol and the Octopus (New York: Dell, 1968), p. 12.

CHAPTER 5

THE HIPSTER AND THE RETURN TO POLITICS

Why Are We in Vietnam?

In Advertisements for Myself, Mailer spoke of the debilitating effects of social communication, which require the
artist to "accept the sluggish fictions of society for at least
nine-tenths of one's expression in order to present deceptive-
ly the remaining tenth which may be new" (AM, p. 287).
He was especially concerned with the forms of social communication provided by cinema, radio, television and the
newspaper, which create a "debased common denominator"
(AM, p. 287). Yet in the melodrama of An American Dream
and Why Are We in Vietnam? which contains, in addition,
an eighteen-year-old narrator with a raucous, slangy voice
who fashions himself a radio disc jockey, Mailer transmutes
the forms of popular culture into art.

For Mailer, a revolutionary vision could be captured
aesthetically if one

> will explore not nearly so far into that jungle of
> political economy which Marx charted and so o-
> pened to rapid development, but rather will engage
> the empty words, dead themes, and sentimental
> voids of that mass-media whose internal contradic-
> tions twist and quarter us between the lust of the
> economy (which radiates a greed to consume into
> us, with sex as the invisible salesman), and the
> quiet of the economy which must chill us with au-
> thority, charities for cancer, and all reminder
> that the mass consumer is only on drunken fur-
> lough from the ordering disciplines of church,
> F. B. I. and war. (AM, p. 437)

Acknowledging the relevance of the passage quoted above to
Why Are We in Vietnam?, Richard Poirier states that the
narrator's voice "manages to incorporate nearly every kind
of cant one can hear on the airways of America."1 However, Poirier does not sufficiently emphasize the radical
stance of the parodist in so many of D. J.'s banal outbursts.
As a narrator, D. J. possesses a spontaneous style that runs
counter to the rehearsed interview or taped television show,
both of which Mailer criticized in The Presidential Papers
and Cannibals and Christians as highly controlled and therefore falsified attempts to present a segment of reality. In
Why Are We in Vietnam? Mailer echoes the style of William
Burroughs, whose prose "has the snap of a whip," with
words that "come out in squeaks, spiced with static, sex
coiled up with technology like a scream on the radar" (CC,
p. 117).

Two years after the publication of Why Are We in Vietnam? Mailer talked about the deterioration of the American
language, which

> has become a conveyer belt to carry each new A-
> merican generation into its ordained position in the
> American scene, which is to say the corporate
> technological world. It can deal with external de-
> scriptions of everything which enters or leaves a
> man, it can measure the movements of that man,
> it can predict until such moment as it is wrong
> what the man will do next, but it cannot give a
> spiritual preparation for our trip to the moon any
> more than it can talk to us about death, or the in-
> ner experiences of real sex, real danger, real
> dread. (EE, p. 289)

Mailer has criticized the prose of American national leaders
for being just so flat. In Cannibals and Christians, if Mailer criticizes Bobby Kennedy for possessing "a dead stick's
prose," he shrinks from Lyndon Johnson's "totalitarian prose"
which dulls consciousness "with sentences which are nothing
but bricked-in power structures" or which "slobbers upon an
audience a sentimentality so debauched that admiration for
recklessness is inspired" (CC, pp. 57, 51). In Miami and
the Siege of Chicago, Hubert Humphrey's phrases are described as "building plots in sub-developments, each little
phrase was a sub-property--the only trouble was that the
plots were all in different towns, little clichés from separate speeches made on unrelated topics in distinctly differ-

ent years were now plumped down next to each other in the
rag-bag map of his mind. "2

However, in Why Are We in Vietnam? D. J. utilizes
the slang of a Harlem "Spade" and a white, hip Texas adolescent. His voice is essentially discordant, which encourages Poirier to state that the style of this novel "is mimet-
ic of the arts of the absurd" in its emphasis on discontinuity
and interruption through shifts in context, mood, and language. 3 The decreative impulse which surfaced in An American Dream is suggested here, and also in the density of
D. J. 's punning, which often shatters communication because
of the range of associations attached to a given word. 4 D. J.,
then, utilizes the language of Hip which Mailer described
earlier in "The White Negro" and depicts in The Armies of
the Night in his portrayal of the black demonstrators who
"signaled to each other across the aisles, and talked in
quick idioms and out, an English not comprehensible to any
ear which knew nothing of the separate meanings of the same
word at separate pitch ... " (AN, p. 102).

Nevertheless, D. J. manages to present an intelligible,
syncretic vision of America. As in An American Dream,
Mailer's notion of the hipster and his radicalism are embraced by cosmological speculations. While in An American
Dream he points to an extraterrestrial force as a controlling
power in the universe, in Why Are We in Vietnam? Mailer
tends to root these cosmological speculations in material
conditions. If Rojack has a secret romance with the phases
of the moon, D. J. is more attuned to the source of energy
emanating from the center of the earth, the electromagnetic
field. Less concerned with God and the Devil, but still recognizing man as the principal agent in their eternal war,
Mailer places more emphasis on forces grounded in the physical universe which have their human psychological counterparts. In addition, he is more explicitly ambiguous in his
presentation of these forces. That source of power which
Rojack sought to assimilate without the interference of his
repressive past is no longer viewed as beneficent in Why
Are We in Vietnam? Here, God is imaged as a beast who
says to man, "'Go out and kill--fulfill my will, go and
kill'.... "5 While he suggests that D. J. 's sense of God,
like Rojack's suicidal impulses aroused by the power of the
moon, might be the externalization of repressed feelings,
there is too much evidence in Why Are We in Vietnam?,
which is corroborated in his later work, that Mailer now
believes man to possess instinctual murderous impulses
which are grounded in the nature of the universe.

The decision made by D. J. to meet the "wizard" (WV, p. 208) in Vietnam is Mailer's way of describing the intensity of these feelings. For D. J. has developed an acute sensitivity to the hypocrisy and repressiveness of American institutions. Without a fully developed political consciousness, he is closer to a radical vision of America with an emphasis on change, growth, and individual expression than to a conservative approach, which he criticizes in his continual fusillades against the consolidated power of the corporations and the United States government. His ostensible happiness about his coming departure for Vietnam is not based upon a political analysis, but upon the need for the liberation of his most intense feelings, especially his murderous impulses. Mailer's belief, first expressed in Advertisements for Myself, that in a time of crisis the hipster might turn to the Right for power rather than to "the moribund liberalities of the Left" (AM, p. 374), may be suggested here. However, D. J. 's final exclamation, "Vietnam hot dam" (WV, p. 208), is uttered without an awareness of its political implications, but as a joyful anticipation of the possibilities for individual growth in dangerous and violent confrontations.

D. J. , then, is a very special "white Negro. " As the narrator, he continually tries to confuse the reader about his identity, posing the alternatives of a white, hip Texas adolescent who at times may use the facade of a crippled Harlem genius, or the "ideational heat of a real crazy-ass broken-legged Harlem Spade ... " (WV, pp. 57-58). Still, we come to believe in him more as the former since his experience in both the past and the present remind us of his Texas locale. As Barry Leeds suggests, D. J. 's identification with a "Harlem Spade" comes to be "a metaphor for Mailer himself, a hip consciousness standing behind D. J. , critical of Texas values and writing from New York. "6

With his friend Tex Hyde, D. J. is the embodiment of that synthesis of thought, feeling, and action which David Helsa describes as central to Mailer's idea of the hipster. 7 D. J. refers to himself and Tex as "hunter-fighter-fuckers," with "enclaves of high ability in karate, football, sports car, motorcycle, surfboard, and certain notions of the dance, as well as genius inquiries in electronics and applied existentialism" and special powers derived from "crime, closet fucking, potential overturn of incest ... plus ghoul surgery on corpses ... " (WV, p. 157). While they look alike, Tex suggests the more active, ferocious side of D. J. Tex's father is an undertaker who has a voracious sexual appetite which he even satisfies with his corpses. Like Croft's father, Tex's mother is a descendant of people who fought at the Alamo. Her son has "that mean glint in the eye for which Texans are justly proud and famous" (WV, p. 161), a savagery which gives him the power to make the first clean kill on the hunt, the central action of the novel.

If Tex is a "most peculiar blendaroon of humanity and evil, technological know-how, pure savagery, sweet aching secret American youth, and sheer downright meanness as well as genius instincts for occult power ..." (WV, p. 162), D. J. is much more divided. His friends consider him "'highly attractive,'" yet "'mean and vicious'" (WV, p. 14). His initials identify with the rationality of Dr. Jekyll, and he is a self-styled genius, possessing a highly analytical mind. But he also has the emotional energy of his friend Tex and of Mr. Hyde.

While he views himself through the eyes of his mother, Hallie, as a "puma" (WV, p. 11), he has also been buttered by mother-love, like Cummings in The Naked and the Dead. His father, Rusty, however, has encouraged a highly competitive and aggressive mode of life. D. J. remembers how, at the age of five, he received from Rusty a brutal beating which was followed by Hallie's rescue and caresses. In their origins and the quality of their lives, D. J.'s parents reveal the basis for his split personality. Hallie is not only a respectable Dallas hostess with "half Texas ass accent," but also a sexual connoisseur with "half London wickedness" (WV, p. 12) and a repertoire of lovers around the world. Her mother provides the aristocratically sounding "Frenchy Montesquious," half Portuguese and half French, and "the Mulies," the richest family in Arkansas with a vocational love for the Army. In contrast, on her father's side, Hallie demeans her Indian blood. As for Rusty, there is in his heritage a compendium of marshals, a railroad tycoon, and a Harvard professor, as well as bastards, cowboys, one desperado, and even a witch. Like his ancestors who were "Crazy as wolves" (WV, p. 33), Rusty is drawn to his most powerful feelings, yet he possesses the mask of rationality which is essential to his quest for power as a corporation executive.

As a dialectical warring of opposites, D. J.'s personality encourages him to question his own role as the novel's narrator. He refers to the book as "A tape recording of my brain in the deep of its mysterious unwindings" (WV, p. 24).

Either he "can be in the act of writing it, recording it,
slipping it (all unwitting to myself) into the transistorized
electronic isles and microfilm of the electronic Lord ... or
I can be expiring consciousness ... unwinding and unravel-
ings of a nervous constellation just now executed, killed,
severed or stopped ..." (WV, p. 26). Like the hipster,
D. J. is a "wandering troubadour" who relies on an intensely subjective vision which is revealed in his belief that
"There is probably no such thing as a totally false perception" (WV, p. 8). With Marion Faye of "Advertisements
for Myself on the Way Out," he images truth as a spiral in
order to emphasize its elusive and circuitous quality. He
quotes Edison from the work of McLuhan: "'I start with the
intention to increase the speed of the Atlantic Cable, but
when I've arrived part way in my straight line I meet with
a phenomenon, and it leads me off in another direction and
develops into a phonograph'" (WV, p. 8).

D. J.'s development in the novel, then, is away from
any kind of restraint, toward a demonically energetic sense
of himself where his love for the effusion of William Burroughs and the Marquis de Sade takes precedence over his
interest in the highly analytical James Joyce. Like Edison,
D. J. does not rely on logical progression, but on distrac-
tions. He is similar to the "Mailer" of Cannibals and Christians who stated that the "unendurable demand of the middle
of this century" is "to restore the metaphor, and thereby
displace the scientist from his center" (CC, p. 310). He is
a mystery with mental connections "faster than anything afoot"
(WV, p. 24), and relies on the language of Hip which tries
to extract from situations all possible meanings. His punning language, his long sweeping sentences which sometimes
enclose contradictory feelings and thoughts, both are devices
which D. J. uses to squeeze out the richness of experience.

He has an Adamic conception of himself which refutes
the past in an intense recreation of the present. Yet, if he
refuses to imitate the literature of the past, especially clas-
sicists like T. S. Eliot, he is fully familiar with his literary predecessors, some of whom he parodies. He even acknowledges the deficiency in his own narration, which takes
place two years after most of the events and consists of his
thoughts at a Dallas party, given the evening before his departure for Vietnam. For he knows that his memory is
"always more narrative than the tohu-bohu of the present,
which is Old Testament Hebrew ... for chaos and void" (WV,
pp. 60-61). Therefore, he communicates a sense of the very

act of writing in order to place the reader as firmly as possible in the present. In trying to describe the Brooks Range, he tells the reader of his difficulty in finding the right language: "And it rings back at them like a stone on a shield, no, better block that metaphor, drop it altogether, Lady Ethel, it rings back like a finger wet on the rim of the best piece of glass on Park Avenue ..." (WV, p. 177). According to Dennis Donoghue, this emphasis upon artistic choice suggests the only human answer to the force at the center of the universe since the "rough beast" may be translated "into style."8

If D. J. stresses the power of the imagination, like Rojack he is consumed by a sense of the power of God. Ultimately, he considers his narration in cosmological terms by referring to it as a "total tape" (WV, p. 25) received by the Lord, who takes an imprint from the design of our genes through DNA and RNA. But D. J. acknowledges that he may be falsifying his life. We never really know who D. J. is, if we are to believe him in his constant declarations about his shifting identity and his desire to confuse the reader. He is the hipster who is never the same from one moment to the next, content to hover on the edge of mystery where he assimilates contradictory feelings and thoughts.

Certainly one phase of D. J. 's quest is his attempt to purge those feelings which prevent him from the fullest amount of self-expression. The humiliation foisted upon him by his father and the overly protective attitudes of his mother stir him to a rage to reclaim himself that is epitomized in the sexualized brutality with which he views the world. D. J. is forever concerned with his repressed anger toward his father, who not only hurt him as a five-year-old (very possibly for having interrupted conjugal relations), but whose competitive life at the service of corporate power has aroused D. J. 's hatred. At the age of thirteen, D. J. suffered his father's wrath again in the form of a vicious bite on the buttocks. What was initially a friendly football contest turned into a highly competitive situation because Rusty, once an All American college tackle, could not bring his son down. Even though D. J. felt compassion for his father and allowed himself to be tackled, Rusty was so enraged by his earlier failure that "he flung D. J. and ... bit him in the ass, right through his pants, that's how insane he was with frustration ..." (WV, p. 40). Infuriated in turn, D. J. hit Rusty over the head with a pickaxe handle, an act which did not fully resolve his anger because it resulted in his departure for military school.

If he has picked up some of his father's competitiveness and even feels the lure of corporate success, only to
be put off by its suffocating security, D. J. is, nevertheless,
much closer to the hipster's need to purge the desires and
habits imposed by his background. The "corporation is DC,
direct current, diehard charge, no dialectic man, just one-
way street, they don't call it Washington D. C. for nothing,"
but "it's all torn down by the inexorable hunt logic of the
Brooks Range ..." (WV, p. 126) where D. J. confronts his
inmost feelings. Unlike Rusty and his corporate cohorts,
Pete and Bill, who join the hunt to bring back a bear and
thereby win the admiration of their business associates, D. J.
seeks a different kind of power. Like Rojack after the murder of Deborah, D. J. is the hipster who confronts the mysterious forces of the universe and the possibility of his own
death in an attempt to transcend the debilitating effects of
the past. The entire struggle takes place within the context
of his relationship with his father, toward whom D. J. experiences his most intense anger, which reaches a murderous pitch just after an encounter with a bear. However, he
must pass through a series of less intense encounters before he is prepared for his most significant realization.

Just after Tex kills a wolf, D. J. feels highly competitive and senses the anger emanating from the smell of the
dead animal. He is "ready to get down and wrestle with
the wolf and get his teeth to its throat ..." (WV, p. 70).
After drinking its blood, he feels "up tight with the essential animal insanity of things" (WV, p. 70). Later, when
he kills a goat, its pain is "shot like an arrow into D. J. 's
heart ..." (WV, p. 99). He now comes into contact with
"the unspoken unseen unmeasurable electromagnetism and
wave of all the psychic circuits of all the wild of Alaska
..." (WV, p. 100). Like Rojack looking at the moon, he
experiences dread but part of him is still in the "gasoline
of Texas, the asshole sulfur smell of money-oil clinging to
the helicopter ..." (WV, p. 100). The subsequent killing
of a bear arouses D. J. even more, to the point where "some
prehistoric wolf all eight feet big began to stir new boils and
springs and pools in the river of D. J. , in his blood, beasty
audience, in his blood, and he had to get him a wolf in the
form of a bear ..." (WV, p. 119).

But it is only when Rusty and D. J. leave the tour conducted by Big Luke Fellinka and enter the forest alone, without the aid of the ever-present helicopter, that D. J. finally
breaks through to the heart of his rage, his patricidal feel-

ings. On the hunt, they are like "two combat wolves," and "tight as combat buddies" (WV, p. 128). Like the hipster, D. J. feels comfortably close to danger; however, the sense that bear is present arouses in him an even greater fear when he begins to sense the possibility of his own death. Behind the fear is "crazy-ass murder, cause D. J. for first time in his life is hip to the hole of his center which is slippery desire to turn his gun and blast a shot into Rusty's fat fuck face ..." (WV, p. 136). He thinks of the beating which he received at the age of five and of his repressed anger which may have culminated in cancer of the brain. The murderous impulse is dissipated momentarily in the "aromatic antiseptic" (WV, p. 138) of the pines, and is turned upon the bear which then appears. D. J. courageously fires from ten yards away only to have the animal carom down into thicket and brush. There, desiring to touch the wisdom of the bear's primitive urges at the moment of death, D. J. moves closer, while Rusty, hovering in the distance, fires "from the excessive tension" (WV, p. 147). The fact that Rusty, then, takes virtually full credit for killing the bear signals the "end of love of one son for one father" (WV, p. 148).

D. J. 's patricidal impulses are aroused to such an extent that he finds it necessary to leave the tour again and encourages Tex to join him in another untutored journey into the wilderness. He now experiences his feelings in the broadest cosmological context, so that his desire to kill his father becomes rooted in the nature of all animal life. What initially may have been primal feelings which were only vestiges of D. J. 's unexpressed rage in the past are described as psychologically intrinsic to man. In his depiction of D. J., Mailer, according to Roger Ramsey, perhaps was influenced by cultural anthropologists who emphasize the "animal imperative" of aggression. 9

In Intro Beep 9, D. J. presents his idea of the "animal imperative" in the context of his anal preoccupations and then tries to derive an aesthetic from these concerns. He states that excrement is the physical result of impulses which have been frustrated: "... frustration makes crystals of impulse when they are in the mode of liquid chemical matter ..." (WV, p. 152). The aesthetic dimension of this observation resides in D. J. 's conception of beauty, defined as "a crystal," or "the frustrated impulse of a general desire to improve the creation" (WV, p. 152). D. J. , of course, consistently tries to avoid any frustration of impulse. The very form of the novel, which allows D. J. the opportunity to move in a loose associative manner from one idea and event to another in a language that is always terribly suggestive, is the aesthetic outgrowth of this negation of restraint. Like the hipster, D. J. seeks the multiple meanings in a situation and expands or telescopes an idea in order to generate intense feeling in the reader.

Therefore, in the final journey with Tex into the uncharted Alaskan wilderness, D. J. comes into his most intense contact with the force funneling into the North and South poles, as well as flowing in and around the earth. This electromagnetic field ("e. m. f. ") is the physical counterpart of the "Magnetic-Electro fief ['M. E. F. '] of the dream" (WV, p. 170) in man. The "M. E. F. " is the repository of all those impulses and feelings, many of which are repressed during the day, that provide man with the strongest sense of his own reality, but, in their intensity, force him to confront the most profound terror that he is ever to know in awe, dread, and finally death. It is during sleep that the mind slips into "M. E. F. " and becomes "part of the spook flux of the night like an iron filing in the E. M. field ..." (WV, p. 170). The North pole, then, is the "crystal receiver" of all the messages "of the continent" (WV, p. 172). Without weapons, but keeping a minimal supply of equipment, the two boys enter the northernmost area, the Brooks Range, where the whiteness of the mountains suggests the white force at the end of Poe's novel The Narrative of Arthur Gordon Pym and Melville's whale in Moby Dick. There, they make another attempt to move closer to the instinctual center of the universe.

First they meet a wolf and "Two waves of murder, human and animal, meet across the snow ..." (WV, p. 181). In a "psychic struggle" (WV, p. 182) they defeat the wolf, which must then confront an eagle in another murderous encounter. Then a fox is frustrated by its inability to catch a squirrel. Finally, a bear appears and devours a young caribou. Completely free of the "mixed shit" of his Texas background, D. J. confronts again the "essential animal insanity of things" (WV, p. 200). But this is a natural condition and is accompanied by less frightening situations which arouse in D. J. intensely pleasurable feelings. Caribou passing on a ridge, and cranes flying overhead reveal the possibility for communion. And then, under the lights of the Aurora Borealis, Tex and D. J. experience their feelings for each other in the context of a vision of God, "some beast of a giant jaw and cavernous mouth with a full cave's breath and fangs, and secret call: come to me" (WV, p. 202). Their murderous impulses are aroused in the form of a mutual homosexual assault: "... they hung there each of them on the knife of the divide in all conflict of lust to own the other yet in fear of being killed by the other ..." (WV, pp. 203-04). Listening to the voice of God who says, "'Go out and kill--fulfill my will, go and kill,'" they become "killer brothers" (WV, p. 204).

Mailer's concern with "e. m. f. ," "M. E. F. ," and the Aurora Borealis suggests again Reich's conception of orgone energy, a demonstrably visual and even measurable form of electricity. However, when D. J. taps that energy, he experiences the realization that all animal life is instinctually aggressive and murderous; whereas for Reich violence was a secondary drive that resulted from sexual repression. D. J. 's quest, then, is to plunge into the deepest recesses of his personality, beyond the conventional restraints against violence.

As Richard Pearce indicates, D. J. 's trip into the wilderness is a parody of a similar mission by Ike McCaslin in Faulkner's The Bear: Unlike Ike, D. J. discovers "the meaning of the bear-hunt ritual: that it was a preparation for killing."[10] In his earlier work, particularly The Naked and the Dead, Mailer relied upon an analysis of society and the family in order to explain man's aggressive behavior. But in Why Are We in Vietnam?, though still intent upon describing the pressures of environment, Mailer emphasizes "the essential animal insanity of things" and suggests the atavism which characterizes some of the work of American naturalists, especially Frank Norris. The hipster's vision, which had intimations of anarchy, now begins to suggest the Darwinian concept of survival of the fittest. While Mailer does not exclude the simultaneous existence of more positive feelings, the latter are minimized in Why Are We in Vietnam? Unlike the hipster who must feel his violent impulses in order to be able to purge them in preparation for love, D. J. 's sense of the world is so colored by his aggressiveness that his most tender feelings are suffused with anger.

One of the many characters in Mailer's work whose sexuality is tinged with violence, D. J. is like Sergius O'Shaugnessy of "The Time of Her Time," who views his penis as "the avenger" (AM, p. 488). O'Shaugnessy is engaged in a calculated attack through his sexual potency on the totalitarian and repressive aspects of American society, all of which is culminated in his attempt to give Denise Gondelman, an overly intellectual college student, her first orgasm. D. J., however, is not as purposeful and experiences his sexuality in an undifferentiated manner, ready to "fuck anything" but always with a sense of underlying anger. Although riddled with ponderous Freudian jargon, D. J.'s projection of the psychiatrist's analysis may not be that far from the truth: "he's a humdinger of a latent homosexual highly overheterosexual with onanistic narcissistic and sodomistic overtones, a choir task force of libidinal cross-hybrided vectors" (WV, p. 14).

At the center of D. J.'s sexual needs is his own sense that "virility grew with a taint" (WV, p. 137) because of too much mother-love. His one direct sexual experience in the novel is with Tex under the Aurora Borealis. There D. J. hopes to compensate for his overly maternal past by stealing some power from Tex, a product of "ape shit daddy-love" (WV, p. 160), through buggery. Women also provide D. J. with a way of reclaiming himself from having been the "beloved son of perfume on the poo Halleloo" (WV, p. 202). He does not envision any sexual encounter in tender terms, but "prongs," "proctates," "fucks," "humps," and "drills" with a "dong," or a "gun." At the party in Dallas, he divides women into the "young cunt from which you cop the goods," unlike "used cunt" who are "greedy fucking fiends" (WV, p. 156). If women are not "prissy assed," they are "bitches," one of whom possesses a "lobster claw of a cunt" (WV, p. 161). Even "mother nature" is described "as big and dangerous and mysterious as a beautiful castrating cunt when she's on the edge between murder and love ..." (WV, p. 184).

In fact, with the exception of that part of the novel which describes the experience in the Brooks Range, the tone of D. J.'s narration continually gives evidence of his constant preoccupation with sexuality. D. J. tends to metamorphose everything into the hipster's need for the apocalyptic orgasm. Even in these situations, there is a strong suggestion of D. J.'s anger. Encountering danger is compared with meeting "a real hot fuck in an hour ..." (WV, p. 129). Rusty's description of a saxifrage which "'is strong enough to grow and split a rock'" encourages D. J. to imagine that "... it got a hard on, Herbert, and the rock stone pussy cracks ..." (WV, pp. 128, 129). The weather in the Brooks Range "is like a bitch with hot and cold water running in her bush"; there, snow-topped mountains possess "bare ass peaks" (WV, pp. 176, 177). A recently killed deer is "one old jelly flung together by the bullets, one blood pudding of a cocktail vibrated into total promiscuity by the twenty-foot fall down the rocks" (WV, p. 98). Finally, D. J. even formulates his political criticism in sexual terms, since American intervention in the affairs of other countries is referred to as "flying CIA fucks" (WV, p. 30).

Despite his intense anger and sexuality, D. J.'s activities, ruminations, and explosions of feeling are not merely personally idiosyncratic, but expressions of a culture in the throes of serious internal division. Mailer himself has remarked that the book "is saying that America enters the nightmare of its destiny like a demented giant in a half-cracked canoe, bleeding from wounds top and bottom, bellowing in bewilderment, drowning with radio transmitters on the hip and radar in his ear" (EE, p. 221). According to Tony Tanner, in Why Are We in Vietnam? "Mailer continued his exploration into the mystery and source of power, trying to find the intersection point where the pure pre-moral force of non human nature enters into, affects, or works through the human agencies of society."11 Unlike in An American Dream, where Rojack barely teeters on the edge between rationality and the abyss, in Why Are We in Vietnam? D. J. is much more capable of living in close proximity to that subterranean world of uncontrolled feeling. He is therefore less concerned with his own personal equilibrium and more attuned to the alien quality of his environment. D. J. even states that his purpose in writing the novel is to try to show America how to live "in this Electrox Edison World" (WV, p. 8). Through D. J., Mailer is able to present once again his criticisms of corporate America. But this time he utilizes a language so blunt and a tone so bitter and cynical that the criticism becomes his most enraged attack against the forces of totalitarianism.

The nature of the hunt itself suggests the life style of economically prosperous, yet exploitative Americans who are unwilling to face the wilderness without the trappings of civilization, but are quite capable of ruling over oppressed peoples around the world. The hunting party is referred to as a "gaggle of goose fat and asshole" (WV, pp. 98-99). Not only do they sleep on a "dead-ass air mattress" (WV, p. 68), but they have the constant use of a helicopter. The wilderness has been so overrun by man that the bears have changed their living habits. Rusty compares killing bear to bombing

a city. D. J. views the hunted animals as black people who
are designated in traditional demeaning terms. The huge
assortment of guns which are catalogued precisely, the use
of the helicopter, the continual ravaging of the land which
has changed the living habits of the animals, all are obvious
reminders of the Vietnam war and perhaps of other United
States military adventures in the developing countries, as
well as in the American ghettoes.

Despite his criticism of the American militaristic
sensibility, D. J. 's political orientation falls outside any traditional political categories. While demeaning the Russians
by calling them "Red-ass" (WV, p. 29), he has nothing but
disgust for American dignitaries from the Democratic or Republican party such as Dwight Eisenhower, Lyndon Johnson,
and Henry Cabot Lodge. He is especially critical of the U-
nited States intervention in the affairs of other countries, as
he continually refers to the murderous subterfuge of the CIA.
In a section of the novel which describes Rusty's response
to particular aspects of American life, D. J. parodies the
conservative's fear of the growing emancipation and power of
women, blacks, adolescents and Jews; the deterioration of
American products; the increasing power of communism; and
the loss of a religious belief which is being replaced by LSD
and endless copulation.

D. J. , then, "sees right through shit" (WV, p. 49).
As he says, he rejects "all the positive elements in his rich
secure successful environmental scene including social back-
ing, strong sentiment, national roots, loci of power ..."
(WV, p. 34). For his favorite theory "is that America is
run by a mysterious hidden mastermind, a secret creature
who's got a plastic asshole installed in his brain where he
can shit out all his corporate management of thoughts" (WV,
p. 36). The continual use of obscenity in this passage and
throughout Why Are We in Vietnam? is perhaps the result of
what John Aldridge calls D. J. 's militant moralism: "his obscenity functions as the terrible swift sword of conscience
that slices through the pretensions of everything he finds obscene in American society. "[12] While in The Naked and the
Dead obscenity functioned as a means of undercutting the
military hierarchy, in Why Are We in Vietnam? it serves a
broader purpose which Mailer details in The Armies of the
Night. There, he states that in his latest novel "he had
kicked goodbye ... to the old literary corset of good taste,
letting his sense of language play on obscenity as freely as
it wished, so discovering that everything he knew about the

American language (with its incommensurable resources)
went flying in and out of the line of his prose with the hap-
piest beating of wings--it was the first time his style seemed
at once very American to him and very literary in the best
way, at least as he saw the best way" (AN, p. 48).

Because of his position as an executive with Central
Consolidated Chemical and Plastic, Rusty is closest to the
"mastermind." He is viewed by D. J. as the "highest grade
of asshole" who, in turn, obeys the orders of "Mr. Great
Plastic Asshole," and rules over "medium asshole(s)" (WV,
pp. 37, 52) such as Pete and Bill, two corporate sycophants.
In Dallas, Rusty heads Pew Rapports, "the filter with the
purest porosity of purpose" (WV, p. 31). D. J. tells us that
this filter, which is made of plastic, causes cancer of the
lip. He describes its absorptive powers before he contemplates placing it up the rectum of a girl. The anal imagery
here and throughout Why Are We in Vietnam? is not meant
to be adolescently cute. As in An American Dream, Mailer
links his biological and social observations as well as his
psychological and cosmological concerns in a loose metaphorical chain. In this case Mailer emphasizes the wastefulness
of the corporations which, in their desire to make a profit,
will pawn off on the American public a device that not only
causes cancer, but, in the very process of being produced,
requires a bureaucratic and submissive mentality that creates the psychological climate in which cancer can flourish.

If he is particularly aroused by his father, who is
the "cream of corporation corporateness" (WV, p. 29), D. J.
is equally contemptuous of all aspects of America that have
become extensions of corporate power. Therefore he is especially concerned with Rusty's role in perpetuating the power of the American corporation around the world. Rusty's
job has brought him into contact with an endless array of
organizations, including the FBI and CIA. Mailer's analysis
of an America overrun by a ruling elite with its base in the
economic sphere, which was first articulated in The Naked
and the Dead and is reiterated throughout his work, is given
grotesque dimensions in Why Are We in Vietnam? because of
the number and variety of groups with which Rusty has contact.

A comment on the interlocking nature of power in A-
merica, all the people in the novel, with the exception of
Tex, D. J., and perhaps one of the guides on the hunt, a
displaced Indian, are reflections of the corporate voice which

says "nothing unexpected" but says it "with quality" (WV, p.
50). D. J. continually parodies the emotionally drained but
institutionally sanctioned thoughts, feelings, and language of
Americans who are criticized for "the vacation-directed personal vector imperatives" (WV, p. 60) of their minds which
shut up action after Labor Day. Hallie's psychiatrist hides
behind his mechanical psychiatric jargon while harboring secret desires for her "'white buttermilk flesh'" (WV, p. 17).
Kenneth Easterly, the tour guide coordinator, speaks with a
different accent depending upon the background of his custom-
ers, whom he tries to please by turning hunting into one
more salable commodity; "we offer hunting which is reasonable, decent in its risk, fair to the game, and not utterly
deprived of comfort" (WV, p. 64). Big Luke Fellinka, the
chief guide, is imaged as the President of General Motors
and as the former Secretary of Defense, Robert McNamara.
As the Managing Director of Tendonex, Rusty's rival firm,
Al Percy Cunningham will not join the bear hunt, because
he is attempting to obtain the contract to put a plastic Uni-
var valve "into the bottom of the collapsible built-in space
suit chemical toilet in the Gemini" (WV, p. 47) for the
space program. Even the reader receives D. J.'s wrath in
anal terms. Imaged as soft, complacent, blind, and hypocritical, the reader is referred to on the first page of the
novel as "Braunschweiger," a German name for the bour-
geoisie as well as the anally suggestive sausage. There-
after the reader is demeaned with metaphoric references
such as "suck mouth," "syph-head," "hunk head," and "cock
sucker"; names like "Pierrot" or "Fergus" are ironic reminders of the absence of a romantic or hip strain in the
American sensibility.

At the end of the novel, D. J. links his readers and
his father's hunting clan in one sweeping picture of "the U-
nited Greedies of America" whose ambition for success and
status at the expense of developing a real self and the natural environment continually gives "a singe to the dream
field" (WV, p. 206). They "smog the predawning air with
their psychic glut," and "just generally fuck up that M. E. F.
band ..." (WV, pp. 205, 206). If D. J. is present at a
farewell dinner attended by the "Greedies" of Dallas and is
about to leave with Tex for Vietnam at the end of the novel,
he is an outlaw in the land of the enemy and is attempting
to survive with the artistry of the hipster. Even though he
is aware of the "flying CIA fucks," he is nevertheless in
touch with the murderous impulses in all people. Vietnam
gives him the opportunity to witness terrible carnage and to
vent his own violence.

While acknowledging that Mailer parodies the frontier values of aggressiveness in Why Are We in Vietnam?, Richard Pearce ignores the difference between the forms of violence and the impulse itself. 13 In Why Are We in Vietnam? Mailer suggests that one cannot escape violence, because it is rooted in the nature of life. However, he argues that man can decide the forms of expression which this violence will take. Earlier, in The Presidential Papers, he distinguished between "inhuman violence--violence which is on a large scale and abstract" (PP, p. 136), and violence which takes place in an encounter between individuals. Thus, boxing, which falls into the second of these categories, shows "a part of what man was like, it belonged to his ability to create art and artful movement on the edge of death or pain or danger or attack, and it had much to say about the subtleties of human style" (PP, p. 247). Mailer's own publicly aggressive posturing, his love of bullfighting and his admiration of Hemingway all suggest his belief that the violent impulses in man must be fully accepted and integrated.

Therefore D. J. 's decision to go to Vietnam is more than an attempt to relieve himself of the plague of America which Mailer described in Cannibals and Christians. Neither the diversity of American life nor the stultifying nature of his corporate surroundings alone pushes D. J. to his decision. He goes because rooted in human nature is a reservoir of anger that can be tapped, given the right circumstances. As if to emphasize the ambiguity of D. J. 's political allegiances, Mailer creates a narrator who views black people in the most traditionally stereotypic manner, alternately demeaning them as "Nigger washerwom[e]n" (WV, p. 88), or admiring them as supreme sexual studs with remarkable muscular dexterity. Never really referring to problems of poverty, D. J. is more concerned with those social and political experiences which are in any way related to the problem of repression. As Richard Poirier states, "the question addressed by the book is no longer the Marxist one of the exploitation of working time or even of the human sense of time by the profit motive. Rather the question is the dominance of pleasure by inner time. "14 D. J. , then, is Mailer's attempt to create a narrator much more ambiguous than Lovett, O'Shaugnessy, or Rojack. The dialectic is so rich as to be in danger of exploding even the most minimal sense of continuity. Nevertheless, Mailer's presentation of D. J. 's background and the anthropological conception of the aggressive "animal imperative" help to explain what appear to be contradictory feelings and commitments.

As in An American Dream, Mailer's aesthetic achievement in Why Are We in Vietnam? is diminished by his attempt to illustrate his cosmology, which now contains the
idea of the aggressive "animal imperative." Indicating the
relationship between Mailer's system and "the conception of
the 'Great Chain of Being' that dominated traditional Christian cosmology well past the Elizabethan Age," Richard Finholt believes that Mailer "has broken those lingering vestiges of romantic wishful thinking that distort the otherwise
penetrating insights of 'post-Darwinian' determinism."15
But Finholt never proves that Mailer fully explores the philosophical implications of his cosmology. With his heavy emphasis upon intuition in An American Dream, Mailer presents
through Rojack a world view that lacks intellectual solidity.
Moreover, in "The White Negro" Mailer refers to philosophical and psychological ideas in order to support his stress
upon violence, but in Why Are We in Vietnam? he does not
adequately account for the anthropology which he is advanc-
ing. By showing how Mailer's concern with violence in this
novel indicates his submersion in the competitiveness so
characteristic of the American social and economic order,
Fredric Jameson alerts us to the fact that Why Are We in
Vietnam? captures the structure of feeling of the age which
it describes.16 Thus it is in the energy beneath his cosmology and anthropology, particularly in the language which is
used to communicate his system of belief, and in the finely
paced narrative, that the novel reflects Mailer's talent.
That energy, which was implicit in "The White Negro" in
the idea of the hipster as a dialectical warring of opposites,
is fully embodied by the voice of D. J. in Why Are We in
Vietnam?

The Armies of the Night and
Miami and the Siege of Chicago

In The Armies of the Night and Miami and the Siege
of Chicago, Mailer demonstrates his continuing concern with
America's social and political order. Approaching experience from the vantage point of a reporter who is involved
in the events which are described, he captures both the
"Beast" and the "seer" in himself and therefore suggests
the "schizophrenia" in America, imaged in the midst of a
civil war.17 Unlike D. J., however, Mailer ultimately locates himself beyond the conflicts which are described.

Utilizing the full resources of his dialectic, he acknowledges contradictions and yet synthesizes experience into a broad vision that possesses in muted form the cosmological dimensions of his previous work. He describes the
major political figures and the forces which they embody in
the context of his concern with God and the Devil, but he
does not stress his cosmological interests as much as his
metapsychology, with its emphasis on man as "angel" and
"swine." In focusing upon highly emotional events of the
gravest importance for America, Mailer refuses to define
his allegiances simplistically. Like D. J. and Rojack, he
finds himself trapped between the demands of society and
the "rebellious imperatives of the self." He seeks to become a figure who possesses the courage and the holistic
vision of the hipster, without the latter's inevitable isolation
from the center of American life.

According to Raymond Schroth, for Mailer "as for
the transcendentalists, the structure of the universe dupli-
cates the structure of the individual self; all knowledge begins with self-knowledge."18 Like Whitman, Mailer has
maintained the attitude that he is a representative of all A-
mericans who seek to give shape to their inner experience,
which in turn is a reflection of the vast social order. Because it is so complex and confusing, the American social
order is almost impossible to describe. Some approximation of reality can be obtained "In the unconscious of each
of us," where there is "a detailed conception of a vast social novel greater than most of the vast social novels which
have been written. In every last one of us just about lives
a great novelist" (EE, p. 113).

With this emphasis upon the unconscious, in his adop-
tion of the role of the reporter, Mailer does not pretend to
view events objectively. Throughout his earlier work, he
debunked jounalists because of the censorship imposed upon
and accepted by them. In Cannibals and Christians, Mailer
stated that the journalists' work can become interesting when
"what you write is a reflection of your own consciousness
..." (CC, pp. 218-19). Even though he would "look to the
feel of the phenomenon" (AN, p. 25), Mailer is not content
with the hipster's intensely subjective vision. Acknowledging his dual role as actor and writer, he is a dialectician
who tries to describe the various aspects of a situation and
seeks to extract from experience the largest possible meaning. This has led Robert Lawler to describe Mailer's artistic development as the progression of his ability to create a
narrator who is both a participant and an observer. 19

As a witness, Mailer is unwilling to stand aside and allow events to occur without becoming involved himself. Since 1960, in covering the Democratic and Republican conventions and some major prize fights, Mailer has transformed events into aesthetic or existential projections of himself. The Democratic convention of 1960 became a vehicle for the presentation of his idea of the existential political hero in John Kennedy. In 1962, the fight between Sonny Liston and Floyd Patterson was viewed by Mailer in the context of his magical cosmology, where the psychic bullets of Rojack were the weapons of Sonny, "the King of Hip ... " (PP, p. 267). One day after the fight, Mailer managed to confront Liston before other reporters in the hope of promoting a rematch.

Emphasizing Mailer's tendency throughout his career to consciously parade himself before the public, Robert Merideth states that a "compulsive, narcissistic concern for his image conditioned everything he [Mailer] says he did during the Pentagon weekend or at least controls everything he writes about it."[20] This portrayal does not sufficiently take into account Mailer's concern with recreating experience accurately. In The Armies of the Night, Mailer indicates that

> the Novelist working in secret collaboration with the Historian has perhaps tried to build with his novel a tower fully equipped with telescopes to study--at the greatest advantage--our own horizon. Of course, the tower is crooked, and the telescopes warped, but the instruments of all sciences--history so much as physics--are always constructed in small or large error; what supports the use of them now is that our intimacy with the telescopes (yes even the machinist of the barrels) has given some advantage for correcting the error of the instruments and the imbalance of his tower. (AN, p. 219)

Although constantly maintaining the belief that his activities, feelings, and ideas are part of the events which he proposes to describe, he does manage to distance himself to the point where, at times, he is merely a traditional reporter who engages in the laborious task of presenting statistics and facts. This objectivity is quite evident in his more recent work as a journalist, especially his coverage of the 1969 moon shot in Of a Fire on the Moon, which contains long descriptions of a highly technological nature about various aspects of the American space program.

As if to suggest his movement toward greater restraint, Mailer divides The Armies of the Night into two accounts of the 1967 march on the Pentagon, a protest over A-
merica's military presence in Vietnam. Echoing Henry
Adams' portrayal of himself in the third-person in the Edu-
cation, Book One of Armies, subtitled "History as a Novel:
The Steps of the Pentagon," tends to be a personal history
of Mailer's activities during the protest. Book Two, "The
Novel as History: The Battle of the Pentagon," is primarily a journalistic account of that which Mailer did not witness
but obtained from a variety of sources. Utilizing the point
of view of Book One of Armies, in Miami and the Siege of
Chicago Mailer focuses less upon himself, and details the
events of the 1968 Democratic and Republican conventions,
both of which he attended. Nevertheless, he cautions the
reader who would systematically view any part of his work in
the context of such Manichean categories as subjective or
objective. Even within Book Two of Armies, and throughout Miami and the Siege of Chicago, Mailer is intent upon
presenting an "interior" "history" (AN, p. 255). While
"scrupulous to the welter of a hundred confusing and opposed
facts," he will "unashamedly enter that world of strange
lights and intuitive speculation which is the novel" (AN, p.
255).

Therefore he opens Armies with a Time magazine
account of his own role in the demonstrations. Demeaning
Mailer without looking into the complexity of his personality
or his art, the report suggests the daily operation of the
conventional news media which, under the guise of objectivity, presents events in a highly biased manner. If not biased, most reporting fails to describe the emotional aura of
events. In Miami and the Siege of Chicago, Mailer reprints
an account, which initially appeared in the New York Times,
of a demonstration involving the Poor People's Campaign,
led by Ralph Abernathy of the Southern Christian Leadership
Conference. According to Mailer, the account fails to capture the feelings of both the demonstrators and the observers.
For Mailer, then, "there is no history without nuance" (MSC,
p. 56).

Unlike the hipster who has forged a vision out of the
pressures of his experience, the conventional journalist cannot distinguish between his real feelings and the emotional
encrustations of society. The endless process of socializa-
tion tends to turn the journalist's nervous system into a reflex of the most powerful men in America. Mailer rejects

not only the biases of the popular media, but also those of the counter-culture. He has little sympathy for the falsified accounts and platitudinous oratory of some segments of the Left.

What he seeks is a style and vision that can preserve the integrity of the event, and yet enable him to be true to his inmost feelings. Central to the quest is his ability to expose and balance the various tendencies within himself which might either falsify the mood of the event through self-exposure, or (less likely) create a picture, which, in its photographic verisimilitude, loses the "feel of the phenomenon." Therefore he utilizes a density of style, a mixture of the formal and the colloquial, which leads Dwight Macdonald to compare Mailer with James. [21]

As if to suggest his proclivity for emotional expression, Mailer continually describes his momentary states of feeling. Like the hipster who abhors repression, in Armies Mailer seeks to liberate the various selves which he carries "within him like different models of his experience; parts of him were eighty-one years old, fifty-seven, forty-eight, thirty-six, nineteen, etcetera ... " (AN, p. 9). Moreover, depending upon the occasion, he has various voices. In a speech which he gives before the Pentagon march, the accent of his voice shifts both in conscious parody and uncontrollably on a scale that includes the Irish working class, the black militant, the Southern dwarf alter ego of Lyndon Johnson, the corporate executive, and the academic pedant. Tony Tanner states that in the last twenty years Mailer "has constantly sought to expose himself to the influences at work in America without capitulating to any of them, and has constantly sought for appropriate modes of utterance to project his responses to those influences and transform reaction into style. "[22]

It is not surprising that Mailer describes the "architecture of his personality" as resembling "some provincial cathedral which warring orders of the church might have designed separately over several centuries ... " (AN, p. 17). At a party, "boldness, attacks of shyness, rude assertion, and circumlocutions tortured as arthritic fingers working at lace, all took their turn with him ... " (AN, p. 17). If his roles as reporter and participant contribute to this war, so does the fact that he is also the subject of a film which is prepared by the B. B. C. These large roles sometimes contain roles within themselves in an ever expanding chain, so that it is easy to agree with Richard Poirier, who believes that Mailer purposely asks to be viewed "within intricately related fields of force," where he acts "simultaneously as a participant, witness, and writer, who evokes in the clashes of his style a 'war' among the various elements that constitute the life of the country and of the self."[23]

Essential to this war is the existence in Mailer of the "Beast" and "the modest everyday fellow of his daily round" (AN, p. 13). In "The White Negro," Mailer attributes to the hipster "the sophistication of the wise primitive in a giant jungle ..." (AM, p. 343). While he sought to embody an idea of the self in which thought and feeling would be delicately fused, in his fictional portrayals of O'Shaugnessy, Faye, Rojack, and D. J. Mailer describes perilous emotional transactions which seem to be caught in the throes of an endless dialectic. If the "Beast" does not prevail, it maintains command to the extent that the less intense, daily requirements of the self are rarely met. The "Mailer" projected in Armies and Miami and the Siege of Chicago is not engaged in the same apocalyptic struggle of fuse instinct and reason, because that fusion has to some extent taken place, as evidenced in the elaborate explanations Mailer provides for so much of his behavior and emotional response. In Armies, Mailer appears to have settled into the more conventional aspects of life, and this change is epitomized in his "regimental tie" (AN, p. 202), cufflinks, and suit, as well as in his willingness to detail his parental responsibilities and marital affections.

Nevertheless, the "Beast" abhors repression; he

> did not appear so very often, sometimes so rarely as once a month, sometimes not even twice a year, and he sometimes came when Mailer was frightened and furious at the fear, sometimes he came just to get a breath of air. He was indispensable, however, and Mailer was even fond of him for the wild man was witty in his own wild way and absolutely fearless.... He would have been admirable, except that he was an absolute egomaniac, a Beast-- no recognition existed of the existence of anything beyond the range of his reach. And when he appeared, it was often with great speed; he gave little warning. (AN, p. 13)

Urinating on a bathroom floor, taunting an audience, confronting an American Nazi, all are expressions of Mailer's "Beast" in Armies. In Miami and the Siege of Chicago, his "Beast" tends to be held in abeyance until the end of the Democratic convention, when Mailer's sense of his possible cowardice for failing to enter the "battle" with the demonstrators pushes him into a series of confrontations with police, national guardsmen, and a delegate.

Like the hipster, Mailer continually measures himself according to his willingness to confront dangerous situations. According to Richard Gilman, for Mailer the world is "seen as combat, violence that has to be controlled, as a game and a place for the ego with a name."24 While contemplating his fear of the police at the 1968 Democratic convention, Mailer states that "the secret to growth was to be brave a little more than one was cowardly ..." (MSC, p. 185). His conscience tormented by his failure to act with the demonstrators, he suggests that his writing may suffer, since "A professional could always push a work by an exercise of will, yet was writing himself right out of his liver if the work was obliged to protect the man" (MSC, p. 213). Earlier, in Advertisements for Myself, he stated that he shared with Hemingway the belief that "probably I could not become a very good writer unless I learned first how to keep my nerve, and what is more difficult, learned how to find more of it" (AM, p. 265). In Cannibals and Christians, Mailer referred to cowardice as the most destructive quality for a first-rate writer: "if you're continually worrying about whether you're growing or deteriorating as a man, whether your integrity is turning soft or firming itself, why then it's in that slow war, that slow rear-guard battle you fight against diminishing talent that you stay in shape as a writer and have a consciousness" (CC, p. 218).

Even his aesthetics reflect Mailer's need to maintain a courageously aggressive stance in relation to experience. Refusing to tie himself to the literary techniques and traditions of the past, he believes that "Craft protects one from facing those endless expanding realities of deterioration and responsibility" (CC, p. 216). He likes the possibilities inherent in the scriptless film or impromptu public speaking engagement which requires one "to trick or seize or submit to the grace of each moment ..." (AN, p. 28). Writing about Mailer's notion of form, Richard Poirier states that it "is not predetermined by the constituents of an event," but "is what is left of these constituents after they have been allowed to wear each other down. Form isn't simply equivalent to relationships, strifes, or 'wars.' It is the recollection of these, what remains in the memory after the fact. Form is both the record of a war and the physical equivalent of memory. "25 In Armies, Mailer indicates that the writer engages in a war with experience; ultimately, the "cutting edge of the style employed" (AN, p. 170) discloses what one knows of a subject.

Mailer frankly admits that as a writer and as a man "he had been suffering more and more in the past few years from the private conviction that he was getting a little soft ... " (AN, p. 58). Even before the Pentagon march, he virtually forced himself to sign an income tax protest and to capitulate to the request of Mitchell Goodman that he act in complicity with draft resisters. If he is furious at himself for fleeing in the course of a retreat by some of the more militant demonstrators, he is almost transcendentally happy when he retains his poise at the time of his arrest, which results from a conscious choice to commit civil disobedience.

In Miami and the Siege of Chicago, he is not as active. Attending both conventions as a reporter, he worries about getting his story written. The parameters of the Chicago protest are not as neatly defined as in Washington. There is greater danger of widespread disorder in Chicago because of the complete breakdown in communication between the organizers of the demonstration and city officials. Although he rarely participates in any of the protest activities in the parks or the streets, he continually admires the courage of the demonstrators and calls them "the stuff out of which the very best soldiers are made" (MSC, p. 153). He is tormented by the idea that his success as a writer may have vitiated his revolutionary sensibility.

In Armies, after he is arrested and placed in jail, he becomes obsessed with the arguments of Tuli Kupferberg, who refuses to plead "No Contest," thereby giving up the right to return to the Pentagon for six months. Speaking with Kupferberg and other prisoners encourages Mailer to image a ladder of guilt along which one moves, depending upon a willingness to improve one's moral condition at the expense of physical or psychological security; he reiterates Eitel's belief that "'The essence of spirit was to choose that alternative which did not better your position, but made it worse'" (AN, pp. 192-93). Mailer therefore details the fears and the temptations of the protesters who remain at the Pentagon until the very end of the demonstration. Their numbers having dwindled from the thousands to the hundreds, they are in danger of being severely beaten before arrest. He describes their experience as "a rite of passage ... a black dark night which began in joy, near foundered in terror, and dragged on through empty apathetic hours while glints of light came to each alone" (AN, p. 280). Along with several who remain in jail and refuse prison clothing and food until madness nearly sets in, these protesters receive Mailer's greatest admiration.

Yet, always sensing contradictions, Mailer implies that there is a self-destructive ascetic quality in these protesters which recalls the suicidal urge of the beatnik, rather than the murderous impulse of the hipster. While admiring the courage of civil rights workers who went South in the early sixties, Mailer has "the instinctive withdrawal of a meat-eater before an ascetic" (AN, p. 193) in the presence of Jim Peck, one of the first freedom riders. In The Presidential Papers, Mailer implied that participation in nonviolent political movements requires the repression of considerable anger and therefore violates the integrity of the protesters. Shago Martin of An American Dream cynically acknowledges that he once "'did the Freedom Rider bit'" (AD, p. 188).

For Mailer, the individual must accept and find some outlet for his violent impulses and expect a similar commitment from others. While he is very critical of Mayor Daley and his police for their brutal treatment of the demonstrators, he likes the Mayor and the people of Chicago for their "great faces, carnal as blood, greedy, direct, too impatient for hypocrisy, in love with honest plunder. They were big and human and their brother in heaven was the slaughtered pig--they did not ignore him" (MSC, p. 90). At the moment that he is manhandled by the police at the end of the Democratic convention, Mailer feels "close to some presence with a beatific grace" (MSC, p. 220), because he knows that he is ready to fight. His admiration for the fighting demonstrators in Chicago leads him to call them "revolutionary youth--they were no longer the same young people who had gone to the Pentagon at all. They were soldiers" (MSC, p. 194).

If Mailer praises these young people for their courage to live at war for four days in "'a city run by a beast'" (MSC, p. 194), he nevertheless criticizes them for their banal language, their nihilism, their reverence for drugs, and their tendency to uphold the advance of technology. In a passage which recalls the negative side of Hawthorne's am-

biguous portrayal of the revelers in "The Maypole of Merry-
mount," Mailer calls the youth "Middle-class cancer-pushers
and drug-gutted flower children" with "their lobotomies from
sin, their nihilistic embezzlement of all middle-class moral
funds, their innocence, their lust for apocalypse, their un-
believable indifference to waste: twenty generations of buried
hopes perhaps engraved in their chromosomes, and now conceivably burning like faggots in the secret inquisitional fires
of LSD. It was a devil's drug--designed by the Devil to
consume the love of the best, and leave them liver-wasted,
weeds of the big city" (AN, p. 34). In addition, he senses
their unwillingness to acknowledge fully the "Beast" in themselves. Not only have they been weaned away from violence
by their parents, but they often become tediously self-righteous in their endless protests carried on in the name of
peace and freedom.

Without developing his cosmology, in Armies and
Miami and the Siege of Chicago Mailer reiterates his idea
of the aggressive "animal imperative" which was first presented in Why Are We in Vietnam? He senses the anger of
many demonstrators who have been arrested in Washington,
and even believes for a while that he may get into a fight
with one of them. In Miami and the Siege of Chicago, he
describes the music of a rock musician as "the roar of the
beast in all nihilism" (MSC, p. 142). Announcing their allegiance to nonviolence, many of the demonstrators "lived
in the sound of destruction of all order as he [Mailer] had
known it, and worlds of other decomposition as well ..."
(MSC, p. 142). He believes that the emphasis upon liber-
ated expression by the Yippies is shortsighted since he is
not convinced that it will result only in "an outpouring of
love," but foresees also "the burning of his neighbor's barn"
(MSC, p. 141). While Mailer clearly states that the violence of the Chicago protest was the result of police brutality, he suggests that the occasion provided at least some of
the demonstrators with the opportunity of expressing impulses
long denied. Unlike the hipster, who possesses a rare sensitivity to his aggressive impulses, the McCarthy supporters
"have been so refined away from the source of much power--
infantile violence--that their moral powers exhibit a lean-
ness, a keenness, and total ferocity which can only hint at
worlds given up ..." (MSC, p. 91).

As in Why Are We in Vietnam?, Mailer's continual
attempt to call attention to man's darkest impulses in an
archetypal manner tends to push his social criticism into

the realm of metapsychology. He begins Miami and the
Siege of Chicago by describing Miami's "white buildings"
which "covered the earth where the jungle had been" (MSC,
p. 11). Echoing Conrad's Heart of Darkness, in which the jungle becomes the symbolic counterpart of the instinctually destructive urges in man, Mailer describes "The vegetal memories of that excised jungle": "Ghosts of expunged flora,
the never-born groaning in vegetative chancery beneath the
asphalt came up with a tropical curse ..." (MSC, pp. 11-12).
Before detailing the Chicago convention, he elaborates upon
the stockyards where the animals are killed: "Watching the
animals be slaughtered, one knows the human case--no matter how close to angel we may come, the butcher is equally
there" (MSC, p. 89). In opposition to his sense of the na-
ïveté of the Yippies, he states "that society is built on many
people hurting many people, it is just who does the hurting
which is forever in dispute" (MSC, p. 140).

As in "The White Negro," Mailer's discussion of A-
merica's social and political order takes place in the context of his concern with the complexity of man's instinctual
life. He acknowledges once again the pervasive nature of
corporate power and stresses the atrophying of the senses
and the concomitant repression that accompany the spread
of totalitarianism and technology. In Miami and the Siege
of Chicago, without using his earlier designations of "Cannibals" and "Christians," Mailer isolates the forces of power in the Republican and Democratic parties. If the "Cannibals" have become chastened since their overwhelming defeat in 1964, they have in Richard Nixon a candidate who
embodies some of their furor against everything alien to
"WASP" rectitude and rugged individuality. Without a Scranton or an aggressive Rockefeller, the Republican party has
hardened even more into "the party of conservatism and principle, of corporate wealth and personal frugality, the party
of cleanliness, hygiene, and balanced budget ..." (MSC, p.
14).

Mailer no longer emphasizes the Cannibals' hatred of
the "second rate"; instead, he focuses upon the loss of instinctual power in the Republicans because of their endless
quest for power and control over all aspects of American
life. On the night of the nomination, nothing "could begin
to recall that sense of barbarians about a campfire and the
ecstasy of going to war which Barry Goldwater had aroused
in '64" (MSC, p. 68). Now "the mood on the floor was like
the level in the main office of a corporation when the Christ-

mas Party is high" (MSC, pp. 68-69). Watching the delegates, Mailer states that "they were not on earth to enjoy or even perhaps to love so very much, they were here to serve ..." (MSC, p. 35). His physical descriptions of the delegates and Nixon suggest Reich's notion of character armor, the endless defenses erected by the body against feeling. They do not possess the hipster's sense of the power and importance of the body. Thus the "loins and mind" of many of the delegates are "cut away from each other by some abyss between navel and hip" (MSC, p. 35). Nixon appears as a man with "odd stick-like motions," and intent upon "the total unstinting exercise of the will ..." (MSC, p. 41). With the language and rhythm of Eliot's poem about Prufrock, at one point Mailer images Nixon as a man who is completely dedicated to pleasing others in an artificial manner. 26

If Mailer views the Republican party as the ideological marriage of the corporation and the small town, the Vietnam war serves to relieve the tensions and contradictions in each. Emphasizing the breakdown of the small town through the advance of technology, in Armies Mailer suggests that the growth of the megalopolis has brought with it unsupportable repression which can only be relieved by such foreign ventures as Vietnam. The "small towns now traveled on the nozzle tip of the flame thrower, no dreams now of barbarian lusts, slaughtered villages, battles of blood, no, nor any need for them--technology had driven insanity out of the wind and out of the attic, and out of all the lost primitive places: one had to find it now wherever fever, force, and machines could come together ... one had to find it in Vietnam ..." (AN, p. 153). Moreover, the war serves as a cure for the "schizophrenia" which pervades America: "Any man or woman who was devoutly Christian and worked for the American Corporation, had been caught in an unseen vise whose pressure could split their mind from their soul. For the center of Christianity was a mystery, a son of God, and the center of the corporation was a detestation of mystery, a worship of technology" (AN, p. 188). The expression of brutality in Vietnam opened the emotions of "the average good Christian American" (AN, pp. 188-89), who not only could serve Christ by feeling compassion for the endless suffering in Asia, but also would locate himself closer to one of the major bastions of the corporation, his daily newspaper in which the facts of the war were reported. If Mailer's thinking about the Vietnam war has changed, it has only been in the direction of a greater exploration of the

psychological needs which the war serves. In both Armies
and Miami and the Siege of Chicago, he reiterates the arguments which he presented in Cannibals and Christians, only
to expand more in the direction of the psychological, rather
than the political or the social, a change in emphasis which
is characteristic of his entire work.

In his discussion of the Democratic party, Mailer also emphasizes the loss of instinctual power which has resulted from years of political manipulation. Using the metaphor of politics as property, "concrete negotiable power,"
Mailer states that when "a politician is his own man, attached to his own search for his own spiritual truth ... then
he is ill-equipped for the game of politics" (MSC, pp. 106,
107). However, in comparison with their Republican counterparts, members of the Democratic party are closer to the
roots of feeling: "... the dreams and the nose for power
of aristocrat and gentry were mixed with beatings in the alley, burials at sea in concrete boots, and the poll tax with
the old poll tax rhetoric" (MSC, p. 177). If the moral property of the McCarthy and McGovern supporters wars with
the political and economic property of Hubert Humphrey, the
cosmetic front for Lyndon Johnson, Mailer nevertheless believes that there is at this convention "a revel of banquetry,
huzzah and horror, a breath of gluttony, a smell of blood"
(MSC, p. 177), all of which suggests a more restrained version of the party given by that arch hipster, Marion Faye,
in "Advertisements for Myself on the Way Out."

The restraint is particularly evident in the major
sources of power at the convention. Mailer stresses Humphrey's ability to manipulate Johnson's political capital by
catering to the needs of various officeholders, trade union
members, and the people from America's diverse minority
groups. The Democrats' nominee is portrayed as a hollow,
papier-mâché figure, a sales manager who exudes artificial
odors. While sympathetic to McCarthy and McGovern because of their opposition to the Vietnam war, Mailer is dis-
turbed by their willingness to accept so much of the basic
fabric of American life. In Armies, he is especially critical of "liberal academics" who are opposed to the foreign
policy in Asia but have no quarrel "with technology land itself"; "They were servants of that social machine of the future in which all irrational human conflict would be resolved
..." (AN, p. 16). Mailer therefore is not happy with
McCarthy supporters whose "common denominator seemed
to be found in some blank area of the soul, a species of

disinfected idealism which gave one the impression when a-
mong them of living in a lobotomized ward of Upper Utopia"
(MSC, pp. 92-93). He is concerned about McCarthy's blandness, passivity, and moral rectitude, all buttressed by a
general lack of feeling and perhaps even a "profound detestation of the Romantic impulse" (MSC, p. 120). As in Cannibals and Christians, he is partial to Robert Kennedy,
whose death haunts the convention with "his admixture of
idealism plus willingness to traffic with demons, ogres, and
overloads of corruption" (MSC, p. 93).

Mailer's evaluation of America's political leaders is
as critical as it was when he wrote Cannibals and Christians.
After Nixon's election in 1968, Mailer stated that "We are
governed no longer by chieftains, statesmen, or princes--
now managers, experts, and executives, members of what
some have come to call the techno-structure, seem to rule
society" (EE, p. 320). Without a public figure who embodies the existential hero, he details his own political solutions in Armies, Miami and the Siege of Chicago, and the
1969 New York mayoralty campaign.

Indicating his dissatisfaction with the Marxist conception of class, Mailer does not see any revolutionary potential in the proletariat, which he views as "Storm Troop
Junction" (AN, p. 20) and a major pillar of support for the
Vietnam war. The most liberal elements of the Democratic
party suggest the programmatic segment of the Socialist
Left with its emphasis upon the use of technology by a cen-
tralized government which will make the wealth of the few
available to everyone. In their quest for power, according
to Mailer, these groups proceed by the "unbreakable logic
of the next step" (AN, p. 85) and are ultimately trapped by
rigid ideological applications which do not acknowledge the
complexity of experience, especially the subtle workings of
the irrational in our daily lives. He offers a similar criticism in "The White Negro," where his vision of the hipster
is an alternative for those who moved through the thirties
and forties with a revolutionary commitment based upon an
allegiance to Marx.

Mailer now presents more thoroughly his earlier idea
that the war between the privileged and the oppressed has
been superseded by the conflict between those who would
maximize the productive resources of civilization and others,
who are concerned with developing a more instinctive mode
of life. This second war is "the seed contained within" the

first, and transcends class and ideology: "It would take
place between those forces on their side, who are programmatic, scientific, more or less socialist, and near maniac
in their desire to bring technological culture at the fastest
possible rate into every backward land, and those more traditional and/or primitive forces in the revolution of the
Third World who reject not only the exploitation of the Western world but reject the West as well, in toto, as a philosophy, a culture, a technique, as a way indeed of even attempting to solve the problems of man himself' (EE, pp. 293,
294). This emphasis has led Conor Cruise O'Brien to state
that "Mailer is to the right of the Old Left intellectually,
but imaginatively drawn to what is most histrionic in the
new. "27

In that section of the Black Power movement in the
United States which eschews technology in favor of the "wisdom of the blood" (EE, p. 300), Mailer sees the most po-
tent political force. He quotes from Ron Karenga, a militant black nationalist: "'The white boy is engaged in the
worship of technology; we must not sell our souls for money
and machines'" (EE, p. 300). With their primitive lore and
a sense of the powers that they have developed in withstand-
ing the onslaught of racist America, these black people have
developed a movement "as mysterious, dedicated, instinctive,
and conceivably bewitched as a gathering of Templars for the
next Crusade" (EE, p. 303). The counterpart to this movement in the white Left is that large group of youth, especially the Yippies, who are "programmatic about drug-taking,
Dionysiacs, propagandists by example, mystical in focus"
(MSC, p. 134). While Mailer is sympathetic to this group
because they share with the hipster a respect for mystery
and spontaneity and a distrust of ideology, he is concerned
that their vision does not urge some restraint by acknowledging the danger of drugs and the complexity of the human
heart with its propensity for violence as well as for love.

In their failure to fuse intelligence and feeling, the
Left, in general, does not possess "a vision sufficiently complex to give life to the land" (MSC, p. 63). He even states
that it might be good for the Left to live through a prolonged
period of "political exile" and "to study what was alive in
the conservative dream" (MSC, p. 63). Earlier, in Cannibals and Christians, Mailer quoted from Edmund Burke in
order to indicate the manner in which Barry Goldwater debased the best in conservative thought. In Miami and the
Siege of Chicago, Mailer even shows some sympathy for

Richard Nixon. Not only has Nixon confronted the abyss in his 1960 defeat by John Kennedy, but most of his earlier sentimentality has been replaced with some comprehension of the dialectical quality of experience. While opposed to Nixon's highly manipulative public presentation of a foreign policy which emphasizes patriotic anticommunism and a social program which does not meet the needs of the poor, Mailer senses that Nixon's positions are not unalterably fixed. Always concerned with the relationship between a leader and his country, Mailer states that "It might even be a measure of the not-entirely dead promise of America if a man as opportunistic as the early Nixon could grow in reach and comprehension and stature to become a leader" (MSC, p. 173).

Without the same sense of immediate apocalypse that he possessed in his previous political writings and in his fictional projections of the hipster, Mailer is now more patient in his hope for a transformation of American society. In an "Open Letter to Richard Nixon," written after the 1968 election, he states that "Nothing less than the artful balance of old dialogues and new, of revolutionary approaches to particular problems and the delicate restoration of tradition within other kinds of crisis can begin to awaken our world from the chimeras of destruction which now surround us" (EE, p. 321). Throughout Armies and Miami and the Siege of Chicago, he continually speaks of a revolution that may take twenty years to accomplish. While it will be replete with the battles of Washington and Chicago, the revolution will also take place with the aid of electoral politics, and Mailer himself is now willing, once more, to enter the fray.

In 1960, Mailer's first attempt to run for the office of Mayor of New York ended when he stabbed his wife and was placed in a psychiatric hospital for several weeks. The act was at least partially a reflection of Mailer's need at the time to follow in the path of the hipster and to act upon his deepest feelings. Still very much concerned with the importance of emotional expression, Mailer entered the New York mayoral primaries in 1969 but conducted his campaign with much of the dull discipline of a political veteran.

Running for Mayor on a ticket with James Breslin, a candidate for President of the City Council of New York, Mailer developed more fully his idea of the "Left Conservative," which appeared initially in The Armies of the Night. Valuing Marx for the dialectical quality of his thought and his sensitivity to political and social inequality, Mailer also admired Edmund Burke for his reverence for the past, particularly his desire to explore matters to their root, and his emphasis upon individual effort against "chaos, evil, or waste" (AN, p. 185). With such a varied ideological framework, Mailer sought to cut across traditional political boundaries and to form "'a hip coalition of the Left and Right.'"28 He states that "The style of New York life has shifted since the Second World War (along with the rest of the American cities) from a scene of local neighborhoods and personalities to a large dull impersonal style of life which deadens us with its architecture, its highways, its abstract welfare, and its bureaucratic reflex to look for government solutions which come into the city from without (and do not work)" (EE, p. 328). To begin to solve these problems, he suggested that New York should be composed of a number of neighborhoods, each of which would reflect the needs and interests of everyone in the city.

His campaign slogan, "Power to the Neighborhoods," was designed to appeal to both ends of the political spectrum. Mailer sought that point where sections of the black and white "Left" as well as genuine conservatives meet; where regard "for the animal, the oak, and the field" reflects a basic faith in "primitive wisdom," the "half remembered sense of primitive perception and so was close to life and the sense of life" (EE, pp. 300, 301). More specifically, within the framework of Mailer's radical politics, the concept of power to the neighborhoods acknowledged that the problems of the poor are the result of external conditions and cannot be solved without public assistance. 29 And yet the slogan reveals Mailer's conservative belief in the importance of individual initiative and competitive struggle. 30 Criticizing everyone, from liberal Democrats to Bolsheviks, he believed that man's problems could not be solved from "without and above," but "through his own agency."31 In order to realize these aims, if not gathering more than fifty per cent of the vote, Mailer wanted to provide a referendum, the passage of which would allow for alteration of the city charter and would turn New York into the fifty-first state, thereby circumventing "power brokers in the trade unions, the Mafia and real estate" (EE, p. 332) as well as the federal and state government.

While very much concerned about the material poverty of large numbers of people living in New York, Mailer continued to echo the hipster's preoccupation with the need for a transformation of the inner life. Mailer believed "that New Yorkers were spiritually as well as financially bankrupt. And by going through the process of acquiring statehood, they would have a rebirth, a rediscovery of the soul."32 Moreover, as the principle of power to the neighborhoods began to thrive, the people of New York would be able to combat "the first spiritual problem of the twentieth century--alienation from the self ..." (EE, p. 334). Some of Mailer's proposals, such as "weekend jousting matches for adolescents in the city's parks," mirror the hipster's emphasis upon the need for instinctual liberation: in this case the possibility for purging one's violence in a courageous encounter. 33

Despite the seriousness in Mailer's attempt to run for Mayor, a number of critics have questioned his ultimate intentions. According to Richard Poirier, Mailer "did not mean that N. Y. C. should elect him its Mayor so that he could live in Gracie Mansion and negotiate the garbage pickups. Rather he meant: elect me as the Imagination of your future in the otherwise sure prospect of 'monotony and bleakness. '"34 Joe Flaherty states that "Mailer was willing to submerge himself in the political role to a point, but he demanded that one keep both eyes open so that the literary figure, the celebrity, also be kept in focus."35

There is some evidence in Mailer's work for the views advanced by Flaherty and Poirier. In both Armies and Miami and the Siege of Chicago, Mailer reiterates his sense of the importance of the literary contribution in shaping the events of the day, and in the power of the imagination as a source of transcendence. In an interview he conducted with himself just a few weeks before the Pentagon protest, Mailer stated that he was more interested in becoming "President of the literary world" (EE, p. 217) than President of the United States. Early in Armies, he tries to dismiss the need for his own active involvement in the protest activities by pointing out that "One's own literary work was the only answer to the war in Vietnam" (AN, p. 9).

In addition, the possibility of Mailer engaging in any action tends to be undermined because of his ability to see the endless conundrums in a situation. What he is usually left with is an intense perception of the possibilities inherent in any experience. In the Pentagon protest, he even refuses to eat in order to maintain the "undeniable clarity and sweet anticipation of his nerves ..." (AN, p. 106). Once

actively involved in a situation, he senses that he has a
limited number of choices, and experiences a corresponding
loss in perceptual power. Thus one of the reasons he contemplates leaving the Pentagon for a party in New York is
his desire "to take the cumulative rising memories of the
last three days and bring them whole, intact, in sum, as
they stood now, to cast, nay--shades of Henry James--to
fling on the gaming tables of life resumed in New York, and
there amass a doubling and tripling again" (AN, p. 118).

Nevertheless, Mailer is not immune to the demands
imposed by the moral and political nature of a situation.
His endless ruminations in Chicago about his fear of entering battle alongside the demonstrators is evidence enough of
the obsessive quality of his political commitment. In Washington his stay in jail results in a conscious decision to give
up some of his desire of "savoring, installing, banking the
value of the experience by way of some enjoyable revery on
the trip home tonight" (AN, p. 160). In his appearance before the judge, he even risks further imprisonment by engaging in a discussion about the nature of his plea.

With all of his doubt, Mailer is still concerned about
having a direct effect upon the world. He appears to have
renounced his political withdrawal, first articulated in Cannibals and Christians, where he stated that "The compromises
one has to make in acquiring power dull the brain irreparably" (CC, p. 255). In Armies, he feels the necessity to
educate the nation, at the same time that he is tempted by
the security of the writer's distance from events. During
his mayoralty campaign, he indicated his dissatisfaction with
literary people: "When you've got a world that's disintegrat-
ing around you, if you're a man and you're leading a life
that is self-protected to a degree, you really can't feel too
agreeable about yourself. "36

Ultimately, what Mailer seeks is a synthesis of his
roles as writer and actor, reporter and participant. Like
the hipster, he is not satisfied with allowing his ideas to remain untested by experience. Earlier, in Advertisements
for Myself, he stated that his "best sentence" is contained
in the thought, "It is the actions of men and not their sentiments which make history ..." (AM, p. 477). Running for
Mayor of New York in 1969, he had "one basic, simple no-
tion--which is that till people see where their ideas lead
they know nothing ..." (EE, p. 344). In the wider context
of his recent work, he seeks to heal the fracturing of thought,
feeling and action which permeates American life.

Therefore, at the end of Armies, his vision of the
hipster as "the wise primitive in a giant jungle" takes on
national significance as he contemplates the delivery of "a
babe of a new world brave and tender, artful and wild" (AN,
p. 288). While he echoes the end of The Great Gatsby as
he did in Barbary Shore, Mailer's vision has become more
hopeful and has broadened to include psychological and theological ramifications not present in his earliest work. If
his criticism of America becomes tempered momentarily in
his hope for the country, he locates himself as an observer
on the edge of possibility, where America can run with the
Devil into a "most fearsome totalitarianism" or can finally
realize "the idea that God was present in every man not
only as compassion but as power, and so the country belonged to the people ... " (AN, p. 288). His earlier sense
of the failure of American radicalism has been replaced
with a hope for the rebirth of America through a recognition of some of the possibilities inherent in the hipster's
quest.

Notes

1. Norman Mailer (New York: The Viking Press, Inc. ,
    1972), p. 129.

2. Miami and the Siege of Chicago: An Informal History
    of the Republican and Democratic Conventions of 1968
    (Cleveland: World Publishing Co. , 1968), p. 123.
    Hereafter, page references to Miami and the Siege of
    Chicago (MSC) will appear in parentheses after the
    quotation.

3. Poirier, Norman Mailer, p. 132.

4. Ibid. , pp. 132-33.

5. Why Are We in Vietnam? (New York: Putnam, 1967),
    p. 203. Hereafter, page references to Why Are We
    in Vietnam? (WV) will appear in parentheses after the
    quotation.

6. Leeds, p. 201.

7. Helsa, pp. 211-15.

8. "Sweepstakes, " New York Review of Books, 28 Sept.
    1967, p. 6.

9. "Current and Recurrent: The Vietnam Novel," Modern Fiction Studies, 17 (1971), 419-25.

10. "Norman Mailer's Why Are We in Vietnam?: A Radical Critique of Frontier Values," Modern Fiction Studies, 17 (1971), 413.

11. Tanner, City of Words, p. 366.

12. John W. Aldridge, "From Vietnam to Obscenity," Harper's, Feb. 1968, p. 92.

13. Pearce, pp. 409-14.

14. Poirier, Norman Mailer, p. 134.

15. Richard D. Finholt, "'Otherwise How Explain?' Norman Mailer's New Cosmology," Modern Fiction Studies, 17 (1971), 376, 386.

16. "The Great American Hunter, or, Ideological Content in the Novel," College English, 34 (Nov. 1972), 186-95.

17. Earlier, Mailer indicated that the basic theme of The Naked and the Dead was "the conflict between the beast and the seer in man."

18. Raymond A. Schroth, "Mailer and His Gods," Commonweal, 29 May 1969, p. 226.

19. Lawler, p. 60.

20. "The 45-Second Piss: A Left Critique of Norman Mailer and The Armies of the Night," Modern Fiction Studies, 17 (1971), 438.

21. "Politics," Esquire, May 1968, p. 194.

22. Tanner, City of Words, p. 371.

23. Poirier, Norman Mailer, p. 147.

24. Gilman, The Confusion of Realms, p. 153.

25. Poirier, Norman Mailer, p. 15.

26. Mailer, Miami and the Siege of Chicago, p. 76.

27. "Confessions of the Last American," New York Review of Books, 20 June 1968, p. 18.

28. Managing Mailer (New York: Coward-McCann, 1969), p. 19. Flaherty quotes Mailer here.

29. Mailer, Existential Errands, p. 336.

30. Mailer, Existential Errands, pp. 336-37.

31. Leticia Kent, "Shoot-for-the-Moon Mailer: An Interview with Norman Mailer on the Literary Life and Practical Politics," in Running Against the Machine, ed. Peter Manso (Garden City, N. Y.: Doubleday, 1969), p. 258. Kent quotes Mailer here.

32. Flaherty, Managing Mailer, p. 40.

33. This proposal appears on page 212 in Running Against the Machine, edited by Peter Manso. While the proposal appears in an unsigned "position paper," entitled "A Miscellany of Ideas for the 51st State," throughout the campaign Mailer mentioned this idea during some of his public appearances.

34. Poirier, Norman Mailer, p. 78.

35. Flaherty, Managing Mailer, p. 83.

36. Kent, p. 256. Kent quotes Mailer here.

CHAPTER 6

AQUARIUS

Of a Fire on the Moon

        While Of a Fire on the Moon describes America's
successful 1969 moon landing, Mailer considers this event
in the context of his earlier psychological, social, political,
and mystical concerns. However, he does so with all of the
tentativeness that characterizes his dialectical method. Although he presents a welter of facts about various aspects
of the launch, Mailer is keenly aware of the complexity of
the experience and is rarely given to complete certainty a-
bout anything. He communicates his sense of the nature of
technology, the inner lives of the astronauts and himself, as
well as the condition of America by continually offering a
wide variety of explanations for everything which he considers, explanations which at times already have been formulated in a different context in his previous work, especially
through his concept of Hip.

        Mailer indicates that two years before the launch he
"had projected a novel ... about a gang of illumined and
drug-accelerated American guerrillas who lived in the wilds
of a dune or a range and descended on Provincetown to
kill."[1] And yet in Fire, the positive presence of the hipster
is but dimly felt. While they possess tremendous courage
and risk death, the astronauts are without the emotional intensity and unique life style that characterize the "white Negro." Moreover, if Mailer adopts the name Aquarius, the
astrological sign for his birth in January, partially in order
to present himself as the unique embodiment of that Counter-
Culture to which he has given his qualified allegiance since
he began writing, he describes that world more critically

than at any previous time. Just after the moon launch, he returns to Provincetown, his summer home, where he has dinner with a friend, Eddie Bonetti, a former prize fighter and aspiring writer, whose energy in the restaurant is reminiscent of Mailer's hipster. Uncharacteristically, Mailer feels "obliged to act as a middle-class silencer" (FM, p. 439), since Bonetti's loud, drunken voice cuts with its curses into the decor of the room. Then, as Aquarius, he ponders the

> princelings on the trail of the hip, so avid to deliver the sexual revolution that they had virtually strained on the lips of the great gate. They had roared at the blind imbecility of the Square, and his insulation from life, his furious petulant ignorance of the true tremor of kicks, but now it was as if the moon had flattened all of his people at once, for what was the product of their history but bombed-out brains, bellowings of obscenity like the turmoil of cattle, a vicious ingrowth of informers, police agents, militants, angel hippies, New Left totalists ... an unholy stew of fanatics, farouts, and fucked-outs where even the few one loved were intolerable at their worst, an army of outrageously spoiled children who cooked with piss and vomit while the Wasps were quietly moving from command of the world to command of the moon, Wasps presenting the world with the fact after prodigies of discipline, while the army he was in, treacherous, silly, overconfident, and vain, haters and despisers of everything tyrannical, phony, plastic and overbearing in American life had dropped out, goofed and left the goose to their enemies. (FM, pp. 440-41)

Mailer not only condemns failed hipsters, but is also highly critical of the sensibility that is responsible for the launch: if "there was a wild nihilism in his own army ...," the Wasps had put their nihilism into the laser and the computer, they were out to savage or save the rest of the world, and were they God's intended?" (FM, p. 441). Mailer continues to use his theology of Hip in order to indicate the possibility that the trip to the moon may be an act of man in the service of either God or the Devil. He is especially concerned that God's embattled vision will fail to be realized in the moon launch because of technology's emphasis upon reason at the expense of magic. The Devil, once more, is imaged as the embodiment of the "electronic, plastic, surgery and computer" (FM, p. 469).

Unlike his earlier work, in which the theology of Hip appeared as a system of belief to which Mailer or one of his characters adhered, in Fire Mailer indicates his doubts about this theory, and offers it only as one possible way of evaluating events. Like Melville, who in the "Extracts" of Moby Dick offers many definitions of the whale in order to communicate its ultimate incomprehensibility, Mailer not only continually re-evaluates the meaning of the moon launch, but also describes the intricacies of rocketry as well as the journey from numerous scientific and personal vantage points. Moreover, just as Melville describes various aspects of whaling and thereby provides a realistic base for his metaphysical ruminations, Mailer purposely spends much time poring over the endless physical details of the launch in order to ground his speculations in the material world.

It is not surprising, then, that Mailer has quite consciously drawn from Melville's Moby Dick in Fire. In addition to comparing the launch rocket to "a Leviathan," and a "mechanical white whale," he describes the color of the ascending ship as "the white of Melville's Moby Dick" (FM, pp. 55, 219, 100). At one point, he even suggests that to be an astronaut "one might need some of the monomania of Captain Ahab" (FM, p. 330). In addition, if the long section on the whaling industry comprises much of the middle of Melville's novel, Mailer has divided Fire into three parts, the second of which focuses mainly upon the data of the space program. Parts One and Three are concerned much more with the inner lives of people, especially Mailer himself and the astronauts, but are enmeshed in physical reality through intermittent descriptions of various aspects of the space program. As in The Armies of the Night, Mailer has carefully fused subject and object in order to present experience faithfully. That one tends to be overwhelmed by the plethora of scientific detail in Fire is a reflection of Mailer's continual movement away from the intense subjectivity of the hipster. The very size of the event pushes Mailer to the realization "that the world had changed, even as he had thought to be pushing and shoving on it with his mighty ego" (FM, p. 55). Watching the proceedings, he experiences a progressive diminishing of his personality, so that in much of Fire he virtually empties his perceptions of the last vestiges of himself and tediously records facts about the launch and the space program.

As Aquarius, he views himself as "different in spirit
from eight years ago. He has learned to live with questions"
(FM, p. 4). Unlike his willingness in Advertisements for
Myself to prophesy about the future of America, in Fire his
sense of the seventies is blurred by "no intimations of what
was to come ..." (FM, p. 141). Within the context of his
earlier dialectic, his uncertainty has grown to the point
where he now fully acknowledges that he "had long built his
philosophical world on the firm conviction that nothing was
finally knowable ... he had almost no interest in the small
secret behind a small event.... (There was invariably another secret behind that.) He preferred to divine an event
through his senses ..." (FM, p. 7). Throughout Fire, Mailer considers himself a detective who is writing the most difficult book of his life because of the complexity of the experience which he is attempting to describe, an attitude which
persists in his journalism of the seventies. In "The Faith
of Graffiti," he states that "Journalism is bondage unless you
can see yourself as a private eye inquiring into the mysteries
of a new phenomenon. "2

It is perhaps this very complexity which forces Mailer
into thinking dualistically and thus undermining the sense of
incertitude which he seeks to transmit to the reader. As
Donald Kaufmann points out, Mailer is locked "into a kind of
schizophrenic view of virtually everything and everybody in
Fire. "3 He "hardly knew whether the Space Program was
the noblest expression of the Twentieth Century or the quin-
tessential statement of our fundamental insanity" (FM, p. 15).
Since the entire launch is viewed as possibly a contest between God and the Devil, the astronauts are perceived as
"technicians and heroes, robots and saints, adventurers and
cogs of the machine," who mirror the national mood in A-
merica, "the schizophrenia of the land growing more Faustian and more oriental each season with ABM and million-
footed folk-rock festivals at the poles ... (FM, pp. 313,
316). Even details are often rendered in Manichean terms,
so that the digital computer "was a diabolical machine, or
the greatest instrument ever handed to man" ... (FM, p.
352). The imagery which permeates Fire in the numerous
comparisons of various aspects of the rocket, the launch,
the astronauts, and their brief stay on the moon, to a range
of conditions described in terms of birth and religious apocalypse, reinforces this dualistic thinking. Throughout the
book, Mailer considers the rocket as a "cathedral," "madon-
na," or "shrine," in order to remind the reader that the
NASA program was the "last chalice of Good Square Life"

(FM, p. 253). Nevertheless, the trip to the moon has o-
pened new vistas for technology and the imagination and
thereby diminishes the very security which the Square might
hope to find in the religious significance of the event. Its
immensity and newness elicits in Mailer the response of one
witnessing a birth. The Command Module is described as a
"womb for triplets" (FM, p. 239). Within his space helmet,
Armstrong looks "as lashless in appearance as a newborn
cat in a caul" (FM, p. 87). When Aldrin gives instructions
in the spacecraft before the actual walk upon the moon,
"there was an inevitable suggestion of the kind of dialogue
one hears between an obstetrician and a patient in the last
minutes before birth" (FM, p. 123). On the moon, Armstrong lopes like "a just-born calf" (FM, p. 125).

This tendency to view all experience in terms of un-
resolved dichotomies leads Richard Poirier to describe a
significant shift in Mailer's thinking, away from "a supple,
intimate, and daring search within his schematizations for
pressures that would unsettle them" and toward an insistence
"that the events or persons he writes about should fit the
scheme."4 The syncretic vision so characteristic of his recent work remains, especially when Mailer contemplates the
emergence of a theory "which could revolve at some ease
through the metaphors of the moon and find the link of metaphysical reason between cancer, acne, blisterings of paint
and the wrinkled ridges of a soiled and skin-thick milk" (FM,
p. 291). However, this vision almost becomes a parody of
itself because of Mailer's tendency to lift every event to the
symbolic importance of myth, often with the aid of his "philosophy of Hip. "

He does not hesitate to comment on matters which
have preoccupied him in the past by finding the right moment
to make a slight detour from his subject and to fuse that detour with his central concern. Thus he challenges the Freudian conception of the dream as wish-fulfillment by offering
his own theory that the dream may be "a set of simulations
which explore into dread," a notion which leads to "some obvious comparisons with the trip of Apollo 11 to the moon"
(FM, p. 161). In an earlier essay, "Hip, Hell and the Navigator," which Mailer offered as an appendage to "The White
Negro," he stated that the "Navigator," the helmsman in the
unconscious, possesses "an enormous teleological sense" (AM,
p. 386). In Fire, Mailer suggests that each person has "the
services of a novelist" who drew up "new social charts upon
which the Navigator could make his calculations" (FM, p.

157). The dream, then, becomes for Mailer possibly "some psychic equivalent of those equations of celestial mechanics which find it impossible to plot the trajectory of a moving rocket precisely because there are too many unknowns" (FM, pp. 157-58). The grandiosity of the comparison is not diminished when Mailer imposes his idea of Hip on the process of dreaming and describes the dreamer as one who "was exploring the depths of his own ability to perceive crisis and react to it; he was exploring ultimate modes of existence in sex and in violence, in catastrophe and in death" (FM, pp. 160-61).

If the Apollo Mission gives Mailer the opportunity to comment on the nature of the dream, it also allows him to digress in a discussion of the issue of race. The presence of a Black man at a party in Houston becomes the catalyst for Mailer's speculations about the differences between Black and White culture in the context of the space program. He reiterates the argument first elaborated upon in Existential Errands, where he spoke of the allegiance of one section of the Black Left to magic, an allegiance which in Fire is called the "potential greatness of the Black people" (FM, p. 137). While referring to technology as the tool of the White man, whose senses have been gutted, Mailer echoes the racial stereotypy of "The White Negro": the "instinctive apprehension of existence" among Black people is now reflected in their "distaste for numbers ... because numbers were abstracted from the senses ..." (FM, p. 138).

Of paramount importance in Of a Fire on the Moon, then, is Mailer's desire to comment on psychological, social, and political conditions in the United States. Just as the Army served as the microcosm in The Naked and the Dead, in Fire a discussion of the space program is used as the basis for Mailer's vision of America, its people and institutions. The central dichotomy is whether America will consolidate the movement toward "totalitarianism" and perhaps global destruction through the technological advances epitomized in the moon launch, or whether the country has found in the space program a way to encourage people to bring adventure, mystery, awe, and dread into their lives. A similar problem had been posed in The Presidential Papers and Cannibals and Christians, where the hipster is threatened by the homogeneous life style of Americans who willingly submit to the bland progress of technology urged upon them by the corporations.

More specifically, Mailer views the space program within the context of his earlier conception of American history as "two rivers, one visible, the other underground; there has been the history of politics which is concrete, factual, practical and unbelievably dull if not for the consequences of the actions of some ... and there is a subterranean river of untapped ferocious, lonely and romantic desires, that concentration of ecstasy and violence which is the dream life of the nation" (PP, p. 38). In Fire, America has "erupted" from the "pressure between its love of adventure and its fear that adventure was not completely shut down" (FM, p. 59). The trip to the moon provides Americans with an excuse to "take to the road," both imaginatively and literally, since hundreds of thousands come to Florida to view the launch. But they do so rather like Rusty and his corporate cohorts in the Alaskan wild, with "air mattresses which reposed on plastic cloth floors of plastic cloth tents--what a sweet smell of Corporate Chemical, what a vat and void to mix with all the balmy fermy chlorophylls and pollens of nature! America the Sanitary, and America the Wild, went out to sleep in the woods, Sanitary-Lobe and Wild-Lobe nesting together neatly, schizophrenic twins in the skull case of the good family American" (FM, p. 60).

Those who are responsible for the space program, namely the large corporations and their "Praetorian Guard" (politicians and police), hope that the trip to the moon will magically wipe away the "specter of civil war" which was raised during the sixties in the ghettoes and the colleges: they are Jamesian innocents without a culture, who looked for the "single idea" which "could still electrify the land" (FM, pp. 68, 67). But they are also tied to the deadened, unemotional world of technology, where reason must prevail if the secrets of nature are to be unlocked. Werner Von Braun becomes their embodiment: the "real and true tasty beef of capitalism," he is a man of "veritable brawn," who "wheeled whole complexes of caution into every gesture," so that "the very philosophical explosives he contained under such supercompression gave him an air of magic" (FM, pp. 75, 73).

As "the core of some magnetic human force called Americanism, patriotism, or Wasptitude" (FM, p. 315), the astronauts are for Mailer a reflection of America's divided state: they are men whose allegiance to the rational, purposeful, and mannered conceals another life of impulse, especially the aggressive "animal imperative." If Collins is

"the living spirit of good and graceful manners," Armstrong
is "extraordinarily remote," and Aldrin ("all meat and stone")
suggests "the strength of a tank, dull, almost ponderous"
(FM, pp. 25, 22, 23). Nevertheless, there is Aldrin's "hint
of unpredictability," which is matched by Armstrong's "hints
of every forest apprehension from the puma to the deer to
the miseries of the hyena," and Collins' "Hemingway" mus-
tache (FM, pp. 23, 31, 26). These slight glimmerings of
impulse beneath the rational facade suggest another tension
in the astronauts which is common to the age, "to dwell in
the very center of technological reality ... yet to inhabit--
if only in one's dreams--that other world where death, metaphysics and the unanswerable questions of eternity must re-
side ..." (FM, p. 47). By the end of Fire, Mailer concludes

> that probably we had to explore into outer space,
> for technology had penetrated the modern mind to
> such a depth that voyages in space might have be-
> come the last way to discover the metaphysical
> pits of that world of technique which choked the
> pores of modern consciousness--yes, we might
> have to go out into space until the mystery of new
> discovery would force us to regard the world once
> again as poets, behold it as savages who knew
> that if the universe was a lock, its key was meta-
> phor rather than measure. (FM, p. 471)

If he has created a new synthesis out of warring opposites, this vision has not been adequately substantiated.
For it is only Mailer as Aquarius who possesses such strong
intimations that mystery is at the heart of the denatured
space program. Neither the astronauts, the numerous technicians, the other journalists, nor the rest of the people described throughout the book seem to share Mailer's emphasis.
Mailer, then, has superimposed his mystical sense of experience upon an event whose meaning, he believes, has been
limited by the "technologese" of those responsible for it.
Once again he criticizes Marx for having "done his best to
gut the past of every attachment to the primitive, the sacra-
mental, and the magical," a process which has elevated reason and technology to their present "insane eminence" (FM,
p. 131). Mailer feels "obliged to make a first reconnaissance
into the possibility of restoring magic, psyche, and the spirits of the underworld to the spookiest venture in history ..."
(FM, p. 131). In the guise of Aquarius he has resurrected
some of the sensibility of the "white Negro," particularly
Rojack.

Possessing Rojack's sense of the importance of dread and death, Mailer opens Fire with a discussion of Hemingway's suicide, an event which has filled the air with dread that Americans would eliminate through technology, especially the space program. Upon his visit to the Manned Spacecraft Center in Houston, Mailer shares the hipster's contempt for NASA Wasps, "the most Faustian, barbaric, draconian, progress-oriented, and root destroying people on earth" (FM, p. 10), whose deodorized environment and computerized language reflect their inability to live close to dread and death. Unlike these people who view the moon as "friendly," "hospitable," and "dull" (FM, pp. 408, 410), Mailer looks at that body with Rojack's crazed sense of its mysteries. He "had felt the fullness of the moon in his own dread, his intimations of what full criminality he might possess, had felt the moon in the cowardice not to go out on certain nights, felt the moon when it was high and full and he was occasionally on the side of the brave" (FM, p. 436). He calls the moon "the platinum satellite of our lunacy, our love, and our dreams," "the pale graveyard of sleep," and a "centrifuge of the dream, accelerating every new idea to incandescent states" (FM, pp. 152, 245, 284). The trip may disrupt "God knows what Valhalla of angels and demons, what eminences of benignity and eyries of the most refined spook essence ..." (FM, p. 245). Poring over pictures of the moon, Mailer feels "as if he were a medieval alchemist rubbing at a magic stone whose unfelt vibration might yet speak a sweet song to his nerve" (FM, p. 293).

Looking down from the stages of the vehicle assembly building before the ascent, Mailer echoes Rojack again, suggesting that such a vision opened "oneself to a study of the dimensions of one's fear of heights" (FM, p. 54). Like Rojack, who infuses the objects of the natural environment with demonic power, Mailer compares the ascending rocket to a "thin and pointed witch's hat, and the flames from its base were the blazing eyes of the witch" (FM, p. 101). Moreover, in the chapter entitled "The Psychology of Machines," he refers to the "dread" which "inhabited the technology of rockets" (FM, p. 169) because of the number of unexplained phenomena that have occurred in the space program. He suggests that a man's personality may be responsible for a malfunctioning machine. And he even echoes D. J.'s concern with the changes possibly precipitated by the mysterious "field of magnetic force generated out of the depths of molten iron in the core of the earth itself" (FM, p. 277).

Unlike in An American Dream and Why Are We in
Vietnam?, where it is difficult at times to evaluate just how
much Mailer believes in the arcane theories which are advanced through his narrators, in Fire Mailer offers his i-
deas quite tentatively. He recognizes that "he had all the
failures of the occult in all the ages for model, and so he
knew as he wrote that if the riddle of the ages was at the
root of every form--a pure medievalist is Aquarius!--so,
too, was every temptation of insanity. The profligacies of
thought--total irresponsibility of connection, and complete
loss of the ability to convince ..." (FM, p. 293). Moreover, most of Fire is a careful recreation of the event and
the theories of physics and chemistry which are necessary
to understand it, as well as the social and political matrix
within which the event occurs. Yet, in his perception of
some of the limitations of existing scientific theory and the
experimental nature of engineering, Mailer offers up tentative hypotheses culled from his earlier mystical thought.
At that point where he is faced with the uncertainties inherent in the venture to the moon, his thought tends to wander
into the realm of magic. Existential uncertainty gives way
to Rojack's wild intuitions and D. J. 's sense of the spook
flux of the North Pole. Too often in Fire, Mailer's method
of presenting multiple explanations for complex phenomena
degenerates into careless speculation.

St. George and the Godfather

In St. George and the Godfather, Mailer reflects upon
the 1972 Democratic and Republican Conventions and the
events which surround them in a manner similar to his recreation of the 1969 moon launch. Adopting again the persona of Aquarius, he presents himself as "modest and half-
invisible"5 in order to temper the fires of his ego, an attempt which succeeds only partially. Utilizing the mask of
skepticism which he has cultivated in his use of the dialectic, he looks at American politics with the eye of a chronicler of social and political history as well as through the neb-
ulous filter of his mysticism. In this work his mysticism
is fused with an understanding of America based on the sec-
ular significance of religion. It is not that Mailer has come
to embrace a firmer religious perspective than his theology
of Hip, but that his political analysis rests upon his sense
that

In America, the country was the religion. And all
the religions of the land were fed from that first
religion which was the country itself, and if the
other religions were now full of mutation and stag-
gering across deserts of faith, it was because the
country had been false and ill and corrupt for
years, corrupt not in the age-old human proportions of failure and evil, but corrupt to the point
of terminal disease, like a great religion founder-
ing.
        So the political parties of America might be the
true churches of America, and our political leaders
the popes and prelates, the bishops and ministers
and warring clergymen of ideologies which were
founded upon the spiritual rock of America as much
as any dogma. (SGG, p. 87)

Echoing Of a Fire on the Moon, where the launch is
considered to be the result of Wasp discipline and purpose-
fulness, Mailer quickly refers to the landing area for nota-
bles at the Miami Airport as "Blast Site One," and to Mc-
Govern as an "astronaut" because of "that sense he gave off
of Christian endeavor," his "incorruptible filament of charisma which could be a hole if talking of a saint ..." (SGG,
pp. 12, 24). McGovern is a "minister" with a voice which
speaks "of Methodist beds of Procrustes" (SGG, pp. 68, 24).

The other candidates seeking the Democratic party's
nomination for president are also imaged in religious terms.
There is "Father Hubert," "a Renaissance priest of the Vat-
ican who could not even cross a marble floor without pieties
issuing from his skirt" (SGG, p. 19). And Edmund Muskie:
"If he had grave sins and hell was awaiting him, he must
certainly have paid a tithe in purgatory" (SGG, p. 40). When
George Wallace stepped from the plane, "the band played
'The Star Spangled Banner' as slowly as a hymn to the mar-
tyred spirits beyond" (SGG, p. 10).

With Nixon, the only candidate for president in the
Republican party, Mailer speaks of "Nicodemus," "the Godfather," whose podium at the convention "looked like the bastions of a castle and the battlements of a medieval fort, it
looked like some huge white ship in the sky. Speakers at
the altar of that high and immense podium spoke as if from
the heights of the white knights of Christendom" (SGG, p.
204).

If Mailer utilizes religious imagery to describe the candidates for the presidency, he does not do so with the intention of offering an easy explanation for contemporary American political experience. As in his earlier work, he cultivates the hipster's "negative capability," which has become a stance in itself since Fire and the advent of Aquarius. In Part One, which details the Democratic Convention, Mailer states on the opening page that there are "too many questions and (given the probability of a McGovern steamroller) not enough drama to supply answers. He would be obliged to drift through events, and use the reactions of his brain for evidence" (SGG, p. 3). In Part Two, which focuses mainly upon the consequences of the discoveries made about the past of Thomas Eagleton, McGovern's initial choice for vice president, but which concludes with an interview with Henry Kissinger, Nixon's chief advisor and foreign emissary, Mailer is left at the end "with something near to bewilderment" and is prepared "to go down to Miami again to see if there were moral objects still to be delineated in the ongrowing blur of his surest perceptions" (SGG, p. 121). In comparison with these doubts, his firmer conclusions about the Republican Convention result from his early sense that this meeting "would be interesting after all, not for its conflict, and never for its surprise--rather, for the promise of design" (SGG, p. 137). Even this last part, which ends with chapters and subchapters--a recreation of events witnessed by Mailer, interspersed with "Nixon's Maxims," as well as characteristic vignettes gathered from various newspapers and leaflets--not only suggests a highly detailed scenario into which everything can fit, but also allows for an ironic juxtaposition that tends to explode any order earlier conceived of.

Despite this skepticism, Mailer is clear in his political preferences. Where McGovern offers a liberal humanitarianism whose roots lie close to the Unitarian tradition, Nixon is content with chauvinistic pieties that cut across the dead center of American political life. Thus McGovern "inhabited that religious space where men dwell when they are part of the powers of a church and wish to alter that church to its roots" (SGG, p. 87). He emits "a free current of moral decency which proved to be as strong as the agreeable sense of awe one could know at the best of times in a church" (SGG, p. 110). Mailer sympathizes with McGovern's desire to end the Vietnam War, to decrease poverty, and to democratize American politics, all of which are imaged as secularized forms of the Christian impulse to serve one's fellow man. Nixon, however, is content with consolidating his political position by manipulating the American public, even to the point where he may have decided to allow twelve nominating speeches in order to remind the public of the "twelve apostles" (SGG, p. 205). Nixon speaks in a voice that lays "like Bromo Seltzer upon the pumping of the heart," to those who know that America "had to be saved--the heart of God resided in the living life of an orderly America ..." (SGG, pp. 227, 154). They are the "wad," that mass of homogeneous Americans known to Mailer as "the frozen congelations of the mediocre" (SGG, p. 138), whose apathy often prevented them from voting but who could be aroused to condemn anything that touched upon crime, homosexuality, welfare, hippies, or communists. But Nixon also speaks for most corporation directors, advertising executives, and bankers, as well as the remainder of the small number of rich and importantly placed people who are usually responsible for the shape of power in America. Their religion, "like the religion of the wad, was freedom from dread" (SGG, p. 174).

As in his other political writing, Mailer does not define his allegiances simplistically. He admires Nixon's ability to manipulate the American public, in contrast to McGovern's ineptitude. Although he shares McGovern's vision, as in Armies and Miami and the Siege of Chicago, Mailer questions the faith in technology and the absence of feeling which characterize the more radical elements in the Democratic party. Throughout St. George and the Godfather he calls Nixon an artist because of his ability to create the most packaged political convention in American history. With consummate skill, Nixon engineers a display for television by using speakers who represent various ethnic backgrounds, surnames, religious affiliations as well as political positions, and by eliminating virtually all dissent except for the interruptions of minor protest which also are pressed into the scenario.

Unlike Nixon, McGovern has not mastered the art of manipulation. While he tempers his earlier radical positions, he has incurred the wrath of some of his more militant supporters, especially women. Moreover, he has blundered immeasurably in the initial choice of Thomas Eagleton for the vice presidency: first in not finding out about that senator's trips to the Mayo Clinic to receive electric shock treatments; and later, by dropping him from the ticket just when, according to Mailer, many people were positively aroused, especially the "Wallace folk who liked a candidate with a flaw

they could recognize, something homey and down to rights,
a skeleton in the closet at which they had had a peek" (SGG,
p. 96).

But Mailer saves his most serious criticism of Mc-
Govern for the senator's style, "that paucity of pomp and
pleasure which ... moral principles forbid ..." (SGG, p.
22). Just as he criticized Eugene McCarthy in 1968 for his
lack of emotional intensity, Mailer speaks of "a flatness of
affect in McGovern which depresses," especially the "muted
singsong of his conversational voice," "that tight voice of
a thousand restraints which sings of not a thing but its singsong resentment against the fact of its restraint ..." (SGG,
pp. 22, 24). McGovern's voice suggests "the rigor and
rectitude of a bare, arduous, and programmed life" (SGG,
p. 24). Mailer extends this criticism to his description of
McGovern's followers who are part of "a clerical revolution,
an uprising of the suburban, the well-educated, the modest,
the reasonable and all the unacknowledged genetic engineers
of the future. The best of the liberal mind and the worst
were his troops, all the warriors for a reasonable ecology
and a world where privilege could no longer paralyze were
in his army as well as all the social whips for a new state
of collective man opposed to any idea of mystery in any or-
ganism social or human--a spirit of science concentrated into pills to push behavior" (SGG, pp. 26-27).

Here, as in Miami and the Siege of Chicago, Mailer's
social criticism is tied to his metapsychology with its emphasis upon feeling, especially the aggressive "animal imperative," and points to his earlier allegiance to the emotional intensity of the hipster. What charisma McGovern
possesses is "not of personality but of purpose" (SGG, p.
25) and therefore runs counter to the sensibility of the existential political hero who was described in The Presidential
Papers. McGovern is the essence of moral control, "a fine
blade, stern and silver" (SGG, p. 25). Humphrey's stiff-
ness, however, does not serve the same noble political ends.
His talk to the Jewish Senior Citizens "was analogous to
strip-mining the emotions of the aged" (SGG, p. 16). With
"coatings of TV makeup thick as barnacles," he barely conceals the fact that "the separate parts of his face were no
longer flesh so much as jointed shells" (SGG, p. 17). In
this description of Humphrey, Mailer again appears to have
drawn from the work of Wilhelm Reich, which is utilized
even more directly in the portrayal of Nixon, a president
with "hordes" of "character armor": "Several schemes of

armor are stacked all on top of one another, but none complete" (SGG, p. 198). He is a man almost completely cut
off from his feelings and his body. Like Nixon, whose life
has been given over to the various manipulations of his mind,
Agnew is imaged as a "Latin American dictator" who possesses "a peculiar impersonality much as if he is a spirit installed in some flesh-and-body machine which shakes hands"
(SGG, p. 173). Only among the Wallace delegates and their
most bitter opponents, the Black Caucus, does Mailer find
"the warmth and faction" which are so central to the "white
Negro's" quest.

Nevertheless, it is mainly in the absence of theatre
at the conventions, countered by the atmosphere provided by
some of the demonstrators in the streets of Miami and in
Flamingo Park, that Mailer once again has recourse to his
"philosophy of Hip." If part of Nixon's scenario has included a large throng of Young Voters for the President ("YVP-
ers") who "cheer him as if he is the most popular high-
school principal they have ever had," the demonstrators are
a much more heterogeneous group and emit a mood that is
"separate from everything in the Republican convention," a
mood so "sweet, contentious, hassled, frayed, tawdry, bor-
ing, comic, comfortable, menacing, and the faces are always
in opposition, so direct and so spaced out, so handsome, so
full of acne, so innocent, so open, so depraved, so freaky,
so violent, so gentle ..." (SGG, pp. 197, 220). The feelings
generated in the "YVPers" are often close to hysteria, especially when Nixon is nominated:

> Young Voters for the President were storming cen-
> ter stage ... with such a rush of stampede that
> older delegates were in a horror to get out of
> their way for the YVPers might trample them.
> Anything to reach those balloons which were com-
> ing down! Young Voters were there to devour
> balloons, burst them like bits of meat thrown into
> a pond of piranhas, balloons exploded in a cacoph-
> ony of small arms' fire. And the Young Voters
> waved American flags they carried on small sticks,
> waved them violently. The fins of piranhas were
> in on a new kill. It was as of a celebration of all
> the murder you could shake loose in America.
> (SGG, p. 209)

This display is hardly the philosophical psychopath's conscious search into the past in order to release repressed

feeling, but a momentary unconscious outburst which points
to the vast anger secretly harbored by the Republican young.
While in Armies and Miami and the Siege of Chicago Mailer's
sympathies were clearly with the radical youth because of
their energy and social objectives, in St. George and the
Godfather his admiration extends to their ability to govern
themselves, to become "a community of consent" (SGG, p.
219).

Once again Mailer appears to be moving further away
from the unrestraint so characteristic of his earlier radicalism, especially his notion of the hipster, in order to embrace a more politically expedient perspective. He wonders
if this latest round of demonstrations will only serve to help
"dignify the battlements of the white knights of Christendom"
(SGG, p. 218). Unlike the protests of the late sixties in
which he participated, the street action in Miami forces
Mailer to reflect upon its futility, only because "the real
war" had not yet come to America: "if it ever came ...
he would presumably be enough of a man to recognize it.
If he was not, it would be his own karmic ass he fried"
(SGG, p. 168).

Here Mailer's sense of spiritual retribution in a time
of revolutionary crisis points to the mysticism which often
pervades his "philosophy of Hip. " As in Fire, Mailer projects
himself as Aquarius, whose doubt about his perceptions gives
way at times to an encrusted mystical vision which is mirrored in a sensibility that suggests Rojack's. Consider, for
instance, the opening of St. George and the Godfather, which
indicates the method of the entire book: "Greetings to Charles
Dickens across vales of Karma: it was the best and worst
of conventions" (SGG, p. 3). In this instance, the realistic
tradition within which Mailer operates when he writes as a
chronicler of events is merged with his highly subjective vision of supernatural portents. However tentatively this vision may be offered, it still contributes to the tone of the
book.

Moreover, if in his discussion of the activities com-
prising the Democratic Convention and the surrounding events
Mailer continually reiterates the problem of fully comprehend-
ing the events before him, the ground for his understanding
has at least been partially established in his earlier work
through the mysticism and theology embedded in his "philosophy of Hip. " He acknowledges that "he is much more mystical about the presidency than fashion permits ... " (SGG,

p. 23). And he wonders if in the process of voting "the average man might be engaged in some inarticulate transaction
with eternity?" (SGG, p. 6). Part One of St. George and
the Godfather was initially entitled "The Evil in the Room"5
so as to suggest the absence in the McGovern forces of
"malignity" and "vested bile" (SGG, p. 86), the demonic
powers which Mailer has courted since his presentation of
the existential political hero. He states that "no convention
had ever been more in need of the primeval hysteria of an
all-out demonstration which might remind the delegates of
the fires which resided beneath" (SGG, p. 64). He misses
the "Satanic" spirit which he felt in the charisma of the Kennedy's. And he adds, "assassination was not the worst fer-
tilizer for theories of demonology or Satanist perspectives
on the seizure of history" (SGG, p. 23).

In the Wallace campaign, the Women's Caucus, and
the Eagleton affair, Mailer perceives the slight encroachment
of the demonic at the convention. Wallace "brings with him
the clank of chains down in the dungeons of the moon-reach-
ing blood-pumped crazy American desire" (SGG, p. 15).
But with the Women's Caucus, Mailer is parodying rather
than describing the real infusion of mysterious forces, since
he speaks of the form and style of their protest as "totalitarian." He reads a lettered banner declaring WOMEN POW-
ER as OMEN POWER, "a tribute to witchcraft in the new
political cosmos" (SGG, p. 56). The Eagleton affair, Mailer
suggests, may be "the fine hand of the Devil giving a stir of
the broth for Richard Nicodemus, or the worst zodiacal con-
catenation ever handed a presidential poker player ..." (SGG,
p. 102). However, Rojack's magical world is more directly
reflected among the radical demonstrators, that "medieval
people's band of lepers and jesters who put a whiff of demonology on the screen, or lay an entertaining shiver along the
incantations of their witches" (SGG, p. 218).

In the "dread" conjured up within the "wad" by the
spectacle of these "barbarians," Nixon finds further fuel for
political manipulation. Nixon's bombing of the North Viet-
namese, according to Mailer, is psychologically akin to the
bombing of "the barbarisms beating in the young": "evil was
a plague of creeping things and the bombs were DDT to the
cess-dumps of the world" (SGG, p. 154). Unlike the hipster
who lives close to dread, Nixon's entire campaign is based
upon eliminating the terror of the unknown, the mysterious,
and the irrational. Mailer compares the President's personality to the vacuousness of the television tube which, in turn,

has been utilized to transmit to the American people proceedings that in no way will shake the blandness of their lives. Since he gives a mystical cast to the argument first presented in The Presidential Papers about the effect of the president upon the nation, by describing that office as "primitive," inspiring "the tribes of America to pick up the modes and manners of their chief," Mailer worries about "the damage to temperament, bravado, and wit which the emotional austerities of Nixon had laid on the nation" (SGG, p. 23). Mailer even suspects that the Democrats, with their philanthropic proposals such as welfare reform, are discouraging individual initiative, an idea which was central in his 1969 mayoralty campaign. He reiterates his skeptical allegiance to Marx by questioning the possibility of arriving at a clear economic analysis of poverty because of the biases of the researcher as well as the complexity of the producer and the consumer. Thus Mailer likes "'An existential economy'" which stays "closer to greed, ego, stamina, and desire" (SGG, p. 55).

Mailer's vagueness in his analysis of economic conditions is a reflection of the weakness inherent in his mystical thought and his metapsychology. After The Naked and the Dead he has been inclined to de-emphasize material poverty in his analysis of American life and has focused upon the emotional results of living in a "totalitarian" society. His conception of the "wad," then, is a social stereotype based upon his sense of the inner life of a rather large group of people and in no way does justice to the infinite political, economic, and even psychological differences among them. Moreover, in discussing the significance of the inner life and the emotional aura about events, he at times has had recourse to arcane theories. In St. George and the Godfather, as in Fire, he skeptically advances these ideas which are an outgrowth of his mysticism and his theology of Hip.

Despite his constant qualifications, Mailer does not prevent his supernatural vision from obfuscating his social criticism. In the name of feeling, in opposition to the excesses of technology, in favor of a more humane perspective than that offered by the social sciences, where jargon and the most rigid forms of thinking often blur any sense of what it means to be human, Mailer seeks the epiphany within events, but he has a tendency to be trapped by the vagaries of his position. At his best he is able to tame the hipster's intense subjectivity by locating himself at a point approximately equidistant from the welter of fact inherent in social and political experience and the emotional reverberations which events create. It was in Advertisements for Myself that Mailer first expressed his desire to describe "the psychic anatomy of our Republic." In much of St. George and the Godfather, as well as in The Armies of the Night and Miami and the Siege of Chicago, this desire is realized when he tempers his mystical and theological interests and provides magnificent metaphorical resonance for his social and political observations.

Notes

1. Of a Fire on the Moon (Boston: Little, Brown and Company, 1970), pp. 460-61. Hereafter, page references to Of a Fire on the Moon (FM) will appear in parentheses after the quotation.

2. "The Faith of Graffiti," Esquire, May 1974, p. 77.

3. "Mailer's Lunar Bits and Pieces," Modern Fiction Studies, 17 (1971), 452.

4. Poirier, Norman Mailer, p. 160.

5. St. George and the Godfather (New York: The New American Library, 1972), p. 3. Hereafter, page references to St. George and the Godfather (SGG) will appear in parentheses after the quotation.

6. "The Evil in the Room," Life, 28 July 1972, pp. 26-41.

CHAPTER 7

MAILER AND WOMEN: The Prisoner of Sex

     The Prisoner of Sex is the culmination of Mailer's
thinking about the relationship between men and women, and
the nature of the sexual process.   However, as in much of
his earlier writing, his discussion often grows out of or
leads into other issues, so that one is left again with a syncretic vision which defies neat systematization.   Observations that cut across a variety of fields, from psychology
and sociology to biology, theology, and literary criticism,
are woven together in a language rich in metaphor and allusion.   What holds the observations together is Mailer's
consistent use of a persona who, though possessing a variety of names, reflects the sensibility of Aquarius, the narrative vehicle of Fire and St. George and the Godfather.   The
distaste for technology which permeated so much of his previous work is intensified considerably in The Prisoner of
Sex, at the same time that the mysteries of sexuality are
dialectically emphasized.

     Unlike most of his work, particularly his fiction,
where men play the dominant role, often through the hipster
who is a male persona, in Prisoner Mailer spends much
time detailing his attitudes toward women, at times with the
unacknowledged aid of his "philosophy of Hip." In fact, his
failure to account sufficiently for the experience of women
is one of the major limitations of his earlier writing.
Throughout his career, Mailer has virtually admitted that he
has been unable to capture the complexity of any woman.
His honest confusion is revealed in Of a Fire on the Moon,
where he states that he "spent his formative years and young
manhood in searching for the true nature of women ... " (FM,
p. 7).   He is even more direct in a recent interview when

he remarks that "the greatest vanity we have as men is to assume we know what is going on in women. "[1]

It is not surprising, then, that all of Mailer's novels are really about men. When women appear, they tend to be trapped in conventional roles, serving the men maternally or sexually. Mailer's comments about his wives are no more illuminating. In The Armies of the Night, after describing his inability to understand Beverley Bentley, his fourth wife, he worries about his skill as a novelist, which depends in part on his "knowledge of women" (AN, p. 171). Burdened with the difficulty of comprehension, he searches for a metaphor and suggests that each of his marriages has been the equivalent of living in a major culture. He speaks of Beatrice Silverman, from whom he had learned something "of Jewish genius and of revolutionaries and large indiscriminate love for the oppressed"; of Adele Morales with her "love of painting and sensuality and drama and Latin desperation"; of Lady Jean Campbell, who provided "A love affair with England"; and of Beverley Bentley, an actress from the Southern part of the United States. [2] He talks of how exciting it has been to live with women of such varied backgrounds, but worries about "the vortex of all postmarital pain, " the children who "come out of a vision in the marriage. "[3] He refers to the "unspoken vision you have with your woman, some feeling that you have something together which should be embodied in a child. "[4] And he is obsessed with the singularity of a love affair, since "every time you give something to another woman, the beginning of a different vision is being sent to a different place. It can only work successfully when you have people whose souls are neatly separated. I believe we all have divided souls, but few of us have souls that are divided formally.... But most of us have double personalities that are more amorphous. "[5]

The mysticism which clouds much of Mailer's work, particularly An American Dream, is evident here. But in his biography of Marilyn Monroe it becomes the very basis of his perception. He acknowledges that his investigation strays toward "the borders of magic. "[6] Therefore Marilyn's fear becomes "Nothing less than some intimation of the death of her soul...."[7] And her soul is compounded of her ambitiousness, imaged in Napoleonic terms, and that innocent promise which she exudes. She is not only "one of the world's most formidable monsters of publicity, " but also America's "sweet angel of sex. "[8]

The grandiosity of Mailer's vision of Marilyn may be a fusion of the separate strains of feeling that Leslie Fiedler suggests characterize male American novelists, who almost always portray women as "monsters of virtue or bitchery."9 In a psychoanalytic study, Andrew Gordon has stated that "The standard female in Mailer is aggressive, belittling to men, dominating, and castrating to the touch such as Guinevere in Barbary Shore, Dorothea and Lulu in The Deer Park, the infamous Denise, the Jewess in "The Time of Her Time," Deborah the Great Bitch of An American Dream, and Alice Jethroe in Why Are We in Vietnam?"10 However Gordon's formulation fails to take into account Elena Esposito of The Deer Park, Cherry in An American Dream, Marilyn, and the numerous, if fleeting, portraits of women in Mailer's journalism.

Even with its faults, Marilyn reveals Mailer's sympathy for Monroe, a woman whose family possessed a legacy of insanity that at times was reflected in her relationships with people and that finally immobilized her in rapacious Hollywood. He speaks with great admiration of her vibrancy and courage to survive. Commenting on her life in the fifties, he says that she may have been "on some secret cat-like search through sex in these less recorded years and had many a one-night stand while searching for experience, communication, actor's enrichment, and identification. ... "11

The intensity of her experience is mirrored in the lives of Elena Esposito and Cherry. In Marilyn, Mailer compares the relationship between Monroe and Fred Karger, her singing coach on the film Ladies of the Chorus, to that of Elena and Charles Francis Eitel in The Deer Park. Although Marilyn also may have provided the model for Lulu Meyers, the successful actress in The Deer Park whom Mailer describes as "some fairy princess of sex" (DP, p. 35), Lulu is much more vacuous than Elena, who shared with Monroe an unschooled delicacy of feeling and intelligence. And with his interest in names (he suggests that there may be some significance in the similarity of his own initials and Marilyn's), one can hardly think it coincidence that Mailer names his heroine Cherry in An American Dream and Marilyn played "Cherie," a Southern cabaret singer in Bus Stop. In An American Dream, Cherry is a much more sophisticated Southerner, but nevertheless a singer with a torturous past. At the end of that novel, an air of mystery surrounds her death, as thick as that attributed by Mailer to Marilyn's last night in Brentwood. On the edge of madness in the Nevada desert, Rojack phones Cherry and from the vast space her voice comes back, "Marilyn says to say hello."

In Elena and Cherry, Mailer has created his closest female counterparts to the male hipster. Both have been through numerous affairs with men of varied backgrounds and have utilized these experiences to develop a sensibility which pushes toward the unification of thought and feeling that Mailer has continually valued. If Mailer has provided Cherry and Elena with an individuality that is not characteristic of his other fictional female characters, he has been trapped nevertheless by cultural stereotypes of femininity. Just as he lifts Monroe's sexuality to mythic proportions, Mailer luxuriates in descriptions of women's physical beauty, which they deftly use to attract men. And even if Elena and Cherry are attempting to advance in the world of show business, their lives are really consumed by their relationships with members of the opposite sex. Marilyn's relationships with Joe DiMaggio and Arthur Miller, both of whom offered a minimal kind of security while thriving periodically on her presence, are echoed in The Deer Park, where Elena as well as Lulu Meyers move from one symbiotic relationship to another, and in An American Dream, where Cherry has catastrophic experiences with men who are importantly placed.

Only in his journalism is Mailer occasionally really convincing in his portraits of women. When he offers vignettes of the wives of the politicians or the astronauts, Mailer appears to be less at the mercy of his own imaginative inclinations which have been shaped by the full weight of his emotional life. Whether he is describing Jackie Kennedy's pathetically false presentation during her tour of the White House, Pat Collins' canned interview with reporters upon the landing on the moon, or Pat Nixon's mechanical projection of herself at the 1972 Republican convention, Mailer is able to capture the nuances of the situation, especially the emotional aura about the past and present life of the women. If he misses the richness of their inner experience, he does capture a sense of their personalities by generalizing from a glance, a gesture, or a word.

Despite the accuracy of these portrayals, Mailer's culturally shaped sexual prejudices are revealed quite often in his journalism. This dilemma is particularly evident in the sexual metaphors which he furnishes for so much experience. During the 1968 Republican convention, the heat in

Miami is so bad that "the sensation of breathing, then living, was not unlike being obliged to make love to a 300-pound woman who has decided to get on top. Got it? You could not dominate a thing" (MSC, p. 12). In his description of the 1971 Ali-Frazier heavyweight championship fight, Mailer refers to Ali on the floor as "singing to the sirens in the mistiest fogs of Queer Street ..." (EE, p. 35). 12 Trying to outmaneuver Henry Kissinger in an interview in 1972, he feels "Like a virgin descending the steps of sexual congress" (SGG, p. 116). In these passages, Mailer's preoccupation with the relationship between sexuality and man's need to maintain power, sometimes through the use of violence, has given rise to the legitimate criticism by many, especially feminists, that he has cultivated what Kate Millett calls "a malign machismo. "13

However, the feminists fail to acknowledge that Mailer does not believe in violence and domination as intrinsically desirable modes of sexual response. Consider, for instance, Mailer's conception of Monroe's place in DiMaggio's world: It is a "world where women can be mothers, sisters, angels, broads, good sports, sweethearts, bitches, trouble or dynamite, but are always seen at a remove, as a class apart. "14 Here "the highest prize" is "the most beautiful woman available on your arm and living there in her heart loyal to you. Sexual prowess is more revered than any athletic ability but a good straight right. "15 Mailer is not only highly critical of this code, but also of the "psychology of the stud" whose heartless vanity never fully conceals "the terror that some other dude might be a little better. "16 Kate Millett is quite misleading when she suggests that Mailer fully advocates the kind of sexuality practiced by Rojack on Ruta in An American Dream and by Sergius on Denise in "The Time of Her Time. "17 He indicates that the quality of the sexual encounter in each of these instances is bad precisely because of the furious demands placed by the man upon the woman.

What is very disturbing about Mailer is that he is morally careless when he suggests the benefits that may result when men seek to grow by using women. If he challenged conventional moral standards in Advertisements for Myself when he suggested that there were infinite differences among rapists, 18 he is even more defiant in his discussion of the importance of the act of violence. He states that "if a boy beats up an old woman, he may be protecting himself by discharging a rage which would destroy his body if it were left to work on the cells, so he takes it out on the old woman. The boy may be anything from a brute to Raskolnikov. It requires an exquisite sense of context and a subtle gift as a moralist to decide these matters at times. "19 It is within this framework, I believe, that Mailer would have us understand his stabbing of his second wife, Adele Morales, and the murder of Deborah by Rojack in An American Dream.

The horrifying implications of both these experiences would seem to deny the possibility for any rapprochement between feminists and Mailer. And yet the most positive statement about sexuality in his work is that brief moment of tenderness experienced by Rojack with Cherry, in which two people meet on a plane of equality, where love and lust intermingle beyond the spurious demands of ego. That Rojack is able to maintain virtually no emotional equilibrium after Cherry's death is indicative of Mailer's belief that their kind of sexuality is precarious at best and extremely hard to develop.

For Mailer, the need to dominate and the act of violence are unavoidable components of a sexual relationship; whereas for the feminists, both are an outgrowth of the male-dominated, competitive American social order. In Cannibals and Christians, Mailer states that Lady Chatterley's Lover tries to capture the essence of sex and yet has nothing to say about the violence which is part of sex" (CC, p. 198). But in Prisoner, he admires Henry Miller, who "captured something in the sexuality of men as it had never been seen before, precisely that it was man's sense of awe before woman, his dread of her position one step closer to eternity (for in that step were her powers) which made men detest women, revile them, humiliate them, defecate symbolically upon them, do everything to reduce them so one might dare to enter them and take pleasure of them. "20 Mailer's major quarrel with the feminists, then, is based upon their tendency to emphasize the natural similarity of men and women and to stress the use of technological devices as a means of control over various aspects of the sexual process. Where the feminists suggest that cultural conditioning is the most significant element in shaping notions of masculinity and femininity, Mailer stresses biological endowment and human choice. Just as he condemns the homogeneity of American life in the context of his discussion of totalitarianism, he seeks to prove that men and women are essentially different--a fact which, if acknowledged, could lead to the development of rich, diverse personalities and the most profound kind of sexual experience.

It is Kate Millett who is the focus of Mailer's criticism. Much of The Prisoner of Sex is a response to her book, Sexual Politics, in which she presents an analysis of women's subjugation and the feminist movement, centering upon America and England in the nineteenth and twentieth centuries, and then relates to her discussion the literature of Henry Miller, D. H. Lawrence, Jean Genet, and Norman Mailer. Focusing his remarks mainly upon her literary criticism, Mailer calls Millett a "Left Totalitarian," an unfair evaluation that results in part from his legitimate concern with her tendency to distort through quoting out of context.

Unlike Millett, who criticizes Miller for advocating a male dominated "fuck fest" in which women are piled up like cars on a scrap heap, Mailer praises Miller for his ability to distinguish qualitatively between the infinite forms of sex, from the tender, deeply emotional encounter, to the mechanical, highly depersonalized "in-out." And he finds her hypocritical since she "approves by implication" of the "vibrators and plastic dildoes" used in the laboratory, at the same time that she detests the "foul woman-hating billygoat bulb of old Henry" (PS, p. 114). Yet he dislikes Miller's repetitious use of the same material. A sexual revolutionary in the twenties, Miller held convictions which today are "the same old literary fields of flesh and cunt" (PS, p. 124). Unlike Millett, Mailer accepts too easily Miller's limited emphasis upon women as instruments in man's endless search for sexual satisfaction. When he dismisses the fact that Miller's fictional world does not possess a woman of the stature of Nora in Ibsen's A Doll's House, Mailer suggests a fundamental limitation in his own vision of sexuality.

With Lawrence, Mailer challenges Millett's attempt "to conceal the pilgrimage, hide the life, cover over that emotional odyssey which took him from adoration of the woman to outright lust for her murder, then took him back to worship her beauty, even her procreative beauty" (PS, p. 141). He is particularly sensitized to Lawrence's attempt to become a man in the face of his father's hatred and mother's love, "the classic family stuff out of which homosexuals are made" (PS, p. 154). He acknowledges Lawrence's compensatory "absolute domination of women by men, mystical worship of the male will, detestation of democracy" (PS, p. 136), all of which Millett details. But Mailer is more sensitized to Lawrence's literary and personal transformation, particularly to the revelations in Lady Chatterley's Lover which provide the basis for what happens between Cherry and Rojack, where "the man and the woman are joined, separate and joined" (PS, p. 160). What he misses in Millett's analysis of Lawrence is her concern that the women in his novels are provided with definitions of the apocalyptic encounter by confident men whose personalities are relatively strong. The men, therefore, are psychologically situated for the journey into the egoless unknown which Lawrence advocates. Mailer's concern that Women's Liberation seeks to give "modern woman a full hard efficient ego" (PS, p. 148) almost totally ignores the devastating consequences of living in a culture where male institutional control and stereotyped notions of femininity seem especially designed to subvert attempts by women to achieve that selfhood without which the journey into the unknown will tend to result in the man's domination.

If Mailer is essentially right to criticize Millett for the indignant manner in which, at times, she pigeonholes blocks of information in order to strengthen her argument, he misses the essence of her challenge. By concentrating upon her literary criticism, he fails to do justice to the vast amount of information from a variety of fields which is brought together in her book. More specifically, in his contempt for her stress upon culturally conditioned notions of masculinity and femininity, Mailer has come to place inordinate emphasis upon biological differences, which he dwells upon in a highly mystical fashion. In addition, his legitimate fear of the consequences of conditioning through the use of technology prevents him from acknowledging the positive elements in Millett's desire to "'urge a dissemination to members of each sex of those socially desirable traits previously confined to one or the other while eliminating the bellicosity or excessive passivity useless in either.'"21 Although Millett is sensitive to individual differences among people and advocates in a rather conventional manner the use of contraceptive devices, Mailer erroneously speaks of her "social lust to make units of people" and believes that her remarks "opened the door to eugenics, and beyond was the stuff of experimental control in the extra-uterine womb" (p. 129).

While much of The Prisoner of Sex appears to be an indictment of Millett, it is primarily in Part Three, "The Advocate," that Mailer focuses upon the views presented in Sexual Politics. Just as he has been intent upon weaving his personal experience into journalistic accounts, in Prisoner he presents in Part One aspects of his own life, particularly his summer "dilemma" in 1969 at the end of his fourth marriage, when he was in Provincetown with his children.   As the "Prizewinner," he was a successful novelist and journalist, winner of a Pulitzer Prize and considered for a Nobel, but he had also become the "Prisoner," condemned to play the role of housewife, a condition which, he implies, should better enable him to comment on the nature of a woman's life.   And he indicates the other experiences which have led him to write The Prisoner of Sex: encounters with Gloria Steinem and Bella Abzug; a reading of Mary Ellman's Thinking About Women; a request from the Editor of Time for his opinions on Women's Liberation; and finally the appearance of Kate Millett's Sexual Politics.

By the time Part Two opens, Mailer has firmly established the perspective he will bring to the book, the combination of fact and feeling woven intricately together amidst endless detours before any argument reveals its protean shape.   Part Two, "The Acolyte," is his closest approximation to the bald rendering of fact.   Here he summarizes and evaluates the literature of the women's movement.   If he criticizes most feminists for their "dull and piteous tracts, whining and catarrhal styles" (PS, p. 39), he paternalistically acknowledges the sense of "authority," the "direct speech," the stylistic "gusto" of a few.   He offers the views of Valerie Solanis, who believes that the male is "a biological accident"; the polemics of Linda Phelps, who argues for a revolutionary transformation of the economic system; and the legalese of NOW, an organization which seeks to remedy the oppression and exploitation of women through constitutional amendment.   He quotes from Dana Densmore and Ti-Grace Atkinson about contraception and then offers comments on the nature of female sexuality by Kate Millett, Mary Jane Sherfey, W. H. Masters, Anne Koedt, Frank Caprio, and Germaine Greer.

This presentation of the views of others is but a prelude to Part Four in which, as the "Prisoner," he draws upon his evaluations in the previous sections and even upon his earlier writing in order to detail his conception of the nature of men and women and the sexual process.   Despite the tentativeness, so characteristic of the dialectical method of Aquarius, who, in Prisoner through the mask of various personae, can speak of his ideas as "wild," "loose," or even "lamentable," Mailer offers a vision of sexuality which tends to be a clever reaffirmation of cultural stereotypes in the guise of a narrow biology and an obfuscating mysticism, all wrapped in a thick metaphorical blanket.

Mailer is indeed the "Prisoner" of sex, because he
is inclined to believe that there are certain conditions which
men and women must fully acknowledge as virtually unalter-
able sexual truths. And he tends to arrive at these convictions not on the basis of "scientific evidence" but "on the
metaphorical feel" (PS, p. 132). If he begins with science
and a belief in the reproductive system as the basis of fundamental differences between men and women, he quickly
shifts to metaphysics when he states that a woman's capacity to bear children makes her closer to God, the creative
power in the universe. It is within this context that one
should approach Mailer's statement that "the prime responsibility of a woman probably is to be on earth long enough
to find the best mate possible for herself, and conceive
children who will improve the species" (PP, p. 130). Without a womb (the inner space of conception and therefore the
harbinger of the future), man is further from the source of
creation, to which he is connected by his mother. Cut off
from nature, the male confronts woman's procreative powers
with awe and is condemned to jealously maintain his own
limited, present domain.

It is not that Mailer considers it easy to become a
woman, since he refers to the "sentimental suspicion" that
"one need merely lie back and all Heaven will come into the
cunt" (PS, p. 86). His unwillingness to accept the argument
by some feminists that the vaginal orgasm is an illusion created by the arousal of the clitoris is based on his belief that
the orgasm has less to do with physiology than with the
"character of the soul" (PS, p. 88). Yet implicit in Mailer's
ideas is the notion that a woman's character can develop more
easily because of her inborn capacity to bear children. A
male must compensate for his inability to conceive a child.
His "primary quality" is "an assertion," for in order to
transcend his basic alienation he must seek to "step out of
nature, be almost as if opposed to nature ... man was a
spirit of unrest who proceeded to become less masculine
whenever he ceased to strive ..." (PS, p. 132).

If Mailer's notion of masculinity and femininity is
biologically grounded, both terms take on their more conventional cultural significance in "The Metaphysics of the Belly,"
which was included in The Presidential Papers. Here, without an adequate consideration of biological and psychological
matters, Mailer idiosyncratically attributes masculine and
feminine qualities to food, the digestion of which depends upon a corresponding emotional state in the eater. Thus "bull's

balls," which are equal to virility, can only be digested by
a man who is willing to receive the masculine element present within them, at the same time that he offers up something feminine in himself. Masculinity, of course, is equated with power, strength, the ability to command, and desire
to alter life, the consequences of which are often to increase
responsibility or danger; whereas femininity is identified with
compliance and passivity.

Still, it is within his biological perspective that it is
possible to account for Mailer's inadequate portrayal of women in his fiction. Given his emphasis upon her childbearing capacity, it would not make sense for Mailer to take a
woman through the various forms of conflict which a major
character must experience in a meaningful novel. Moreover,
in his fictional portrayals, he suggests that aggressiveness
in a woman leads to highly destructive results both for herself and for the man with whom she is involved. In this context, Mailer's metaphorical reconstruction of Marilyn Monroe
as a Napoleonic figure with "a blank eye for power unattached
to any notion of the moral"22 is highly suspect. After stating
that "her competetive instincts" were "equal to a great prize-
fighter's," Mailer extends his sympathy to John Huston, the
director of The Misfits, who did "not want the aesthetic
slant of his film to be nudged by her competitive tit."23 One
wonders here just how much Mailer has been guided not only
by his own obsession with power, but also by the disjunction
between his conception of the nature of women and the actual
presence of Monroe.

Speaking of the "range of hostilities" that a woman can
exercise toward a man, Mailer rejects Freud's notion of uni-
versal penis envy, which he replaces with the idea of "penis
contempt." If he agrees with Kate Millett that "penis envy
was a slander upon the complexity of the female," he speaks
of that "look" in a woman's eye which "bemoans the fact she
is not a man, since if she were a man, or better still, a
woman with command of a phallus entrusted to her, she would
know how to use it ..." (PS, p. 86). But the woman, according to Mailer, cannot know of the complex whimsicality of
the phallus, which so often is "not quite under Central Control" (PS, p. 86). One of man's major quests is to learn
how to balance the impulses of his phallus and the strictures
of his will.

Thus it is significant that in his more successful fictional portrayals of women, such as Elena and Cherry, fe-

male sexual responsiveness is predicated upon conventional notions of feminine passivity. Even that brief magnificent moment between Cherry and Rojack is prefaced by a battle of wills in which Cherry gives way first. It is not that Mailer advocates the "insertion of women into a role Betty Friedan will call so tellingly 'The Feminine Mystique'" (PS, p. 179). But his argument with "that old insane shoe" is based primarily upon the desexualization of women that has taken place in a "hygienic," technological society. When he says that he seeks "a balance which would offer men vision and women 'the power of the soul'" (PS, p. 181), he would have both sexes settle fully into a biological design based upon the uniqueness of the womb.

Mailer, then, never creates a complete female hipster. The hipster is continually asserting himself, moving with grace and speed through social, political, and psychological traps in an attempt to maintain selfhood. Unlike women, whose childbearing capacity can take them out of the fray without undue psychological harm, men (even if they are not hipsters) can only settle into their basic biological design by moving in the aggressive direction outlined in "The White Negro."

Furthermore, just as he attributes characteristics of the hipster to the soul in his metaphysical dialogue "The Political Economy of Time," in Cannibals and Christians, Mailer has created a biology of Hip in which the sperm carrying an x-bearing female chromosome or y-bearing male is set against the ovum in a battle for survival as intense as the psychological war waged by the hipster in his relationship with a woman. According to Richard Poirier, the sperm, especially the y-chromosome, "is Hip," while "the ovum is relatively Square."24 Mailer emphasizes the fact that the y-bearing male cell is quick and possesses a shorter survival time than the x-bearing female cell, which is sturdy. Whatever its chromosomal make-up, the sperm is engaged in an arduous journey before it ultimately penetrates the ovum. Only one of approximately four hundred million sperm cells reach their destination, where they must confront "a cameo of the female, sensitive as any other female flesh to the presence of the man who would enter!" (PS, p. 207).

Mailer's reasoning here is obviously much too loose. But he does not stop there. He considers the quality of the sperm and ovum to be a reflection of the vast potentialities of their makers. And he sees some relationship between the quality of passion during intercourse, particularly the nature of the orgasm, and the kind of child that is produced. In St. George and the Godfather, he can only give qualified support to the idea of abortion, since embryos so extinguished "were more likely to be the product of extraordinary fucks than the legal infant who saw the first light in a hospital" (SGG, p. 58). He saves his most virulent opposition for contraception, especially the pill, which, by denying choice "so invaded the undeclared rights of the fuck whose romantic imperative is to prevail--against all odds!" (SGG, p. 58).

According to Mailer, the orgasm achieved while making love with a member of the opposite sex is the supreme statement of selfhood for both men and women. It is then that "a man can become more male and a woman more female," for the womb mirrors and returns "what is most forceful or attractive in each of them" (PS, pp. 171, 172). For his entire career, Mailer has been almost obsessively intent upon describing the "apocalyptic orgasm," but usually has managed to lose himself in his excretory preoccupations. Ironically enough, he was disappointed in Bertolucci's Last Tango in Paris, because the film aroused in him the expectation that all aspects of sexuality would be described and faithfully recorded, but only delivered Paul's (and Brando's) frustrations, imaged in brutal anal terms. 25

Yet in An American Dream and Why Are We in Vietnam?, Rojack and D. J. respectively are haunted by their homosexual impulses, particularly the need to engage in violent buggery. In this context, there is no loss of artistic control in either novel. Mailer is quite aware of what he is doing with his characters. About himself he is a little more vague, although certainly quite suggestive. Speaking in 1954, he wonders "if there were not something suspicious in my intense dislike of homosexuals" (AM, p. 226). More recently, he has indicated that "I've always had a puritanical attitude about homosexuality, almost as if I couldn't afford to begin to get homosexual, because God knows where it would stop. You know about that old Talmudic notion, that if you want to restrain an impulse don't just build a fence around the impulse itself, build a fence around the fence. "26

What he is left with, then, is the Sartrean decision to retain his "maleness" by choosing not to engage actively in homosexuality, which he equates with passivity and defeat. With his emphasis upon choice, Mailer even suggests that at times the process of conception can be controlled psychologi-

cally by a woman who, without external help, could avoid
giving birth "with any man whose sperm was not superbly
suited to the ovum on which she built her view of how life
should be if she were to create it" (PS, p. 200). To use
contraceptive devices, to engage in masturbation or homosexual activity, is to destroy the meaning of sexuality since
the possibility of conceiving a child is the most significant
aspect of the encounter. His often quoted statement that
"The ultimate direction of masturbation always has to be insanity" (PP, p. 141) is his metaphorical way of speaking of
the "confrontation between fucking and reality" (PS, p. 190).
Masturbation, he believes, is an act which nourishes one's
fantasies: it helps to destroy a sense of reality not only by
eliminating an active partner, but by denying the possibility
of a child's birth. Contraception can also be harmful, particularly to the woman for whom "the chemicals of contraception" transform the ovum whose "arts" wander "through
the body, arts which find no home in the flesh--who will accept the thought that the most unlocatable madness or depression can seep out of the death of such arts?" (PS, p. 197).
And he believes that contraception is an example of technology's use of reason at the expense of the imperatives of the
emotional life, especially obligation and guilt.

A number of critics have legitimately remarked that
Mailer sounds curiously puritanical when he states that the
sexual experience has become "utterly lobotomized away from
the sense of sin" (AN, p. 14). Where Mailer once viewed
the orgasm as the supreme act, which might cut the individual loose from the instinctual restrictions imposed by the
family and society, now he is much more cautious when
speaking about the liberating powers of sexuality. Sex for
him is not the modern day "gymnasium of love," but a more
selective act whose reverberations echo forever in the deepest chambers of the self and even of the cosmos. The current fascination with the "polymorphously perverse" is never
an issue for Mailer. Even in "The White Negro," where he
states that the vast possibilities of sexuality are often lost
in a repressive childhood, his focus is always upon the geni-
tal orgasm. He makes no attempt to align himself with radical followers of Freud, such as Norman O. Brown, and to
resurrect the diffuse sexuality of the infant, whose entire
body is a source of pleasure and pain in a world where socially constructed notions of masculinity and femininity are
overshadowed by the satisfaction of need. The hipster's
search to repossess his instinctual life stops, then, at a
point beyond which the very notion of heterosexuality might

be challenged in the name of an androgynous ideal. For Mailer, that ideal is a perversion of the differentiation of the sexes, a biological fact which has grave implications. Perhaps his greatest fear is that in our technological society, which "wants humans to become units," the notion of bisexuality, if embraced, might only encourage a never-ending promiscuous display.

Throughout the sixties, therefore, particularly in An American Dream, Mailer began to explore the white Negro's desire for the apocalyptic orgasm within the context of the sacredness of the sexual experience, linked now to a belief that there are "two kinds of death," "Final death as some species of oblivion, and transcendental death," in which one's guilt in the past is outweighed by one's courage. 27 In Miami and the Siege of Chicago, his sense of guilt over having enjoyed an extra-marital "dalliance" is reflected in his compulsion to confess to his wife out of the feeling that this "would be a warrant of magic to aid Senator [Robert] Kennedy" (MSC, p. 94), who had just been shot.

With this rather mystical emphasis, Mailer links his conception of sexuality to theology and to politics. The Prisoner of Sex is his attempt to affirm once again his sense that "there is design in the universe, that humans embody a particular Intent": "he preferred to believe that the Lord, Master of Existential Reason, was not thus devoted to the absurd as to put the orgasm in the midst of the act of creation without cause of the profoundest sort, for when a man and woman conceive, would it not be best that they be able to see one another for a transcendent instant, as if the soul of what would then be conceived might live with more light later?" (PS, pp. 190, 86-87). If he does not belabor his theology of Hip, he continually states that the sexual act must be understood in the context of the mysterious creative powers at the center of the universe. "A step, or a stage, or a move or a leap nearer the creation of existence," the woman is "a victim of a relationship to certain murmurings of eternity" through her womb, which is the "unaccountable liaison with the beyond" (PS, pp. 60, 61-62, 61). More so than men, women are at the mercy of the mysterious forces which haunt Rojack and D. J., for the womb runs counter to the methods of technology and seems "to obey some private compact with the moon" (PS, p. 61). In the act of sex, "great forces beyond [man's] measure seem to be calling to the woman" (PS, p. 117). One feels the pull of these forces in An American Dream in Rojack's sense of Deborah and

Cherry, in The Armies of the Night and Of a Fire on the
Moon when Mailer describes his relationship with Beverley
Bentley, and in Marilyn through his emphasis upon the intensity of feeling in Monroe who "belonged to the occult
church of the film, and the last covens of Hollywood."28

It is on the basis of his emphasis upon the mysterious
powers of the womb that Mailer challenges contemporary conceptions of revolution dependent upon reason and technology
as method and mode. Unlike past revolutions, which "had
been the attempt of the exploited to define themselves as
men, ... present attempts (since power was now technological) were to achieve command of techniques ..." (PS, p.
67). He criticizes not only Women's Liberation but other
contemporary revolutionary struggles, questioning the "revolution by reason" begun in the Renaissance, "not a war to
liberate man, but to pollute him by the wastes of his vanity,
huge scientific vanity now destroying every natural act of
nature" (PS, p. 56). He fears that the revolution "may become the first bureaucracy of sex, and the technicians of
genetics its intelligentsia" (PS, p. 223). At one point, he
even describes some feminists as "a squadron of enraged
Amazons, an honor guard of revolutionary (if we would only
see them) vaginas" (PS, p. 13). Therefore, as in Existential Errands, he suggests that the revolution might be in its
"final fission" between the artists, prophets, adventurers,
and guerillas on the one side and the engineers, program-
mers, technicians, and "organized echelons of the nonviolent"
(PS, p. 223) on the other. If he maintains his allegiance to
the former section of the Left, he warns of the "murderous
inflammation of the will" (PS, p. 55) that can accompany
revolution--another reminder of his modified belief in the
purgative powers of violence elaborated upon in his idea of
the "philosophical psychopath."

But Mailer's major quarrel is with non-violent manifestations of the will. Like Lawrence, who was deeply opposed to the rise of industrialism, which turned man away
from his deepest emotional resources, Mailer is concerned
with man's interest in the machine, an interest which has
turned from use to identification. Thus he calls modern day
virility "a quality blank as plastic, an abstract power over
the employment of techniques" (PS, p. 67). Yet unlike Lawrence, Mailer maintains a more dialectical perspective when
he states that man's interest in technology also provides a
way to acquire "masculinity" through a willingness to work
with the incomprehensible "forces" of uncharted science.

The woman, however, is already close to her femininity, because she possesses the power to conceive. Despite the fact that he speaks of the womb as a "damnable disadvantage" in the social struggle with men, "a cranky fouled-up bag of horrors for any woman who would stand e-qual to man on modern jobs" (PS, p. 60) which require severe routinization, Mailer has advocated more political and economic rights for women. In the course of his 1969 mayoralty campaign, he stated that "'women in any administration I could run would have more voice, more respect, more real opportunity for real argument than any of the other candidates would offer ..." (PS, pp. 22-23). Nevertheless, it is because liberation is a necessary precondition for a "free search" "to look for a mate" (PS, p. 232) that Mailer can agree with some of the ideas of the feminists. In the end, he indicates that "he would agree with everything they asked but to quit the womb ..." (PS, p. 233).

It is this emphasis upon the womb which prevents Mailer from adequately exploring the experience of women. The Prisoner of Sex unfortunately provides resonance for his fictional and non-fictional portrayals in which a woman's sexuality tends to be emphasized at the expense of her other qualities, and a man is condemned from birth to prove his masculinity in various apocalyptic confrontations. In Prisoner, Mailer allows too many ideas which are offered as tentative explanations to become unproven declarations about the biological, psychological, and social implications of sexuality. And then there are his theological and cosmological hypotheses, which seem arcane, anachronisms culled from the book of a medieval alchemist. If his exploration is much more complex than most critics have acknowledged, Mailer has been unable adequately to analyze and integrate his genuine feelings, his culturally shaped prejudices, and the findings of others. He advances too many idiosyncratic notions, some of which are culturally sanctioned, in the context of his heavy stress upon the dangers of technology and the mysteries of the sexual process.

Notes

1. Buzz Farbar, "Mailer on Marriage and Women," Viva, Oct. 1973, p. 146.

2. Armies, p. 170.

3. "Mailer on Marriage and Women," p. 76.

4. Ibid.

5. Ibid.

6. Marilyn (New York: Grosset and Dunlap, 1973), p. 20.

7. Marilyn, p. 17.

8. Marilyn, pp. 90, 15.

9. Leslie A. Fiedler, Love and Death in the American Novel (New York: Criterion Books, 1960), p. xix.

10. "The Naked and the Dead: The Triumph of Impotence," Literature and Psychology, 19, No. 3-4 (1969), 5.

11. Marilyn, p. 78.

12. Mailer believes that any defeat for a man is a movement, however slight, toward passivity and homosexuality.

13. See page 11 of this book.

14. Marilyn, p. 97.

15. Marilyn, p. 99.

16. "Mailer on Marriage and Women," p. 76.

17. See Sexual Politics, pp. 9-16, 324-25.

18. See page 10 of this book.

19. "Talking of Violence," Twentieth Century, 168 (Winter 1964-65), 110.

20. The Prisoner of Sex (Boston: Little, Brown and Co., 1971), p. 116. Hereafter, page references to The Prisoner of Sex (PS) will appear in parentheses after the quotation.

21. The Prisoner of Sex, p. 129. Here Mailer quotes Millett in the context of his distaste for her attempt to "push past the argument that sex was not so much in the organs as the mind."

22. *Marilyn*, p. 43.

23. *Marilyn*, pp. 200, 201.

24. Poirier, *Norman Mailer*, p. 118.

25. "A Transit to Narcissus," *New York Review of Books*, 17 May 1973, p. 6.

26. "Mailer on Marriage and Women," pp. 147-48.

27. "Mailer on Marriage and Women," p. 146.

28. *Marilyn*, p. 16.

CHAPTER 8

EPILOGUE: MAILER AND AMERICA

Having lived through the depression of the thirties, the military holocaust of World War II in the forties, the Cold War period of the fifties, and the rebellions emanating from the ghettoes and the campuses during the sixties, it is not surprising that Norman Mailer has been continually concerned with the relationship between American institutions and the inner lives of the American people. At various points in his career, Mailer has explored the nature of the family and its immediate extensions, the school and the church, as well as the government with its ties to the large corporation, the Army, and the police. If his analyses and his proposals for reform have been a strange compendium of sentiments which cut across the political spectrum, Mailer has generally aligned himself with the Left. This alignment, as well as his entire intellectual and aesthetic development, cannot be separated from the fact that he is of Jewish origin and has lived most of his life in an urban area under financial conditions which have varied according to his literary success.

His Jewishness has been a matter of social and psychological importance, rather than a reflection of his theology. Despite his interest in Hasidic tales, which have helped to shape his mystical inclinations, Mailer has not particularly drawn from Judaic tradition in his fiction. Unlike Saul Bellow, Bernard Malamud and Philip Roth, contemporaries whose work reveals a preoccupation with many aspects of Jewish life, Mailer has tended to project both himself and his characters within a different framework. In his notion of the hipster, he has created a variety of personae, none of whom conveys the sense of a Jewish background.

172

Leslie Fiedler has suggested that in the "white Negro" Mailer has created an alter ego whose passion and activity are a reflection of those elements that he has failed to integrate fully in himself: Fiedler points out that Mailer's incomplete eight-part novel was to be "a study of how an inadequate Jew, baffled sexually and artistically, invents, in his troubled sleep, the synthetic Ubermensch."[1] That "Ubermensch" is fully drawn in "The Time of Her Time" as the Irish Sergius O'Shaugnessy, a more forceful version of his namesake in The Deer Park. Both characterizations point the way to the abundant energy in Mailer's projection of the hipster in his future work, and can be contrasted with Sam Slovoda, the dreamer in the unfinished eight-part novel, who is projected in the segment, "The Man Who Studied Yoga," as a sexually and aesthetically crippled Jew.

Unlike the hipster, whose quest requires feats that seem barely human, Slovoda is more convincing as a character, because he stumbles and struggles in ways that are easily recognizable. But Mailer is not content to populate contemporary American fiction with one more battered antihero. In his stress upon the need for self-transcendence, he provides some of his characters with mythic stature without sufficiently acknowledging that he is doing so.

It is this fact, in part, which forces Robert Solotaroff to argue that Mailer has not been able to find the "objective correlative" of his vision. Mailer, he says, "will only write major fiction when he cleans up ... his habit of subordinating the subject matter to his ego instead of his ego to the subject matter."[2] We have only to look at An American Dream, where, given his emphasis upon the existence of powerful outside forces operating upon man, Mailer creates a narrator whose feelings often seem excessive. Solotaroff suggests that the real hero of An American Dream is Stephen Rojack Norman Mailer: both were Harvard graduates, former members of the Progressive party, television celebrities, as well as five feet eight and aspiring boxers.[3] More important, Mailer transformed his stabbing of Adele Morales, his second wife, into the murder of Deborah by Rojack.

Speaking of Philip Roth's novel Letting Go, Mailer has said that "Virtually every writer, come soon or late, has a cramped-up love affair which is all but hopeless.... But the obsession is opposed to art in the same way a compulsive talker is opposed to good conversation. The choice

is either to break the obsession or enter it" (CC, p. 122).
According to Brock Brower, Mailer manipulated his second
wife "until she was almost a living projection of his Hip
dares."[4] By 1961 his philosophy had also become an obsession, an intellectual superstructure which he would utilize to
understand many aspects of experience. Despite periodic
changes in emphasis, his thinking had begun to harden into
a stale formula. Mailer then further complicated the problem by exploring his own personal tragedy in An American
Dream through the use, once again, of his "philosophy of
Hip."

     Ironically enough, the stabbing itself was not merely
a grotesque way of testing a philosophical credo. Whereas
in "The White Negro" Mailer speaks of the need for a conscious purgation of violence, his act reflects the extent to
which he dissociated his anger. He could say afterwards,
"'I felt somehow it was phony.... It wasn't me,'"[5] despite
the fact that on the evening preceding the deed he gave a
party during which he became involved in several fights with
crashers from the street. It is very tempting to believe
that Mailer's inability to understand his own roaring emotions is in part responsible for his failure to explore Rojack's situation in a credible manner. For all of its symbolic intent, An American Dream still relies upon a realistic base which at times is unpardonably violated, given the
carelessness of Mailer's approach to Rojack's inner experience. Without offering any qualification, Mailer asks us to
believe that Rojack is a man on the brink of madness not
because he attributes his own feelings to objects and other
people, but because he is engaged in a heroic battle with
forces from the beyond.

     It is no wonder that his journalism is Mailer's most
significant aesthetic achievement. For he is forced by the
very nature of the genre to stay close to the emotional aura
surrounding people and events. Yet even here, his feelings
often compel him to invest his subject with unwarranted
significance. Think of John Kennedy, the "prince" of Hip;
Sonny Liston, the agent of the Devil; or Mailer himself, the
"General."[6] This kind of inflation is quite evident in Mailer's public appearances, particularly when he resorts to an
Irish brogue and the pose of a tough barroom brawler, or
Hemingway prize fighter. And yet, for one who has been so
intent upon describing himself in the context of his non-fiction,
particularly his journalistic accounts, it is quite remarkable
that Mailer has said virtually nothing about his early life with

his parents in Brooklyn. His few statements are quite revealing. In Advertisements for Myself, he indicates that he
"started as a generous but very spoiled boy" (AM, p.
21), an idea which is echoed in Armies where he speaks of the
one personality which "he found absolutely insupportable--
the nice Jewish boy from Brooklyn. Something in his ade-
noids gave it away--he had the softness of a man early ac-
customed to mother-love" (AN, p. 134). As Germaine
Greer[7] has suggested, through his impassioned plea in The
Prisoner of Sex for D. H. Lawrence, whose mother loved
her son "outrageously," Mailer perhaps describes his own
dilemma. Lawrence, according to Mailer, sought all his
life to develop a will equal to his mother's, a desire which
could never be fully realized with another woman but which
came to fruition in his artistic work. Mailer, who continually presents himself as a "general" in his non-fiction,
states that "Hitlers develop out of such balance derived from
imbalance, and great generals and great novelists (for what
is a novelist but a general who sends his troops across
fields of paper?)" (PS, p. 153).

This dynamic might also help to explain Mailer's public posturing, that continual attempt to throw himself into a
relationship with public figures such as President John Kennedy and his wife Jackie, Sonny Liston and Gore Vidal, as
well as his skirmishes at the Pentagon and in the streets of
Chicago. In these encounters, Mailer tends to project the
image of a beleaguered man who has little possibility of
actually impinging upon another person or institution. His
conception of ego, which he develops in the context of his
presentation of the 1971 Ali-Frazier heavyweight championship fight, is appropriate here: "Ego is driving a point
through to a conclusion you are obliged to reach without
knowing too much about the ground you cross between" (EE,
p. 5). But unlike heavyweight fighters or astronauts whose
training prepares them for the voyage into the unknown,
Mailer is usually ill-equipped for the adventures which he
engages in, and he winds up, more often than not, as a
jester without an audience. Aside from the psychological
needs which are fulfilled in these public displays, what he
obtains is a sharpening of his senses, particularly his acute
consciousness of social reality, all of which he utilizes in
his writing.

It was after the publication of The Naked and the Dead
that Mailer felt himself "moved from the audience to the
stage" (AM, p. 92). He was especially concerned with his

ability to arouse emotion in others because of his recent
fame. Others, he believed, were constantly measuring themselves against him, so that he found it "exhausting to live in
a psychic landscape of assassins and victims" (AM, pp. 92-93).
It is easy to see why he would sympathize (perhaps identify)
with Lawrence, who sought to dominate since "dominance was
the indispensable elevator which would raise his phallus to
that height from which it might seek transcendence" (PS, p.
155). Always in Mailer's notion of the hipster there is the
sense of a figure being projected whose activity and emotional intensity are attempts to reclaim a self which has been
thwarted not only by the emotional demands of another person
but by existent social boundaries.

In fact, Mailer's hipster is really a description of a
heroic figure who is more appropriate for an earlier era.
Daniel Hoffman has stated that common to the unique mythic
archetypes that infuse American literature of the nineteenth
century are the qualities of "metamorphosis, adaptability,
and indomitable self-mastery."8   With his heavy emphasis
upon individual expression and exploration, Mailer has acknowledged his affinity for that "turn-of-the-century American capitalism, the only prosperous middle-class power ever
built on a series of outrageous gambles ..." (FM, p. 183).
However, the period of laissez-faire with its "itch for exploitation and nose for growth" ended long ago, and instead
there is corporate capitalism, "the marriage of huge profit
with huge service, of teamwork ..." (FM, p. 183). The individual has become lost in today's social order, where there
is a "detestation of contradiction" (FM, p. 183) and a love
of uniformity. Thus Samuel Hux shows how the nineteenth-
century mythical figure of the American as Adam, who refused "to worship reason" but relied upon "the primacy of
the will and choice, the life of creation (of environment and
values)," and an "incessant individualism," has been transformed by Mailer into a hero who "far from feeling an ad-
vantage in being free from the past, feels resentment, hope-
lessness, and deprivation."9

The hipster, then, is an extremely marginal figure.
Grace Witt has indicated that in his hero "Mailer has retained the courage and individualism of the frontiersman,
added sex as the most important aspect of existence, and
coupled sex with the violence of the bad man."10 In "The
White Negro," Mailer describes the "frontiersmen in the
Wild West of American night life," the "new breed of adventurers, urban adventurers who drifted out at night looking for action ..." (AM, pp. 338, 341).

As an urban phenomenon, the hipster is a product of
the continuing shift in American life away from the country
to the city. Mailer's own experience, which has been mainly confined to New York, with brief interludes in Boston and
Paris, has provided him with a rich canvas from which to
project his hero. From the men on the platoon in The Naked
and the Dead, most of whom are city bred, to the Brooklyn
boarding house in Barbary Shore, to Rojack's haunted New
York experience in An American Dream, Mailer has shown
what it is like to live in the city. Despite the lengthy journey to Alaska in Why Are We in Vietnam?, even D. J. is a
strange synthesis of Harlem and Dallas. And Desert D'Or
in The Deer Park is really an extension of Hollywood and
Los Angeles.

In The Presidential Papers, Mailer states that the
city does not afford the frontiersman the physical latitude
which he once possessed, but offers the possibility for psychological development. If the city is "dynamic, orgiastic,
unsettling, explosive, and accelerating to the psyche" (PP,
p. 43), this impression has been created through the com-
bined effects of a dissonant physical landscape and the proximity of a variety of people. Confronted with an intractable
external world on which he impinges with minimal results,
the hipster has become more inward than the Backwoodsman.
He utilizes the differences in class, racial origin, political
orientation, religion, and occupation among the people whom
he meets in order to unlock his own repressed feelings.
The attempt to rid oneself of the historical and geographical
past which was central to the American Adam's quest in the
nineteenth century has become for the hipster primarily an
inner journey in which he tries to purge himself of society's
restrictions upon intense feeling.

Whatever the precise nature of his inner quest, the
hipster has not been concerned with accumulating wealth.
If Mailer initially projected the "white Negro" as "the lazy
proletariat" (AM, p. 373), he has been increasingly inclined
to provide him with a secure economic base from which to
make the journey within. After recording the poverty of urban America throughout The Naked and the Dead and in
brief passages in Barbary Shore and The Deer Park, Mailer
has not written in detail about oppressive economic conditions in the United States.

This transformation can be partially accounted for in
terms of the circumstances of Mailer's life. Christopher

Lasch has stated that in order to comprehend Mailer "it is
first necessary to understand the sociology of literary success in America."11 Although he obtained quick fame with
the appearance of The Naked and the Dead, Mailer did not
have the literary and financial security which could only come
after the publication of additional books. If his artistic talent was questioned, each succeeding book added to his notor-
iety and wealth.

    With The Deer Park Mailer confronted a major crisis
when his initial publisher, Rinehart, wanted to change a passage which described the sexual activity of a call girl and a
producer. When he refused in the name of artistic integrity,
Mailer found himself forced into the position of running from
one publishing house to another. Since he was given to "in-
sulting a few publishers en route as if to discover the limits
of each situation" (AM, p. 232), he became an enfant terrible. Ultimately Putnam's decided to publish the book "without conditions, and without a request for a single change"
(AM, p. 231). But Mailer confronted another crisis when
his concern about his public reception so shaped his imaginative life that he was no longer able to ascertain clearly
whether his decision to rewrite sections of The Deer Park
was the result of his aesthetic beliefs. He did state that
"I was beginning to avoid new lines in the Putnam Deer Park
which were legally doubtful, and once in a while, like a
gambler hedging a bet, I toned down individual sentences
from the Rinehart Deer Park, nothing much, always a matter of the new O'Shaugnessy character" (AM, p. 242).

    The failure of the novel to achieve an "enormous
sale" left Mailer with his confidence shaken and the feeling
that "he would be open like all others to the attritions of
half-success and small failures" (AM, p. 247). In an attempt to say "good-by to the pleasure of a quick triumph,
of making my apologies for the bad flaws in the bravest effort I had yet pulled out of myself, and certainly for declaring to the world (in a small way, mean pity) that I no longer
gave a sick dog's drop for ... the authority of the public's
literary mind, those creeps and old ladies of vested reviewing" (AM, p. 248), Mailer included in The Village Voice an
advertisement which consisted of brief clips from some of
the most critical reviews of The Deer Park. Although the
advertisement was bought in 1955, Mailer unwittingly set
himself up for the publication in 1959 of Advertisements for
Myself in which he capitalized upon the skirmishes with publishers, critics, and the public in the preceding years by
making himself the focus of his work.

The shift away from a description of socio-economic
conditions to an emphasis upon the nature of inner experience, all of which was reflected in his first three novels,
is revealed more fully in this collection, in which Mailer
dwells upon his own problems as a writer. By 1960 Mailer
had become a full-fledged public personality and was virtually assured a large audience for anything that he published.
Thus, when he wrote the pieces that comprise The Presidential Papers, he had become quite secure financially, a fact
which helped to shape his sensibility. It is in this work that
Mailer articulates more emphatically than at any previous
time his belief that individual consciousness, rather than the
economic system, should be the focus of radicals intent upon
social change.

However, despite his later stress upon inner experience, Mailer always maintained a political perspective.
While after The Naked and the Dead he no longer confined
himself to the naturalistic tradition with its emphasis upon
the power of environment to shape people's lives, Mailer
developed a more profound analysis of American culture because of his ability to delineate the emotional results of living in a predominantly authoritarian, repressive, and exploitative society. Moreover, his initial shift from a rich portrayal of external reality in The Naked and the Dead to a
greater preoccupation with inner experience in Barbary Shore
was not only a reflection of his changing political sentiments,
but an indication of his attempt to grow aesthetically. Realists like Farrell, Steinbeck and Dos Passos could only provide him with a method of understanding experience which
could be accounted for in logical and rational terms. But
it is Mailer's contention in "The White Negro" that

> The Second World War presented a mirror to the
> human condition which blinded anyone who looked
> into it. For if tens of millions were killed in con-
> centration camps out of the inexorable agonies and
> contractions of super-states founded upon the always
> insoluble contradictions of injustice, one was then
> obliged also to see that no matter how crippled and
> perverted an image of man was the society he had
> created, it was nonetheless his creation, his col-
> lective creation (at least his collective creation
> from the past) and if society was so murderous,
> then who could ignore the most hideous of ques-
> tions about his own nature? (AM, p. 338)

Even in The Naked and the Dead Mailer had explored the nature of the self. But he changed aesthetically only when he no longer believed as much in the importance of social, political, and economic analysis as a means of understanding individual behavior. In this context, Norman Podhoretz has stated that "To write realistic fiction a novelist must believe that society is what it seems to be and that it reveals the truth about itself in the personalities it throws up, the buildings it builds, the habits and manners it fosters; all the writer need do is describe these faithfully, selecting whatever details seem to him most sharply revealing and significant, and the truth will be served. But Mailer's point in Barbary Shore is precisely that our society is not what it seems to be. It seems to be prosperous, vigorous, sure of itself, purposeful, whereas in fact it is apathetic, confused, inept, empty, and in the grip of invisible forces that it neither recognizes or controls."12 These forces are operating on both sides of the organized political spectrum. In Barbary Shore, political disquisition points to the failure of capitalism and the limited possibilities of socialism, given the murderous compromises of the Russian bureaucracy and the projection of a totalitarian future in the United States.

The "libertarian socialism" which he devised was a reaction against the organizational and ideological rigidities of the Left in both countries. Stressing "respect for the varieties of human experience," he believed "that society must allow every individual his own road to discovering himself" (AM, p. 225). This direction is hinted at in Barbary Shore where the narrator, Lovett, is an amnesiac with an existential and Kafkaesque view of the world that is matched by his Troskyist political perspective. And Lovett's mentor is McLeod, whose earlier allegiance to organized political power in Russia and the United States has been transformed because of his unwillingness to overlook the grave limitations in each, especially the refusal to reconcile the demands of the state with the need for full individual development.

By the time The Deer Park was published, Mailer called himself a "Marxian anarchist." His interest in Marx appears to have been equaled by his affinity for Wilhelm Reich. The ending of The Deer Park with its hymn to sexuality suggests Reich's concern with the importance of the orgasm in human experience. Like Reich, Mailer modified his allegiance to Marx when he found the thinking and organizational vehicles of Left-wing radicals too constricting. His interest in Reich's notion of orgone especially helped to push him into an increasing reliance upon mysticism and theology. In fact, it appears that Mailer transformed some of Reich's more spectacular clinical work into rather amorphous mystical speculation. He projected outward the hipster's concern with the accumulation of energy and created a cosmological vision in which the world consists of a vast network of interrelated fields of force. Yet Mailer's mysticism never turned into the form advocated by Lawrence, who at one point in his career came to embrace primitive and religious modes with an authoritarian cast. Even in his discussion of John Kennedy as the existential political hero, what Mailer sought was not a blind veneration of presidential authority but a new awakening of the American people. Mailer thought that Kennedy's energy might inspire a large number of Americans to become more passionate and unique. Even before his assassination, Kennedy failed to meet the standards set for "The Hipster as Presidential Candidate." This failure, together with the "Caesarean" presidency of Lyndon Johnson, encouraged Mailer to deemphasize his concern with political reality. Therefore his "Marxian anarchism" became lost in his interest in psychological growth.

Neither Rojack in An American Dream nor D. J. in Why Are We in Vietnam? provides political alternatives. But they do continue the attack on the major political systems that Mailer began in Barbary Shore. Each of these heroes is concerned with coming closer to that Reichian energy at the heart of the universe, an attempt which is thwarted by conventional society and established power. Appropriately, their search for this energy is communicated in a language rich in metaphor and allusion, and through a plot which involves encounters that are barely credible renditions of "the violent and the orgiastic."13

D. J.'s departure for Vietnam is indicative of the fact that as much as Mailer was moving away from his earlier political interests he could not avoid the military conflict in which the United States was heavily engaged during the mid-sixties. A few years earlier, in 1964, he reported upon the Republican convention. That account, together with a number of other articles dealing with political matters during the Johnson Administration, appeared in Cannibals and Christians. Ultimately the turbulence of the mid-sixties in the American ghettoes and colleges as well as overseas in the form of United States military involvement in the affairs of other countries, particularly Vietnam, helped focus Mailer's attention once again upon social and political reality.

However, after 1966, his journalism reveals that his political thinking has shifted considerably. George Lukács describes "critical realists" who in their opposition to capitalist society tend to emphasize the individual and his personal conflicts and from this base work "towards wider social significance," and "socialist realists" who are more likely to try "to discover an Archimedian point in the midst of social contradiction" from which character becomes intelligible.[14] Mailer has been increasingly intent upon describing himself, a few fictional characters, or the major political figures in order to detail the condition of America. At the same time, his earlier belief in socialism has waned. Within the framework of his new perspective as a "Left Conservative," Mailer has come to advocate a series of proposals which suggest his admiration for laissez-faire capitalism. As a conservative, he believes that man must solve social and political problems without subordinating himself to any organization. As a radical, he recognizes that these problems cannot be solved by private effort alone. No longer referring to himself as a socialist in the New York mayoralty campaign of 1969, his proposals for reform emphasize the need for individual initiative in a society which has grown too large and bureaucratic. His campaign slogan, "power to the neighborhoods," is designed to encourage limited forms of collective involvement in an attempt to preserve the integrity of the self.

Mailer himself believes that he has retained a revolutionary perspective within the framework of Marx's dialectical method and sensitivity to political and economic oppression, as well as Reich's understanding of the restrictions imposed by society upon the full development of the individual's emotional life. But in stripping Marx of his heavy emphasis upon economics and in carelessly utilizing Reich, Mailer's understanding of America is weakened. Unlike Marx, who attempted to root all contradictions in an analysis of the material conditions of society, especially economic reality, Mailer has failed to analyze meticulously the individual components which comprise the paradox, ambiguity and tension that he sees in all aspects of experience. He luxuriates in dialectics, a kind of Paterian delight in the imaginative resources an individual can bring to the contradictions in everything. In Armies, after he is arrested, he speaks of his desire "to steep essences of this experience at his leisure" and calls himself an "emotional connoisseur, let us say even like Huysmans' Des Esseintes" (AN, p. 160).

This tendency is particularly evident in his discussion
of the nature of men and women in The Prisoner of Sex.
There he has offered a careless assortment of his own intuitions and cultural stereotypes, most of which are unconvincing. Despite his emphasis upon the inherent differences
between the sexes in Prisoner, even in that book Mailer continues to speak of the importance of social and political reality in shaping people's lives. In the early seventies he has
become highly pessimistic about the revolutionary possibilities
within the United States. He speaks of "the revolution" which
"called again, close to farce, that ill-mannered, drug-leached,
informer-infested, indiscriminate ripping up of all the roots,
yes, spoiled young middle-class heroes with fleas in their
beard and rashes doubtless in the groin were accelerating
each other now to accelerate America into the straightest
fascism of them all" (PS, p. 44). But then he adds that
"he could not condemn them. Society left to itself, bliss-
fully void of revolutionaries, would expire in a welter of the
most liberal sentiments and the foulest air, die in the total
ecological disruption of the universe, if indeed the insane economic imbalances of the cities did not burst forth first" (PS,
p. 44).

Mailer, then, remains a cultural analyst with a political commitment that defies precise categorization. His attempt to introduce metapsychological, as well as mystical,
theological, and cosmological speculations into his analysis
of American society has left him quite vulnerable to attack
by theorists who are more intent upon understanding the nature of political reality through analysis of specific material
conditions. Nevertheless, although The Armies of the Night
ends with Mailer's preoccupation with God and the Devil,
that work is not seriously hampered by his unconvincing cosmology. Unlike An American Dream, which contains a magical world, medieval in its intensity, in Armies experience
is rooted in material reality. If Mailer presents the idea of
the aggressive "animal imperative" in Armies and Miami and
the Siege of Chicago without adequately exploring the alternative explanations for the "beast" in man, he does not allow
this idea to interfere seriously with his ability to render the
nuance of event and character. He is not so fortunate in Of
a Fire on the Moon and St. George and the Godfather, where
his heavy reliance upon mysticism clouds his understanding
of events and people.

Mailer is at his best when he can draw upon, yet not
be bound by, the intellectual heritage which he utilizes so

freely. With his "philosophy of Hip," he has incorporated
in his writing important psychological, social, and political
observations. Too often, however, his aesthetic of "writing
more pages about fewer episodes" (AM, p. 379) neither contributes to the artistry of his work nor results in a comprehensive vision. In Barbary Shore and The Deer Park his
ideas do not emerge organically from described experience
but are appended to the thoughts and discussions of various
characters. With the cosmology of An American Dream and
the anthropology of Why Are We in Vietnam? Mailer under-
cuts his significant aesthetic achievement.

This attempt to extract the largest possible meaning
from events is part of Mailer's attempt to move beyond the
realistic tradition, an attempt which never fully succeeds.
The process of aesthetic experimentation, so crucial to Mailer's notion of himself as an artist, is really part of a larger
quest for self-transcendence. But in his search for a hero
who would possess mythic stature, Mailer often inflates character in ways that are dissatisfying. He is most successful
as a novelist, and as a journalist, when he captures the
texture of event and character by metaphorically detailing the
complex relationship between instinctual and institutional power.

Finally, despite his inability to consider adequately
the experience of women in his self-consciously masculine
"philosophy of Hip," Mailer has developed a strategy for living under "totalitarianism." While his discussion of sexuality and violence is inadequate, even in his early work he
knew that Hip "was a vast human and historical distance from
the philosophy which may follow it" (AM, p. 314). Although
continuing to cultivate "a malign machismo," he has transformed his attack against the corporate fabric of American
life. He no longer emphasizes, as he did in "The White
Negro," the instinctual tenacity of a few, but the blunted
sensibility of all Americans. His recent restraint in The
Armies of the Night, Miami and the Siege of Chicago, Of a
Fire on the Moon, and St. George and the Godfather does
not suggest a belief that America has changed to accommo-
date his values. Rather, at times in this journalism, he
has employed his sense of the dialectic both aesthetically and
ideologically without succumbing to the terrible pressure of
his inner experience or to the torturous nature of American
life.

Notes

1. <u>Waiting for the End</u> (New York: Stein and Day, 1964), p. 100.

2. Solotaroff, p. 259.

3. <u>Ibid.</u>, pp. 130-31. I am highly indebted to Solotaroff for his discussion of the relationship between Mailer's life and the fictional portrayal in <u>An American Dream</u>.

4. "In this Corner, Norman Mailer, Never the Champion Always the Challenger," <u>Life</u>, 24 Sept. 1965, p. 112.

5. <u>Ibid.</u>, p. 100. Brower quotes Mailer here.

6. Mailer's latest hero appears in "The Faith of Graffiti" in the guise of Sisyphus again. He is CAY 161 who, along with his compatriots, stealthily seeks to carve his ego into the impenetrable walls of New York City. Mailer turns Cay's mundane confrontations with the transit authorities and the police into "existential" encounters, which give him the stature of one whose voice possesses a "Delphic" ring, an "unexpected resonance--as if the idol of a temple has just chosen to break into sound." Perhaps we can forgive Mailer for this excess since it precedes Cay's observation that the name is "the faith." Unwittingly, Cay has provided the title of the work. But the actual process of implanting one's insignia is compared not only to the first attempts of cave painters whose hands pushed "forward into the terror of future punishment from demons filled with fury at human audacity," but to the attempts of all the artists who ever lived, whose works reverberate telepathically with the sensibilities of Cay and his friends. See <u>Esquire</u> article, p. 79.

7. "My Mailer Problem," <u>Esquire</u>, Sept. 1971, p. 92.

8. <u>Form and Fable in American Fiction</u> (New York: Oxford University Press, 1965), p. 34.

9. Hux, pp. 83, 195. Richard Warrington Baldwin Lewis was the first to elaborate fully upon the idea of the American Adam in his book <u>The American Adam: Innocence, Tragedy, and Tradition in the Nineteenth Century</u> (Chicago: University of Chicago Press, 1955).

10. Witt, p. 207.

11. The New Radicalism in America (1889-1963): The Intellectual as a Social Type (New York: Knopf, 1965), p. 335.

12. Podhoretz, pp. 378-79.

13. In Advertisements for Myself, Mailer speaks of Barbary Shore as a novel which suggests that his "vision" "was leading toward the violent and the orgiastic" (AM, p. 106).

14. Realism in Our Time: Literature and the Class Struggle, trans. John and Necke Mander (New York: Harper and Row, 1964), p. 94.

BIBLIOGRAPHY

List of Works Consulted

Aaron, Daniel. Writers on the Left. New York: Harcourt, Brace & World, 1961.

Aaron, Jonathan. "Existentialist Sheriff." The New Journal, 10 Dec. 1967, pp. 6-7.

Adams, Laura. Norman Mailer: A Comprehensive Bibliography. Metuchen, N. J. : Scarecrow, 1974.

Aldridge, John. After the Lost Generation. New York: McGraw-Hill, 1956.

_____. "America's Young Novelists." Saturday Review, 12 Feb. 1949, pp. 6-8, 36-37, 42.

_____. "From Vietnam to Obscenity." Harper's, Feb. 1968, pp. 91-96.

_____. In Search of Heresy. New York: McGraw-Hill, 1956.

_____. "Perfect Absurd Figure of a Mighty, Absurd Crusade." Saturday Review, 13 Nov. 1971, pp. 45-46.

_____. "A Review of An American Dream." Partisan Review, 32 (Spring 1965), 180-81.

_____. Time to Murder and Create. New York: David McKay Co. , Inc. , 1966.

_____. "Victim and Analyst." Commentary, Oct. 1966, pp. 131-33.

187

_____. "What Became of Our Postwar Hopes?" New York Times Book Review, 29 July 1962, pp. 1, 24.

Alexander, S. "Not Even Good Pornography." Reporter, 20 Oct. 1955, pp. 46-48.

Allen, Walter. The Urgent West: The American Dream and Modern Man. New York: Dutton, 1969.

Alvarez, A. "Norman X." Spectator, 7 May 1965, p. 603.

_____. Under Pressure: The Writer in Society: Eastern Europe and the U. S. A. Harmondsworth, Middlesex, England: Penguin Books, 1965.

"Americana: Of Time and the Rebel." Time, 5 Dec. 1960, pp. 16-17.

Angoff, Allan. "Protest in American Literature Since the End of World War II." College Language Association Journal, 5 (1961), 31-40.

Arnavon, Cyrille. "Les Cauchemars de Norman Mailer." Europe, Jan. 1969, pp. 93-116.

Auchincloss, Eve, and Nancy Lynch. "An Interview with Norman Mailer." Mademoiselle, Feb. 1961, pp. 76-77, 160-63.

Auchincloss, Louis. "The Novel as a Forum." New York Times Book Review, 24 Oct. 1965, p. 2.

"Authors: Two Bucks--20 Dances." Newsweek, 12 March 1962, p. 10.

"Backstage with Esky." Esquire, April 1953, pp. 15-16.

"Backstage with Esquire." Esquire, Nov. 1960, pp. 75-76.

Balakian, Nona. "The Prophetic Vogue of the Anti-heroine." Southwest Review, 47 (Spring 1962), 134-41.

Baldwin, James. Nobody Knows My Name: More Notes of a Native Son. New York: The Dial Press, 1961.

Beaver, Harold. "A Figure in the Carpet: Irony and the American Novel." Essays and Studies, 15 (1962), 101-14.

Bell, Pearl K. "The Power and the Vainglory." New Leader, 8 Feb. 1971, pp. 16-17.

Berman, Ronald. America in the Sixties: An Intellectual History. New York: The Free Press, 1968.

Bersani, Leo. "The Interpretation of Dreams." Partisan Review, 32 (Fall 1965), 603-08.

Bittner, William. "The Literary Underground." Nation, 22 Sept. 1956, pp. 247-48.

Blotner, Joseph. The Modern American Political Novel, 1900-1960. Austin: University of Texas Press, 1966.

Bone, Robert. "Private Mailer Re-enlists." Dissent, 7 (Autumn 1960), 389-94.

Braudy, Leo. "Advertisements for a Dwarf Alter-ego." The New Journal, 12 May 1968, pp. 7-9.

_____, ed. Norman Mailer: A Collection of Critical Essays. Englewood Cliffs, N. J.: Prentice-Hall, Inc., 1972.

Breit, Harvey. "Talk with Norman Mailer." New York Times Book Review, 3 June 1951, p. 20.

Breslow, Paul. "The Hipster and the Radical." Studies on the Left, 1 (1960), 102-05.

Brookeman, C. E. "Norman Mailer." Times Literary Supplement, 3 Oct. 1968, p. 1104.

Brower, Brock. "In this Corner, Norman Mailer, Never the Champion, Always the Challenger." Life, 24 Sept. 1965, pp. 94-117.

Brustein, Robert. "Who's Killing the Novel?" New Republic, 23 Oct. 1965, pp. 22-24.

Bryant, Jerry. "The Last of the Social Protest Writers." Arizona Quarterly, 19 (Winter 1963), 315-25.

_____. The Open Decision: The Contemporary Novel and Its Intellectual Background. New York: The Free Press, 1970.

Buchanan, Cynthia. "Existential Errands." New York Times Book Review, 16 April 1972, pp. 27-28.

Burdick, Eugene. "The Innocent Nihilists Adrift in Squaresville." Reporter, 3 April 1958, pp. 30-33.

_____. "The Politics of the Beat Generation." Western Political Quarterly, 12 (1959), 553-55.

Burg, David F. "The Hero of The Naked and the Dead." Modern Fiction Studies, 17 (1971), 387-401.

Burgess, Anthony. The Novel Now. London: Faber and Faber, 1961.

Carroll, Paul. "Playboy Interview: Norman Mailer." Playboy, Jan. 1968, pp. 69-72, 74, 76, 78, 80, 82-84.

Chase, Richard. The American Novel and Its Tradition. Garden City, N.Y.: Doubleday, 1957.

_____. "Neo-Conservatism and American Literature: Traditional Impulse and Radical Idea." Commentary, March 1957, pp. 254-61.

_____. "Novelist Going Places." Commentary, Dec. 1955, pp. 581-83.

_____. "Radicalism in the American Novel: A Reclamation of Values." Commentary, Jan. 1957, pp. 65-71.

Christian, Frederick. "The Talent and the Torment." Cosmopolitan, Aug. 1963, pp. 63-67.

Cleaver, Eldridge. "Notes on a Native Son." Ramparts, June 1966, pp. 51-52, 54-56.

Clecak, Peter. "Social Criticism and Illusions of the Open Society." Massachusetts Review, 10 (Spring 1969), 247-79.

Clurman, Harold. "Theatre." Nation, 20 Feb. 1967, pp. 252-53.

Cook, Bruce. The Beat Generation. New York: Charles Scribner's Sons, 1971.

_____. "Norman Mailer: The Temptation to Power."
Renascence, 14 (Summer 1962), 206-15, 222.

Corrington, John William. "An American Dreamer." Chicago Review, 18 (1965), 58-66.

Cowan, Michael. "The Americanness of Norman Mailer."
Norman Mailer: A Collection of Critical Essays. Ed.
Leo Braudy. Englewood Cliffs, N. J. : Prentice-Hall,
Inc. , 1972.

Cowley, Malcolm. "The Literary Situation 1965 (A Seminar
at the Southern Literary Festival)." University of Mississippi Studies in English, 6 (1965), 91-98.

Culey, Thomas F. "The Quarrel with Time in American
Fiction." American Scholar, 29 (Autumn 1960), 552,
554, 556, 558, 560.

Current Biography: 1948. New York: H. W. Wilson Co. ,
1948.

Dabney, Louis. "The American Novel in the Age of Conformity." Nation, 23 Feb. 1957, pp. 167-69.

Darack, Arthur. "Man Against His Times." Saturday Review, 3 Sept. 1966, p. 35.

Davis, David Brion. "Violence in American Literature."
Annals of American Academy of Political and Social
Sciences, 364 (March 1966), 28-36.

Davis, Ronald L. "All the New Vibrations: Romanticism
in the 20th-Century America." Southwest Review, 54
(1969), 256-70.

Decter, Midge. "Mailer's Campaign." Commentary, Feb.
1964, pp. 83-85.

DeMott, Benjamin. "Docket No. 15883." American Scholar,
30 (Spring 1961), 232-37.

_____. "Inside Apollo 11 with Aquarius Mailer." Saturday Review, 16 Jan. 1971, pp. 25-27, 57-58.

_____. "Jewish Writers in America." Commentary,
Feb. 1961, pp. 127-34.

Dickstein, Morris. "A Trip to Inner and Outer Space." New York Times Book Review, 10 Jan. 1971, pp. 1, 42-43, 45.

Didion, Joan. "A Social Eye." National Review, 20 April 1965, pp. 329-30.

Dienstfrey, Harris. "The Fiction of Norman Mailer." On Contemporary Literature. Ed. Richard Kostelanetz. New York: Avon, 1964.

Dommergues, P. "Rencontre avec Norman Mailer." Les Langues Modernes, 3 (May 1967), 61-66.

Donoghue, Denis. "Sweepstakes." New York Review of Books, 28 Sept. 1967, pp. 5-6.

Donohue, H. E. F. Conversations with Nelson Algren. New York: Hill and Wang, 1964.

Duhamel, P. Albert. "Love in the Modern Novel." Catholic World, April 1960, pp. 31-35.

Dupee, F. W. "The American Norman Mailer." Commentary, Feb. 1960, pp. 128-32.

Eble, Kenneth. "The Individual at Mid Twentieth Century: A Symposium. America's Lonely Writers." Western Humanities Review, 12 (Autumn 1958), 350-57.

Ehnmark, Anders. "Rebels in American Literature." Western Review, 12 (1958), 43-56.

Eisinger, Chester E. Fiction of the Forties. Chicago: University of Chicago Press, 1963.

_____. Introduction to The Naked and the Dead. New York: Holt, Rinehart and Winston, 1968.

Ellman, Mary. Thinking About Women. New York: Harvest, 1968.

Epstein, Joseph. "Mailer Rides Again: Brilliant, Idiosyncratic, Unquotable." Book World, 10 Sept. 1967, pp. 1, 34.

Fallaci, Oriana. "Interview with Norman Mailer." Writer's Digest, Dec. 1969, pp. 40-47.

Farbar, Buzz. "Mailer on Marriage and Women." Viva, Oct. 1973, pp. 75-76, 144, 146, 148, 150, 152.

Fenton, Charles. "The Writers Who Came Out of the War." Saturday Review, 3 Aug. 1957, pp. 5-7, 24.

Fiedler, Leslie. "Antic Mailer--Portrait of a Middle-Aged Artist." New Leader, 25 Jan. 1960, pp. 23-24.

_____. "The Breakthrough: The American Jewish Novelist and the Fictional Image of the Jew." Midstream, 4 (Winter 1958), 15-35.

_____. "The Jew as Mythic American." Ramparts, Autumn 1963, pp. 32-48.

_____. Love and Death in the American Novel. New York: Criterion Books, 1960.

_____. "Master of Dreams." Partisan Review, 34 (Summer 1967), 353-54.

_____. The Return of the Vanishing American. New York: Stein and Day, 1968.

_____. Waiting for the End. New York: Dell, 1964.

Finholt, Richard D. "'Otherwise How Explain?' Norman Mailer's New Cosmology." Modern Fiction Studies, 17 (1971), 375-86.

Finkelstein, Sidney. Existentialism and Alienation in American Literature. New York: International Publishers, 1965.

_____. "Norman Mailer and Edward Albee." American Dialog, 2 (Feb.-March 1965), 23-28.

Finn, J. "Virtues, Failures and Triumphs of an American Writer." Commonweal, 12 Feb. 1960, pp. 551-52.

"First Person Singular." Time, 23 Feb. 1968, p. 81.

Fitch, R. E. "Mystique de la Merde." New Republic, 3 Sept. 1956, pp. 17-18. Reply. Time, 1 Oct. 1956, p. 94.

Fitzgerald. F. Scott. The Great Gatsby. New York: Charles Scribner's Sons, 1925.

Flaherty, Joe. Managing Mailer. New York: Coward-McCann, 1969.

_____. "When Norman Mailer Ran for Mayor." Book World (Chicago Tribune), 28 Dec. 1969, pp. 1, 3, 4.

Flint, Joyce Marlene. "In Search of Meaning: Bernard Malamud, Norman Mailer, John Updike." Diss., Washington State, 1969.

Foster, Richard. "Mailer and the Fitzgerald Tradition." Novel, 1 (Spring 1968), 219-30.

_____. Norman Mailer. Minneapolis: University of Minnesota Press, 1968.

Fremont-Smith, Eliot. "Family Report." New York Times, 28 Oct. 1968, p. 45.

_____. "A Nobel for Norman?" New York Times, 22 Aug. 1966, p. 31.

_____. "Norman Mailer's Cherry Pie." New York Times, 8 Sept. 1967, pp. 1, 34.

Fuller, Edmund. Man in Modern Fiction: Some Minority Opinions on Contemporary American Writing. New York: Random House, 1958.

Galligan, Edward L. "Hemingway's Staying Power." Massachusetts Review, 8 (Summer 1967), 431-39.

Gamberg, Herbert. "The Modern Literary Ethos: A Sociological Interpretation." Social Forces, 37 (Oct. 1958), 7-14.

Garraty, John. "A Century of American Realism." American Heritage, 21 (June 1970), 12-15, 86-90.

Geismar, Maxwell. American Moderns, from Rebellion to Conformity. New York: Hill and Wang, 1958.

Gelfant, Blanche H. The American City Novel. Norman: University of Oklahoma Press, 1954.

Gelmis, Joseph. The Film Director as Superstar. Garden City, N. Y.: Doubleday, 1970.

Gilbert, James. Writers and Partisans: A History of Literary Radicalism in America. New York: John Wiley, 1968.

Gilman, Richard. The Confusion of Realms. New York: Random House, 1969.

_____. "What Mailer Has Done." New Republic, 8 June 1968, pp. 27-31.

_____. "Why Mailer Wants to be President." New Republic, 8 Feb. 1964, pp. 17-20, 22-24.

Gittelson, N. "Norman Mailer: Devil in the Fire." Harper's Bazaar, July 1971, pp. 14, 16.

Glicksberg, Charles I. "Norman Mailer: The Angry Young Novelist in America." Wisconsin Studies in Contemporary Literature, 1 (Winter 1960), 25-34.

_____. "Sex in Contemporary Literature." Colorado Quarterly, 9 (Winter 1961), 277-87.

Gold, Herbert. "How to Tell the Beatniks from the Hipsters." The Noble Savage, 1 (Spring 1960), 132-39.

Goldman, Lawrence. "The Political Vision of Norman Mailer." Studies on the Left, 4 (Summer 1964), 129-41.

Goodman, Walter. "On the (N. Y.) Literary Left." Antioch Review, 29 (Spring 1969), 67-75.

Gordon, Andrew. "Confrontation with Norman Mailer." The San Francisco Phoenix, 23 Nov. 1972, pp. 3, 20.

_____. "The Naked and the Dead: The Triumph of Impotence." Literature and Psychology, 19, No. 3-4 (1969), 3-13.

_____. "A Psychoanalytic Study of the Fiction of Norman Mailer." Diss., Berkeley, 1973.

Grant, L. "Norman Mailer, Dialogue with a Non-Mayor." Ramparts, Dec. 1969, pp. 44-46.

Graves, R. "Norman Mailer at the Typewriter: Writing on the Moon Landing." Life, 29 Aug. 1969, p. 1.

Greenfield, Josh. "Line Between Journalism and Literature Thin, Perhaps, but Distinct." Commonweal, 7 June 1968, pp. 362-63.

Greenway, J. "Norman Mailer Meets the British Brigade." National Review, 27 July 1971, p. 815.

Greer, Germaine. "My Mailer Problem." Esquire, Sept. 1971, pp. 90-93.

Gross, Theodore L. The Heroic Ideal in American Literature. New York: The Free Press, 1971.

Guttmann, Allen. "Jewish Radicals, Jewish Writers." American Scholar, 32 (Autumn 1963), 563-75.

Halberstam, M. "Norman Mailer as Ethnographer." Trans-Action, March 1969, pp. 52-53.

Hampshire, Stuart. "Mailer United." New Statesman, 13 Oct. 1961, pp. 515-16.

Hardwick, Elizabeth. "Bad Boy (a review of An American Dream)." Partisan Review, 32 (Spring 1965), 291-94.

Harper, Howard M., Jr. Desperate Faith: A Study of Bellow, Salinger, Mailer, Baldwin and Updike. Chapel Hill: University of North Carolina Press, 1967.

Hassan, Ihab. "The Avant Garde: Which Way Is Forward?" Nation, 18 Nov. 1961, pp. 396-99.

_____. "Focus on Norman Mailer's Why Are We in Vietnam?" American Dreams, American Nightmares. Ed. David Madden. Carbondale: Southern Illinois University Press, 1970.

_____. "The Novel of Outrage: A Minority Voice in Postwar American Fiction." American Scholar, 34 (1965), 239-53.

_____. Radical Innocence: Studies in the Contemporary American Novel. New York: Harper & Row, 1961.

Bibliography / 197

_____. "The Way Down and Out: Spiritual Deflection in Recent American Fiction." Virginia Quarterly Review, 39 (Winter 1963), 81-93.

Hastings, Michael. "Who Is Killing Us?" Time and Tide, 12 Oct. 1961, p. 1704.

Healy, Robert C. "Novelists of the War: A Bunch of Dispossessed." Fifty Years of the American Novel. Ed. Harold C. Gardiner, S. J. New York: Charles Scribner's Sons, 1951.

Helsa, David. "The Two Roles of Norman Mailer." Adversity and Grace. Ed. Nathan A. Scott, Jr. Chicago: University of Chicago Press, 1968.

Hicks, Granville. "Lark in Race for Presidency." Saturday Review, 16 Sept. 1967, pp. 39-40.

_____. "They Needn't Say No." Saturday Review, 2 July 1960, p. 14.

_____. "Vision of Life Is His Own." Saturday Review, 7 Nov. 1959, p. 18.

Hoffman, Daniel. Form and Fable in American Fiction. New York: Oxford University Press, 1965.

Hoffman, Frederick J. "Dogmatic Innocence: Self Assertion in Modern American Literature." Texas Quarterly, 6 (Summer 1963), 152-62.

_____. The Modern Novel in America. Chicago: Henry Regnery Co., 1963.

_____. The Mortal No: Death and the Modern Imagination. Princeton: Princeton University Press, 1964.

_____. "Norman Mailer and the Revolt of the Ego: Some Observations on Recent American Literature." Wisconsin Studies in Contemporary Literature, 1 (Fall 1960), 5-12.

Howe, Irving. "Mass Society and Post-Modern Fiction." Partisan Review, 26 (Summer 1959), 420-36.

_____. "The New York Intellectuals." Commentary, Oct. 1968, pp. 29-51.

_____. "Some Political Novels." Nation, 16 June 1951, pp. 568-69.

_____. A World More Attractive: A View of Modern Literature and Politics. New York: Horizon Press, 1963.

Hux, Samuel Holland. "American Myth and Existential Vision: The Indigenous Existentialism of Mailer, Bellow, Styron, and Ellison." Diss., Connecticut, 1965.

Hyman, Stanley Edgar. "Norman Mailer's Yummy Rump." The New Leader, 15 March 1965, pp. 16-17.

Jameson, Fredric. "The Great American Hunter, or, Ideological Content in the Novel." College English, 34 (Nov. 1972), 180-97.

Jones, James. "Letter Home." Esquire, Dec. 1963, pp. 28, 30, 34, 40, 44.

Kael, Pauline. "Current Cinema." New Yorker, 20 Jan. 1968, pp. 90, 92-95.

Kahn, E. J., Jr. "When the Real Norman Mailer Stands Up, Please Don't Lay a Hand on Me." Holiday, March 1968, pp. 34, 36-37.

Kaufmann, Donald L. "The Long Happy Life of Norman Mailer." Modern Fiction Studies, 17 (1971), 347-59.

_____. "Mailer's Lunar Bits and Pieces." Modern Fiction Studies, 17 (1971), 451-54.

_____. Norman Mailer: The Countdown. Carbondale: Southern Illinois University Press, 1969.

Kaufmann, Stanley. "An American Dreamer." New Republic, 16 Sept. 1967, p. 18.

Kazin, Alfred. "The Alone Generation." Harper's, Oct. 1959, pp. 127-31.

_____. "How Good Is Norman Mailer?" Reporter, 26 Nov. 1959, pp. 40-41.

_____. "Imagination and the Age." Reporter, 5 May 1966, pp. 32-35.

_____. "The Jew as Modern Writer." Commentary, April 1966, pp. 37-41.

_____. "The Literary Sixties, When the World Was Too Much With Us." New York Times Book Review, 21 Dec. 1969, pp. 1-3, 18.

_____. "New York Jew." New York Review of Books, 14 Dec. 1972, pp, 4, 6, 8, 10, 12.

_____. "The Trouble He's Seen." New York Times Book Review, 5 May 1968, pp. 1-2, 26.

Kent, Leticia. "Shoot-for-the-Moon Mailer: An Interview with Norman Mailer on the Literary Life and Practical Politics." Running Against the Machine. Ed. Peter Manso. Garden City, N.Y.: Doubleday, 1969.

Kermode, Frank. "Rammel." New Statesman, 14 May 1964, pp. 765-66.

Kerr, Walter. "Norman Mailer's Wicked 'Deer Park.'" New York Times, 1 Feb. 1967, p. 27.

Knickerbocker, Conrad. "A Man Desperate for a New Life." New York Times Book Review, 14 March 1965, pp. 1, 36, 38-39.

Krim, Seymour. "Get Out of My Head!" New York, 21 April 1969, pp. 35-42.

_____. Shake It for the World, Smartass. New York: Dial, 1970.

Lakin, R. D. "The Displaced Writer in America." Midwest Quarterly, 4 (Summer 1963), 295-303.

Langbaum, Robert. "Mailer's New Style." Novel, 2 (Fall 1968), 69-78.

Lasch, Christopher. The New Radicalism in America (1889-1963): The Intellectual as a Social Type. New York: Knopf, 1966.

Lawler, Robert W. "Norman Mailer: The Connection of New Circuits." Diss., Claremont, 1969.

Lawrence, D. H. The Collected Letters of D. H. Lawrence. 2 vols. Ed. Harry T. Moore. New York: The Viking Press, Inc., 1962.

Leeds, Barry H. The Structured Vision of Norman Mailer. New York: New York University Press, 1969.

Lehmann-Haupt, Christopher. "Mailer's Dream of the Moon." New York Times, 7 Jan. 1971, p. 33, and 8 Jan. 1971, p. 29.

_____. "Norman Mailer as Joycean Punster and Manipulator of Language." Commonweal, 8 Dec. 1967, pp. 338-39.

Leverenz, David Langmuir. "A Psychoanalysis of American Literature." Diss., Berkeley, 1969.

Levine, Richard M. "When Sam and Sergius Meet." New Leader, 8 July 1968, p. 1050.

Lewis, R. W. B. The American Adam: Innocence, Tragedy, and Tradition in the Nineteenth Century. Chicago: University of Chicago Press, 1955.

_____. "Recent Fiction: Picaro and Pilgrim." A Time of Harvest: American Literature 1910-1960. Ed. Robert Spiller. New York: Hill and Wang, 1962.

Lifton, Robert Jay. "Protean Man." Partisan Review, 35 (Winter 1968), 13-27.

Lucid, Robert F., ed. Norman Mailer: The Man and His Work. Boston: Little, Brown and Co., 1971.

Ludwig, Jack. Recent American Novelists. Minneapolis: University of Minnesota Press, 1962.

Lukács, George. Realism in Our Time: Literature and the Class Struggle, trans. John and Necke Mander. New York: Harper and Row, 1964.

Macdonald, Dwight. "Art, Life and Violence." Commentary, June 1962, pp. 169-72.

_____. "Our Far-flung Correspondents: Massachusetts vs. Mailer." New Yorker, 8 Oct. 1960, pp. 154, 156, 158, 160-66.

_____. "Politics." Esquire, May 1968, pp. 41-44, 194, 196, and June 1968, pp. 46, 48, 50, 183.

McPherson, Myra. "Mailer Muses on Activism." San Francisco Chronicle, 11 May 1970, p. 4.

Maddison, Michael. "Prospect of Commitment." Political Quarterly, 32 (Oct. 1961), 353-62.

Maddocks, M. "Norm's Ego Is Working Overtime for You." Life, 10 May 1968, p. 8.

Mailer, Norman. Advertisements for Myself. New York: Putnam, 1959.

_____. An American Dream. New York: Dial, 1964.

_____. The Armies of the Night: History as a Novel, The Novel as History. New York: The New American Library, 1968.

_____. Barbary Shore. New York: Rinehart, 1951.

_____. The Bullfight: A Photographic Narrative with Text by Norman Mailer. New York: Macmillan, 1967.

_____. Cannibals and Christians. New York: Dial, 1966.

_____. Deaths for the Ladies (and other disasters). New York: Putnam, 1962.

_____. The Deer Park. New York: Putnam, 1955.

_____. The Deer Park: A Play. New York: Dial, 1967.

_____. Existential Errands. Boston: Little, Brown and Co., 1972.

_____. "The Faith of Graffiti." Esquire, May 1974, pp. 77-79, 88, 154, 157-58.

_____. The Fight. Boston: Little, Brown and Co., 1975.

_____. Genius and Lust: A Journey Through the Major Writings of Henry Miller. New York: Grove Press, 1976.

_____ . The Idol and the Octopus. New York: Dell, 1968.

_____ . The Long Patrol: 25 Years of Writing from the Work of Norman Mailer. Ed. Robert Lucid. New York: World Publishing Co. , 1971.

_____ . Maidstone. New York: The New American Library, 1971.

_____ . Marilyn. New York: Grosset and Dunlap, 1973.

_____ . Miami and the Siege of Chicago: An Informal History of the Republican and Democratic Conventions of 1968. Cleveland: World Publishing Co. , 1968.

_____ . The Naked and the Dead. New York: Rinehart, 1948.

_____ . Of a Fire on the Moon. Boston: Little, Brown and Co. , 1970.

_____ . "Of a Small and Secret Malignancy. " Esquire, Nov. 1977, pp. 125-48.

_____ . The Presidential Papers. New York: Putnam, 1963.

_____ . The Presidential Papers. 1963; rpt. Harmondsworth, Middlesex, England: Penguin Books, 1968.

_____ . The Prisoner of Sex. Boston: Little, Brown and Co. , 1971.

_____ . St. George and the Godfather. New York: The New American Library, 1972.

_____ . "Search for Carter. " New York Times Magazine, 26 Sept. 1976, pp. 19-21, 69-70, 72-78, 80-85, 88-92.

_____ . The Short Fiction of Norman Mailer. New York: Dell, 1967.

_____ . Some Honorable Men: Political Conventions, 1960-1972. Boston: Little, Brown and Co. , 1976.

_____ . "Talking of Violence. " Twentieth Century, 168 (Winter 1964-65), 109-14.

_____. The White Negro. San Francisco: City Lights Books, 1957.

_____. Why Are We in Vietnam? New York: Putnam, 1967.

"Mailer for Mayor." Time, 13 June 1969, pp. 21-22.

"Mailer Opening." New Yorker, 2 Oct. 1971, p. 33.

"Mailer's America." Time, 11 Oct. 1968, pp. 81-82.

Malin, Irving. Jews and Americans. Carbondale: Southern Illinois University Press, 1965.

_____, and Irwin Stark, eds. Breakthrough: A Treasury of Contemporary American-Jewish Literature. New York: McGraw-Hill, 1964.

Manso, Peter, ed. Running Against the Machine. Garden City, N. Y. : Doubleday, 1969.

Martien, Norman. "Norman Mailer at Graduate School." Norman Mailer: The Man and His Work. Ed. Robert F. Lucid. Boston: Little, Brown and Co. , 1971.

Maxwell, Robert. "Personal Reactions to a Presidential Candidate." Minnesota Review, 5 (Aug. /Oct. 1965), 244-54.

Merideth, Robert. "The 45-Second Piss: A Left Critique of Norman Mailer and The Armies of the Night." Modern Fiction Studies, 17 (1971), 433-49.

Middlebrook, Jonathan. Mailer and the Times of His Time. San Francisco: Bay Books, 1976.

Miller, Jonathan. "Black Mailer" (a review of The Presidential Papers). Partisan Review, 31 (Winter 1964), 103-07.

Millett, Kate. Sexual Politics. Garden City, N. Y. : Doubleday, 1970.

Millgate, Michael. American Social Fiction: James to Cozzens. New York: Barnes and Noble, 1964.

"Misshapen Image." Time, 29 Nov. 1963, pp. 106, 109.

Moore, William. "Norman Mailer in Full Cry." San Francisco Chronicle, 26 Oct. 1972, p. 7.

Mordecai, Richard. "Norman Mailer." Encounter, July 1955, pp. 61-64.

Morel, Jean-Pierre. "Pourquois Sommes-Nous au Vietnam?" Etudes, 329 (Nov. 1968), 574-80.

Mount, D. N. "Mailer Lights Another Fire." Publisher's Weekly, 15 Feb. 1971, p. 55.

Mudrick, Marvin. "Mailer and Styron: Guests of the Establishment." Hudson Review, 17 (Autumn 1964), 346-66.

Muggeridge, Malcolm. "Books." Esquire, Dec. 1966, pp. 104, 106, 108.

Muste, John M. "Norman Mailer and John Dos Passos: The Question of Influence." Modern Fiction Studies, 17 (1971), 361-74.

Nadon, Robert. "Urban Values in Recent American Fiction: A Study of the City in the Fiction of Saul Bellow, John Updike, Philip Roth, Bernard Malamud, and Norman Mailer." Diss., Minnesota, 1969.

Newfield, Jack. "Bobby Hero." Cavalier, Aug. 1966, pp. 31, 82-85.

Nichols, D. "Secret Places of the Groin." Nation, 5 Nov. 1955, pp. 393-95.

Noble, David W. The Eternal Adam and the New World Garden: The Central Myth in the American Novel Since 1830. New York: George Braziller, 1968.

"Norman Mailer's March." Times Literary Supplement, 19 Sept. 1968, p. 1050.

Oates, Joyce Carol. "Out of the Machine." Atlantic, July 1971, pp. 42-45.

O'Brien, Conor Cruise. "Confessions of the Last American." New York Review of Books, 20 June 1968, pp. 16-18.

"Odd Couple." Newsweek, 12 May 1969, pp. 37-38.

"Of Time and the Rebel." Time, 5 Dec. 1960, pp. 16-17.

Olmstead, Robert Taft. "The American Novel of World War II as Social Criticism." Diss., Stanford, 1970.

"Pasta Fazoul." Newsweek, 29 Aug. 1966, pp. 73-74.

Pearce, Richard. "Norman Mailer's Why Are We in Vietnam?: A Radical Critique of Frontier Values." Modern Fiction Studies, 17 (1971), 409-14.

Pearce, Roy Harvey. The Continuity of American Poetry. Princeton, N. J.: Princeton University Press, 1961.

Phillips, William. "Notes on the New Style." Nation, 20 Sept. 1965, pp. 232-36.

Pickerel, Paul. "Thing of Darkness." Harper's, April 1965, pp. 116-17.

Pilati, J. "On the Steps of City Hall." Commonweal, 16 May 1969, pp. 255-56.

Podhoretz, Norman. "Norman Mailer: The Embattled Vision." Partisan Review, 26 (Summer 1959), 371-91.

Poirier, Richard. "Good Form and Bad." Saturday Review, 22 April 1972, pp. 42-46.

_____. "Morbid-mindedness." Commentary, June 1965, pp. 91-94.

_____. Norman Mailer. New York: The Viking Press, Inc., 1972.

_____. "Norman Mailer: A Self-Creation." Atlantic, Oct. 1972, pp. 78-85.

_____. The Performing Self. New York: Oxford University Press, 1971.

_____. "Ups and Downs of Mailer." New Republic, 23 Jan. 1971, pp. 23-26.

Prescott, Orville. In My Opinion: An Inquiry into the Contemporary Novel. New York: Bobbs-Merrill, 1952.

Pritchard. William H. "Norman Mailer's Extravagances." Massachusetts Review, 8 (Summer 1967), 562-68.

Pritchett, V. S., and Joyce Carol Oates. "With Norman Mailer at the Sex Circus." Atlantic, July 1971, pp. 40-45.

Radford, Jean. Norman Mailer: A Critical Study. London: Macmillan. 1975.

Rahv, Philip. "Crime Without Punishment." New York Review of Books, 25 March 1965, pp. 1-4.

Rainer, D. "Fattening for the Slaughter." New Republic, 31 Oct. 1955, p. 25.

Ramsey, Roger. "Current and Recurrent: The Vietnam Novel." Modern Fiction Studies, 17 (1971), 415-31.

Reich, Wilhelm. Character Analysis, trans. Vincent R. Carfagno. 3rd ed. New York: Farrar Straus, 1972.

Resnik, Henry S. "Hand on the Pulse of America." Saturday Review, 4 May 1968, pp. 25-26.

Richardson, Jack. "The Aesthetics of Norman Mailer." New York Review of Books, 7 May 1969, pp. 3-4.

Richler, Mordecai. "Norman Mailer." Encounter, July 1965, pp. 61-64.

Rideout, Walter B. The Radical Novel in the United States: 1900-1954. Cambridge: Harvard University Press, 1956.

Roddy, J. "Latest Model Mailer." Look, 27 May 1969, pp. 22-28.

Rodman, Selden. "Deaths for the Ladies (and other disasters)." New York Times Book Review, 8 July 1962, p. 7.

Rosenthal, Melvyn. "The American Writer and His Society-- The Response to Estrangement in the Works of Nathaniel Hawthorne, Randolph Bourne, Edmund Wilson, Norman Mailer, and Saul Bellow." Diss., Connecticut, 1968.

Roth, Philip. "Writing American Fiction." Commentary, March 1961, pp. 223-33.

Rubin, Louis. "The Curious Death of the Novel." Kenyon Review, 28 (June 1966), 305-25.

Sale, Roger. "Watchman, What of the Night?" New York Review of Books, 6 May 1971, pp. 13-17.

"Savage Ending." Newsweek, 5 Dec. 1960, p. 33.

Schickel, R. "Stars and Celebrities." Commentary, Aug. 1971, pp. 61-65.

Schott, W. "Mailer Writes Dirty about Aurora Borealis." Life, 15 Sept. 1967, p. 8.

Schrader, George A. "Norman Mailer and the Despair of Defiance." Yale Review, 51 (Dec. 1961), 267-80.

Schroth, Raymond A. "Between the Lines: Norman Mailer." America, 30 Nov. 1968, p. 558.

_____. "Mailer and His Gods." Commonweal, 29 May 1969, pp. 226-29.

_____. "Mailer on the Moon." Commonweal, 7 May 1971, pp. 216-18.

Schulz, Max F. "Mailer's Divine Comedy." Contemporary Literature, 9 (Winter 1968), 36-57.

_____. Radical Sophistication: Studies in Contemporary Jewish-American Novelists. Athens: Ohio University Press, 1969.

Scott, James B. "The Individual and Society, Norman Mailer versus William Styron." Diss., Syracuse, 1964.

Scott, Nathan A. Three American Moralists. Notre Dame, Ind.: University of Notre Dame Press, 1973.

Shaw, Peter. "The Conventions, 1968." Commentary, Dec. 1968, pp. 93-96.

_____. "The Tough Guy Intellectual." Critical Quarterly, 8 (Spring 1966), 13-28.

Sheed, Wilfrid. "Genius or Nothing." Encounter, June 1971, pp. 66-71.

_____ . "Miami and the Siege of Chicago: A Review." New York Times Book Review, 8 Dec. 1968, pp. 3, 56.

_____ . "One-Man Dance Marathon." New York Times Book Review, 21 Aug. 1966, pp. 1, 33.

Sisk, John P. "Aquarius Rising." Commentary, May 1971, pp. 83-84.

Smith, William James. "The Stage." Commonweal, 10 March 1967, pp. 657-58.

Sokoloff, B. A. A Comprehensive Bibliography of Norman Mailer. Folcroft, Pa.: Folcroft Press, 1970.

Sokolov, Raymond A. "Flying High with Mailer." Newsweek, 9 Dec. 1968, pp. 84, 86-88.

Solotaroff, Robert. Down Mailer's Way. Urbana: University of Illinois, 1974.

Solotaroff, Theodore. The Red Hot Vacuum. New York: Atheneum, 1970.

Spatz, Jonas. Hollywood in Fiction: Some Versions of the American Myth. The Hague: Mouton and Co., 1969.

Spender, Stephen. "Mailer's American Melodrama." The Great Ideas Today, 1965. Ed. Robert Hutchins and Mortimer Adler. Chicago: Encyclopaedia Britannica, Inc., 1965.

Stark, John Olsen. "Barbary Shore: The Basis of Mailer's Best Work." Modern Fiction Studies, 17 (1971), 403-08.

_____ . "Norman Mailer's Work from 1963 to 1968." Diss., Wisconsin, 1970.

Steiner, George. "Naked But Not Dead." Encounter, Dec. 1961, pp. 67-70.

Stevenson, David. "Fiction's Unfamiliar Face." Nation, 1 Nov. 1958, pp. 307-09.

_____. "The Lost Audience." Nation, 2 Aug. 1958, pp. 58-59.

_____. "Styron and the Fiction of the Forties." Critique, 3 (Summer 1960), 47-58.

"Surveying Supernation." Newsweek, 26 Feb. 1968, p. 62.

Swados, Harvey. "Must Writers Be Characters?" Saturday Review, 1 Oct. 1960, pp. 12-14, 50.

_____. "The Writer in Contemporary American Society." Anger and Beyond, 55 (1966), 62-75.

Swenson, May. "Deaths for the Ladies (and other disasters)." Poetry, May 1963, p. 118.

Tanner, Tony. "The American Novelist as Entropologist." London Magazine (British), Oct. 1970, pp. 5-18.

_____. City of Words: American Fiction 1950-1970. London: Jonathan Cape, and New York: Harper & Row, 1971.

_____. "The Great American Nightmare." Spectator, 29 April 1966, pp. 530-31.

_____. "On the Parapet: A Study of the Novels of Norman Mailer." Critical Quarterly, 12 (1970), 153-76.

"The Talk of the Town." New Yorker, 23 Oct. 1948, pp. 23-27.

Thompson, John. "Catching Up on Mailer." New York Review of Books, 20 April 1967, pp. 14-16.

Thorp, Willard. American Writing in the Twentieth Century. Cambridge: Harvard University Press, 1960.

Toback, James. "At Play in the Fields of the Bored." Esquire, Dec. 1968, pp. 150-55, 22, 24, 26, 28, 30, 32, 34, 36.

_____. "Norman Mailer Today." Commentary, Oct. 1967, pp. 68-76.

Trilling, Diana. "Norman Mailer." Encounter, Nov. 1962, pp. 45-56.

Twentieth Century Authors, First Supplement. Ed. Stanley
    Kunitz. New York: H. W. Wilson Co., 1955.

Velde, Paul. "Hemingway Who Stayed Home." Nation, 20
    Jan. 1964, pp. 76-77.

Vidal, Gore. "The Norman Mailer Syndrome." Nation, 2
    Jan. 1960, pp. 13-16.

Volpe, Edmund. "James Jones--Norman Mailer." Contem-
    porary American Novelists. Ed. Harry T. Moore.
    Carbondale: Southern Illinois University Press, 1964.

Wagenheim, Allan J. "Square's Progress: An American
    Dream." Critique, 10 (1967), 45-68.

Wain, John. "Mailer's America." New Republic, 1 Oct.
    1966, pp. 19-20.

Waldmeir, Joseph J. "Accommodations in the New Novel."
    University College Quarterly, 11 (Nov. 1965), 26-32.

_____. American Novels of the Second World War. The
    Hague: Mouton, 1969.

_____. "Quest Without Faith." Nation, 18 Nov. 1961,
    pp. 390-96.

Waldron, Randall H. "The Naked, the Dead, and the Ma-
    chine: A New Look at Norman Mailer's First Novel."
    PMLA, 87 (March 1972), 271-77.

Warfel, Harry R. American Novelists of Today. New York:
    American Book Co., 1951.

Weales, Gerald. "The Park in the Playhouse." Reporter,
    6 April 1967, pp. 47-48.

Weatherby, W. J. Squaring Off: Mailer vs. Baldwin. New
    York: Mason/Charter, 1977.

Weber, Brom. "A Fear of Dying: Norman Mailer's An A-
    merican Dream." Hollins Critic, June 1965, pp. 1-6.

Weinberg, Helen. The New Novel in America: The Kafkan
    Mode in Contemporary Fiction. Ithaca, N.Y.: Cornell
    University Press, 1970.

West, Paul. "Romantic Identity in the Open Society: Anguished Self Scrutiny Among the Writers." Queen's Quarterly, 55 (1959), 578-85.

"What Might Have Been." Newsweek, 9 Nov. 1959, pp. 126-27.

Whitman, Walt. Prose Works 1892. 2 vols. Ed. Floyd Stovall. New York: New York University Press, 1964.

Widmer, Kingsley. The Literary Rebel. Carbondale: Southern Illinois University Press, 1965.

Willingham, Calder. "The Way It Isn't Done: Notes on the Distress of Norman Mailer." Esquire, Dec. 1963, pp. 306-08.

Wilson, Robert Anton. "Negative Thinking: The New Art of the Brave." Realist, Dec. 1960, pp. 5, 11-13.

Winegarten, Renee. "Norman Mailer--Genuine or Counterfeit?" Midstream, Sept. 1965, pp. 91-95.

Winn, Janet. "Capote, Mailer and Miss Parker." New Republic, 9 Feb. 1959, pp. 27-28.

Witt, Grace. "The Bad Man as Hipster: Norman Mailer's Use of the Frontier Metaphor." Western American Literature, 4 (Fall 1969), 203-17.

Wolfe, Tom. "Son of Crime and Punishment." Norman Mailer: The Man and His Work. Ed. Robert F. Lucid. Boston: Little, Brown and Co., 1971.

"Women's Lib: Mailer vs. Millett." Time, 22 Feb. 1971, p. 71.

Wood, Margery. "Norman Mailer and Nathalie Sarraute: A Comparison of Existential Novels." Minnesota Review, 6 (1966), 67-72.

Woodley, R. "Literary Ticket for the 51st State." Life, 30 May 1969, pp. 71-72.

Woodress, James. "The Anatomy of Recent Fiction Reviewing." Midwest Quarterly, 2 (Autumn 1960), 67-81.

Wustenhagen, Heinz. "Instinkt Kontra Vernunft: Norman Mailers Ideologische und Asthetische Konfusion." Zeitschrift für Anglistik und Amerikanistik, 16, No. 4 (1968), 362-89.

INDEX

NOTE: To save space, book titles in the index are shortened to their essential elements, as follows: